DESIGN YOUR FUTURE

This book presents a compelling, science-based guide for navigating life's many transitions: from first jobs to midlife pivots to purposeful retirements. Based on insights from over 10,000 people across all ages and career stages, it blends identity work, prototyping, and psychological capital to foster sustainable, purpose-driven career paths. Drawing on design thinking, positive psychology, and behavioral science, each chapter encourages reflection, exploration, and growth, supported by a practical toolkit featuring methods such as the Magic Circle, Life Loops, and the Stairway to Heaven. Readers are equipped to overcome procrastination, redesign habits, explore bold dreams, and build a portfolio life that reflects personal evolution. Whether you're feeling stuck, restless, or ready for something new, *Design Your Future* will help you take action with confidence and joy. This book is not about making the perfect plan; it's about designing your next brave step.

SEBASTIAN KERNBACH is a professor associated with the University of St. Gallen, Stellenbosch Business School at Stellenbosch University, and Stanford University. He is a global Life Design pioneer and winner of the HSG Impact Award. He advises organizations such as NASA, the UN, and the IOC, and presented Life Design as proactive career and transition competence at the UN Goals House at the World Economic Forum.

MARTIN J. EPPLER is Professor of Communications Management and Director of the Institute for Media and Communications Management at the University of St. Gallen. He is the author of 25 books and over 300 articles, and has served as an advisor and trainer to organizations including the UN, the European Central Bank, Porsche, and IBM.

DESIGN YOUR FUTURE

The Innovative Career and Transition Guide

SEBASTIAN KERNBACH
University of St. Gallen

MARTIN J. EPPLER
University of St. Gallen

Shaftesbury Road, Cambridge CB2 8EA, United Kingdom

One Liberty Plaza, 20th Floor, New York, NY 10006, USA

477 Williamstown Road, Port Melbourne, VIC 3207, Australia

314–321, 3rd Floor, Plot 3, Splendor Forum, Jasola District Centre, New Delhi – 110025, India

Cambridge University Press is part of Cambridge University Press & Assessment, a department of the University of Cambridge.

We share the University's mission to contribute to society through the pursuit of education, learning and research at the highest international levels of excellence.

www.cambridge.org
Information on this title: www.cambridge.org/9781009737340
DOI: 10.1017/9781009737333

© Sebastian Kernbach and Martin J. Eppler 2026

This publication is in copyright. Subject to statutory exception and to the provisions of relevant collective licensing agreements, no reproduction of any part may take place without the written permission of Cambridge University Press & Assessment.

When citing this work, please include a reference to the DOI 10.1017/9781009737333

First published 2026

A catalogue record for this publication is available from the British Library

A Cataloging-in-Publication data record for this book is available from the Library of Congress

ISBN 978-1-009-73734-0 Hardback
ISBN 978-1-009-73731-9 Paperback

Cambridge University Press & Assessment has no responsibility for the persistence or accuracy of URLs for external or third-party internet websites referred to in this publication and does not guarantee that any content on such websites is, or will remain, accurate or appropriate.

For EU product safety concerns, contact us at Calle de José Abascal, 56, 1°, 28003 Madrid, Spain, or email eugpsr@cambridge.org

Contents

List of Figures	page vii
List of Tables	ix
Foreword by Dr. Hans Groth, Chairman, World Demographic & Ageing Forum	xi
A Message from the Authors	xiii

PART I WELCOME TO LIFE DESIGN

1 Introduction	3
2 Life Designer Stories	9
3 Why Life Design Matters	14

PART II LIFE DESIGN BUILDING BLOCKS

4 Life Design Abilities	27
5 Life Loops Framework	40
6 Life Design Levels	60

PART III LIFE DESIGN TOOLBOX

7 Methods	73
8 Ideation Methods	91
9 Prototyping Methods	104
10 Learning Methods	128
11 Perseverance Methods	138

PART IV LIFE DESIGN SECRETS: WHAT 10000+ PEOPLE TAUGHT US

12 Method Mix by Transition Type	153
13 Special Methods: Sustainable Life Design	179
14 Silent Truths: What We Don't Say Out Loud	207

PART V HORIZONS OF LIFE DESIGN

15 Life Design as a Catalyst for Scaling Change	235
16 Life Design and the Future (of the Planet)	252
Conclusion: A Life Design Manifesto	269

Further Reading	272
Index	285

Figures

3.1	Life Design integrates past, present, and future.	*page* 16
3.2	Life Design as interdisciplinary, science-based approach.	18
3.3	Implications of longevity: from three-stage-life to multistage-life.	19
4.1	Life Design abilities.	29
5.1	From small loop to big loop: self-efficacy through Life Design.	41
5.2	Life Loops framework.	43
5.3	Expand problem space to increase solution space.	48
5.4	Redesigning the morning routine.	54
6.1	Applying Life Design on different levels of life.	61
P.1	Methods per phase (Core and Extended Toolboxes).	72
7.1	Three Good Things.	74
7.2	The Strengths Portfolio.	81
7.3	Connecting the Dots.	88
7.4	Observation sheet for Connecting the Dots.	89
8.1	The Core of Creativity.	94
8.2	Opportunity Bingo sheet.	97
8.3	Future Scenarios.	101
9.1	The Prototyping Prism.	106
9.2	The Magic Circle.	110
9.3	Ten Ways of Prototyping (for careers, side hustles and big life dreams).	114
9.4	Checklist for Ten Ways of Prototyping.	123
9.5	The Stairway to Heaven.	126
10.1	Growth Journey Map.	130
10.2	PPCO Hollywood Star.	133
10.3	Start–Stop–Continue.	136
11.1	Nudging Nuggets to overcome procrastination.	141
11.2	DJ of the Inner Sound.	144
11.3	The Social Support Map.	148

13.1	The Energy Curve.	183
13.2	Chronotype overview.	184
13.3	The Energy Map.	187
13.4	The Energy–Tension Matrix.	190
13.5	Microstrategies for calm energy.	191
13.6	Visualization examples: career matrix and action matrix.	197
13.7	Life Design Spaces.	198
13.8	Instructions for producing a mini-zine.	200
13.9	Life Design mini-zine.	201
16.1	Human intelligence and artificial intelligence as collaborators.	255
16.2	Ways of using AI in Life Design and along the Life Loop framework (© Nadine Bienefeld).	257
16.3	Beyond linear careers: new types of nonlinear careers.	262
16.4	Design your sustainable impact.	267

Tables

3.1	Myth versus reality of career transitions – and how Life Design helps	page 23
5.1	Life Design approach with morning routine example	55
7.1	Classification of twenty-four character strengths and virtues	80
14.1	Types of career and life portfolios	210
15.1	Life Design for Individuals	236
15.2	Life Design for organizations	242
15.3	Life design impact on society	247

Foreword

In a world dominated by constant distraction, screen overload, and the relentless comparison culture of social media, this book offers something rare: a breath of fresh air with a serene focus on yourself – your strengths, your options, and your path through life. It reads like a retreat, a mini-sabbatical, an invitation to slow down, to reflect, or to reconnect with what truly matters. It serves as a catalyst for personal growth, to spark meaningful conversations with others, and to take active steps for yourself.

Let's be honest: when was the last time you paused long enough to ask yourself what *you* actually want – beyond the likes, the to-do lists and the expectations? What happens when the way you've been taught to plan your life is based on outdated assumptions? What if waiting for clarity is the very thing holding you back?

The World Demographic & Ageing Forum (WDA Forum) had the honor of presenting ideas of a modern – and definitely longer – life span at the United Nations General Assembly, to the Global Coalition on Aging. We positioned them as a key strategy to meet the challenges and opportunities of longer lives all around the world. Our "100-year life" is no longer a distant concept – over 50 percent of people under twenty-five today are expected to live to 100 years. That makes learning how to design one's life not just helpful, but critical, for everybody! If you're likely to live that long, wouldn't you want to learn how to live well – and on your own terms?

Rooted in science and brought to life through visual tools, playful structures, and real-life stories, the "Life Design" approach described in this book empowers you to navigate life transitions creatively and proactively. It's more than having the perfect plan. It's about experimenting, learning, and adjusting – again and again. It's about realizing that you don't have to wait until you're burned out, stuck, or broken to make an urgently necessary life course change. You can start from curiosity. From hope. From a whisper that says, "Something more is possible."

This book isn't just for people in crisis or at a crossroads. It's for anyone who feels the quiet tug of change – whether you're a student searching for your first job, a midcareer professional feeling restless, or someone reimagining what retirement could look like. Life Design – the content and the purpose of this book – meets you where you are, and helps you take the next step with proactivity, purpose, and patience. Have an exciting journey!

Dr. Hans Groth, Chairman,
World Demographic & Ageing Forum

A Message from the Authors

When we began developing Life Design in 2018, we could not have imagined how far this approach would travel – or how deeply it would resonate across the world. What started as a passion project became a book in German by 2020, and by 2022, Life Design was honored with an Impact Award for its contribution to personal and societal well-being. Since then, we've had the privilege of bringing this approach to life in over 100 courses across universities from South Africa to Norway, from Hawaii to Australia. Life Design has found its way into MBA programs at institutions like Stellenbosch Business School and the University of St. Gallen, as well as new executive offerings on Life Design Coaching, Life Design Leadership, and the CAS Life Design.

From NASA to the International Olympic Committee, from the World Economic Forum to multinational corporations, Life Design has helped people at all levels rethink their futures, take ownership of their paths, and align their lives with what truly matters. The World Demographic & Ageing Forum has even recognized Life Design as a key strategy for navigating the challenges – and seizing the opportunities – of longevity and the 100-year life. And now, as we integrate artificial intelligence (AI) into Life Design practices, we are preparing individuals and organizations alike to design futures where technology enhances, rather than diminishes, human potential.

What unites all these journeys – from students and professionals to leaders and lifelong learners – is a shared desire to stop waiting for life to happen and instead start shaping it intentionally. Life today is full of distractions, comparison traps, and overwhelming options. It is easy to fall into passivity – consumed by what's outside of our control, distracted by social media, or paralyzed by too many choices. The truth is: the more control you have over your attention, the more control you have over your future. And it starts with the courage to protect your time and energy. As we often remind ourselves: what we trade our attention for is what our life becomes.

Life Design offers a practical, science-based, and deeply human alternative. It helps you be proactive, build self-efficacy, realize your potential, craft possibilities, and gain clarity – one small step at a time. It is not about grand leaps or dramatic overhauls. Instead, it invites you to engage in meaningful, low-risk experiments that turn uncertainty into opportunity. Our most beloved methods – like the "Magic Circle" and the "Stairway to Heaven" – have empowered people of all ages and stages, from Stanford's Distinguished Careers Institute fellows making high-stakes decisions, to individuals quietly redesigning their mornings or exploring new creative outlets.

This book is a guide to becoming a Life Designer. It's for anyone asking, "What now?" or quietly wondering, "I just don't know anymore . . . ." It's for those seeking to move from question to clarity, from inertia to momentum. Together, we will explore the Life Loops framework, inspired by the Infinity Model of Innovation, and five key Life Design abilities that help you turn reflection into action and action into learning. Whether you are launching your career, navigating leadership transitions, or reinventing yourself at midlife or beyond, Life Design will meet you where you are and help you move forward with curiosity, courage, and creativity.

Our hope is simple: that this book inspires you to design your life with intention, embrace change as a space for creativity and possibility, and navigate the future with confidence. The next chapter of your life is not written yet. Let's design it – one loop at a time.

PART I

Welcome to Life Design

In a world marked by complexity, constant change, greater longevity, and the need for reinvention across all stages of life, navigating (y)our future requires more than just planning. It requires design. In this section, we introduce the foundation of Life Design – a human-centered, science-backed approach to shaping your future with intention, creativity, and care. You'll discover why Life Design matters now more than ever, hear real stories of people who've used it to move from confusion to clarity, and begin to see your own life not as a problem to be solved, but as a portfolio to be explored. Whether you're feeling stuck, in transition, or simply ready for something more, Part I invites you to rethink what's possible – and to begin designing a future that's both meaningful and uniquely yours.

CHAPTER I

Introduction

We are living at the intersection of complexity, longevity, and rapid societal change. In such a world, navigating your career and life paths is no longer a matter of just finding the one right answer or following a prewritten script. It is an act of creativity and will. It is a continuous, evolving process. It is designing your future with Life Design.

This book is not just another guide to planning your career or achieving goals faster. It is an invitation to see your life as something you can shape, prototype, and reimagine – not once, but again and again, in loops of curiosity, courage, and care. It will also challenge dysfunctional beliefs and offer alternatives: You do not have to wait for clarity to act. You find clarity by acting.

Life Design is grounded in science. Its principles draw from cutting-edge research in design thinking, behavioral economics, positive psychology, and knowledge visualization. But more importantly, Life Design is rooted in practice. Over the years, we have run dozens of seminars around the world with thousands of people who wanted to change something in their lives or careers – but didn't know what to change or where to start, or were simply stuck in the status quo.

It is time to design your future. Life Design is more than a method – it is a way of being. At the core of Life Design lies the deep belief in human potential and the ability to live more consciously and proactively despite all distractions. But proactivity does not mean hustling endlessly or constantly doing more. Rather, it means becoming more aware of what is happening in your inner and outer world, stepping out of autopilot, and shifting from being a passive passenger in your life to becoming an active, thoughtful driver. It is about developing agency and self-efficacy – the belief that your actions can shape your path.

Life Design offers the mindset, methods, and micro-actions that help you do exactly that. It begins with simple areas where you have the most control – your morning routines, how you manage your energy, your evening wind-down rituals. It expands into larger areas of life through prototyping – testing ideas in low-risk ways – and builds on the growth mindset by focusing on learning rather than perfection. You'll work with your strengths and signature strengths, tapping into what energizes and motivates you naturally. You'll use those strengths to build a portfolio of activities that give you meaning and pleasure – and to approach even the biggest dreams not as distant someday-goals, but with Life Design and prototyping, starting today. You'll also confront and disarm one of the most common challenges in personal change: procrastination. Rather than shame or ignore it, Life Design invites you to understand it and respond with smart nudges, social support, and more constructive inner dialogues.

At the heart of Life Design is a simple but powerful idea: You move your life forward through loops of action and reflection. These "Life Loops" help you move beyond overthinking and feeling stuck by engaging in small, doable experiments. As the saying goes, "Doing is like thinking – only more intense." By engaging actively with your questions and dreams, you'll strengthen your mental and physical well-being, boost your resilience, and find more energy and fulfillment at work and in life.

Life Design is more than a method. It is a way of being.

- A way of embracing transition and uncertainty.
- A way of holding your dreams lightly but moving toward them boldly.
- A way of turning fear into possibility and procrastination into progress.

What makes Life Design different is its deep respect for human realities. We do not promise rigid formulas or overnight transformations. Instead, we offer a toolkit that is *playful yet disciplined*, structured yet flexible. We celebrate the bumps, doubts, and detours as natural parts of the journey. And we invite you to live your life not as a perfect plan, but as a dynamic, evolving portfolio of experiences that reflect your full humanity.

Life Design is inherently collaborative. You do not have to do this alone. It is better when life transitions are discussed and experienced with fellow travelers – peers who challenge you, support you, and remind you that change is not only possible, but more joyful when shared.

Don't be misled by dramatic media stories of sudden life overhauls – like the investment banker who gives it all up to run a B&B in Tuscany. These narratives often skip the messy, uncertain elements in-between. In reality, change happens through gradual, grounded steps. It's not about leaping blindly into a new life – it's about designing your way forward with prototypes, learning loops, and ongoing reflection.

1 Introduction

So, take a breath. Take stock of where you are. Take hold of the tools offered here. And then: take a step. Any step. Especially a small one. You are not designing a distant, abstract future. You are designing the next small, brave chapter of your life – and from there, the next, and the next.

You do not have to wait for clarity TO start acting.

You find clarity BY acting.

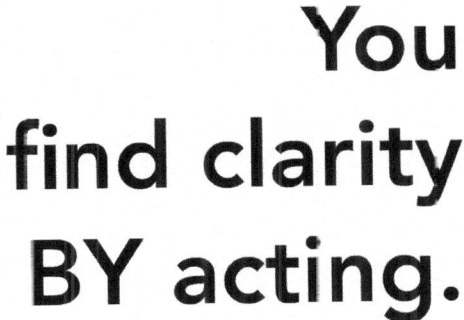

Welcome to your Life Design journey. The next iteration of your life is not predetermined. It is waiting to be shaped – with science, with creativity, and with care. Ultimately, it is all about bringing more of yourself into the future.

Who This Book Is For

This book is written for you. The Life Design approach is especially powerful during times of transition – no matter your age or background. We have worked with people from ages eight to eighty-eight, and we've seen firsthand how the mindset, methods, and Frameworks of Life Design help individuals take charge of their lives with clarity, creativity, and confidence.

From working with many people around the world, we have seen a lot of typical situations, questions, or challenges. Here are three questions we hear very often.

- "How do I start?" They were eager to move but stuck in ambiguity and doubt.
- "How do I get unstuck or progress my career?" They were doing "okay" but knew more was possible.
- "How do I pursue my dreams and ambitions – even wild ones?" They were ready to take a leap, but didn't know how to land.

Wherever you are in your life – early career, midtransition, nearing retirement, or simply asking "What's next?" – this book is for you. It doesn't offer a blueprint, but rather a mindset, a set of tools, and a growing global community of people who are daring to proactively shape their futures.

Whether you're:

- a student wondering what to do after graduation,
- a recent university graduate unsure where to start your career,
- an experienced professional questioning your next move,
- returning to work after a parental leave, illness, or time off,
- approaching retirement and seeking a meaningful "encore" phase,

Life Design gives you the tools to explore, experiment, and evolve at any age and stage.

In this book, you'll meet Life Designers navigating key transitions across the lifespan.

- Early-career (eighteen to thirty): managing too many options, comparison stress, and "fear of missing out" (FOMO); balancing study, travel, and creative ambitions.

- Midlife (thirty to fifty): moving beyond either-or thinking, for example, "Shall I stay, or shall I go?", redefining success, managing career and family, and shifting from burnout to work–life rhythm.
- Best-agers (fifty to ninety): asking "What's next?" and shaping retirement as a vibrant new chapter – integrating past experience with emerging dreams.

How to Use This Book

Just like Life Design itself, you can approach this book in the way that works best for you. Some of you may want to read it cover to cover, page by page. Others might dive straight into the methods section to start applying tools right away.

You may be curious to explore the curated journeys – real questions people have faced and the Life Design tools that helped them move forward. Or perhaps you're here because you want to finally tackle procrastination and need a starting point now.

If all of these options feel overwhelming, no problem. Simply skim through the pages and notice what sparks your curiosity or energy. Let your attention guide you – and enjoy the process.

Download Your Free Workbook

We've created a companion workbook to help you engage more deeply with the material – to download visual templates, expand your reflections, and turn insights into action. Whether you're looking to redesign your mornings, manage your energy, shift small habits, reassess your career direction, build a meaningful portfolio, or pursue bold dreams using the Magic Circle, the workbook offers a structured space to reflect, plan, and move forward.

You can access the workbook at: www.LifeDesignLab.world/workbook.

Get in Touch

At the Life Design Lab at the University of St. Gallen, our mission is to continuously evolve the Life Design approach to unlock human potential and help people bring more of themselves into the future. What began as a university course has grown into a global movement.

Our student programs at the University of St. Gallen are among the most popular, regularly overbooked by more than 300 percent. We also teach Life Design in MBA programs and midlife transition initiatives such as Next at the University of St. Gallen and the Distinguished Careers Institute (DCI) at Stanford University. As a member of the Nexel Collaborative – a global alliance of universities redefining lifelong learning – we co-create the future of education across the lifespan.

To further scale our impact, we are developing new courses, workshops, and programs for students, managers, and best-agers – within universities, organizations, and governments. A recent milestone was the launch of two executive education programs in Life Design Coaching and Life Design Leadership, which together form the Certificate of Advanced Studies (CAS) in Life Design – the first program of its kind in the world.

Our work is grounded in research. We study the impact of Life Design across a range of areas including affect regulation, psychological capital, and the role of knowledge visualization in the design process. We regularly share our findings through publications, conferences, and public events, bridging science and practice.

In collaboration with organizations worldwide – including NASA, the International Olympic Committee (IOC), Nike, Swiss Re, and others – we apply Life Design in diverse organizational contexts. Recently, we partnered with the World Demographic & Ageing Forum (WDA) to explore how Life Design can address the opportunities and challenges of longevity and lifelong transitions. We also joined a panel at the UN Goals House during the World Economic Forum in Davos, discussing the future of career transitions and personal development alongside Moira Forbes and other global leaders.

If our work resonates with you – whether you're an educator, researcher, practitioner, or simply someone navigating change – we'd love to connect. Join us in shaping the future of education, transitions, and human potential through Life Design. Email us at info@lifedesignlab.ch or just visit our website. You can get in touch with us at www.LifeDesignLab.world.

CHAPTER 2

Life Designer Stories

What does it look like to design your future? Let's explore a few stories from people who have shaped their futures in both small and significant ways, before we dive into the building blocks of the Life Design approach – its methods, tools, and curated journeys. The following three stories offer a glimpse how you can prototype yourself. These experiences already show you how Life Design builds self-efficacy and fosters a proactive mindset. You'll meet:

- Nina, a university student drowning in options and self-doubt, who learns to move from chaos to clarity by testing her way forward;
- John, a mid-career professional stuck in either-or thinking, who begins to design a path that blends security with purpose and creativity;
- Ingrid, a seasoned leader confronting the quiet dissatisfaction of "fine," who uses Life Design tools to reimagine the next chapter of her life with joy and intention.

Across stages and ages, these stories show how small experiments, self-reflection, and curiosity can transform uncertainty into momentum – and how Life Design helps people move forward with more energy, alignment, and meaning.

Early Career: From Chaos to Compass

Nina sat at the back of the university library, surrounded by coffee-stained notebooks, half-read brochures, and a dozen open tabs – consulting, UX design, teaching abroad, maybe even starting something of her own. Her thoughts buzzed with possibility and pressure. Everyone else seemed to have a plan. She felt stuck – unsure, overwhelmed, and afraid of choosing the wrong path.

She had already tried a few things. During an internship at a top consultancy, she enjoyed the energy and ambition of her colleagues – but not the long office hours or the feeling that success required sacrificing her personal life. "Why can't I just figure it out?" she scribbled in her journal. "Everyone else seems to know what they're doing."

Skeptical but curious, she signed up for a free webinar on Life Design. That one hour didn't solve everything – but it cracked something open. She wasn't broken. The process was messy. It was supposed to be. Later, as a graduate student, she enrolled in "Design Your Future." There, she began to apply simple but powerful tools that helped her move forward with more clarity and energy. She redesigned her morning routine, replacing reactive habits with reflection and intention. She mapped her energy curve and protected her Prime Time to focus on exploring career ideas. She used scenario thinking as a creative game plan – imagining different versions of her future that went beyond the standard tracks.

Momentum started to build. She prototyped a summer internship in design thinking – chaotic but energizing. She shadowed a friend in education – and felt unexpectedly at home. She joined a storytelling workshop she'd always dreamed of trying – and felt something spark. Not every step was smooth. One pitch flopped. A presentation rattled her nerves. But instead of seeing these moments as failures, she began to treat them as data. What gave her energy? What drained it? What mattered most?

Over time, the fog lifted. Nina wasn't chasing the perfect path anymore – she was creating her own. With each small step, she felt more grounded, more curious, more alive. She didn't have it all figured out – but now she had a mindset, a toolkit, and, most importantly, the confidence to keep moving forward. And for the first time in a long while, she felt genuinely excited about the future.

Mid-Career: From Either-Or to Exploration

John was halfway through his MBA, and the pressure was real. His classmates were racing toward internships at top consulting firms or locking in corporate roles. He had those offers too – prestigious, well-paid, "safe" next steps. But something didn't sit right. A question kept looping in his mind: "Do I stay in the corporate world. . . or take the risk and do my own thing?"

The problem was, neither option truly excited him. He only knew what he *didn't* want – another decade climbing someone else's ladder. But when he asked himself what he *did* want, the answers were blurry. He felt stuck – caught in other people's definitions of success, trapped in either-or thinking, unsure how to move forward.

EARLY-CAREER

From chaos to compass.

MID-CAREER

From either-or to exploration.

LATE-CAREER

From "Is this it?" to "This is it!"

Then, during a workshop on "Designing Your Future," something shifted. He realized he didn't have to make one big, irreversible decision. Instead, he could start small – by building a portfolio of meaningful activities that connected his signature strengths with his evolving interests. He could explore side projects, hobbies, and ideas beyond his core career path – not to abandon structure, but to enrich it.

Despite his packed schedule, John began carving out just a few minutes here and there – in the mornings, between classes, on the weekend. He treated it as creative play, not pressure. A quick sketch of a podcast concept. A thirty-day experiment testing an idea for a learning platform. A one-hour coaching session with an undergrad. None of it felt like a heavy lift. In fact, it gave him energy.

With each joyful micro-step, John gained more clarity. He used the process to reconnect with what energized him, what mattered most, and how to blend rather than choose between paths. He realized he could take a flexible corporate role while developing a meaningful side hustle. He could pursue coaching and creativity without needing a perfect plan.

What started as a stressful dilemma became a design challenge. What felt like being trapped in a binary turned into a more open, exploratory process. John didn't just change direction. He changed his way of making decisions – grounded in curiosity, joy, and alignment. Now, when people ask what's next, he doesn't give a title or a five-year plan. He simply smiles and says, "I'm designing it – one joyful step at a time."

Later Career: From "Is This It?" to "This Is It!"

Ingrid had built a solid career. For more than twenty-five years, she held leadership roles in communications – respected, reliable, and known for delivering results. She had led major campaigns, mentored teams, and earned recognition for her work. Life was good.

But now, in her early fifties, with her children grown and her calendar no longer bursting at the seams, a quiet question kept returning: "Is this it?" She wasn't unhappy. Her job was fine. Life was fine. But "fine" had started to feel like a ceiling.

What about the next five, ten, fifteen years? Could she really imagine the same meetings, the same office routines, the same responsibilities – all the way to retirement? Gardening and travel sounded nice, but not enough. She didn't want to wind down. She wanted to lean in – to something meaningful, something new, something that made her feel alive.

That's when she started exploring Life Design. One of the first methods she used was the Magic Circle – a way to reconnect with her deeper dreams and values. She was surprised by what surfaced: an old, long-held dream of opening a restaurant. It wasn't something she'd talked about in years, but there it was – still glowing quietly in the background.

To explore the idea, Ingrid used the Stairway to Heaven method to break down the vision into concrete, manageable steps. She asked herself: "What's one small, joyful way I can try this without a big investment or irreversible leap?" So, she hosted a series of mini "restaurant nights" in her own home – inviting a few close friends, planning the menu, setting the mood. She cooked, hosted, created atmosphere. And she loved it.

But something even more important happened. Through the experience, Ingrid realized that her dream wasn't really about *owning* a restaurant. What truly mattered to her was being a host, bringing people together, creating warm and welcoming spaces where others could slow down, connect, and enjoy themselves. That insight opened up a world of possibilities – many of them far more flexible and energizing than the original idea. She could create that experience through pop-up dinners, community events, coaching retreats, or simply by bringing more intention to how she gathered people in her life.

That's the beauty of being a Life Designer: you stay curious about what's behind your ideas. You try things in small, low-risk ways. And eventually, you make things happen – sometimes close to what you imagined, sometimes even better.

Today, Ingrid isn't stuck between "keep going" and "blow it all up." She's designing her next chapter – step by step, experiment by experiment, with joy and intention. Work still plays a role – but it's no longer the whole story. And when people ask what she's doing next, she smiles and says: "I'm not retiring. I'm redesigning."

We've seen how Life Design can transform real lives – from Nina's journey out of overwhelm, to John's shift beyond either-or thinking, to Ingrid's joyful reinvention of what comes next. These stories show that Life Design isn't just theory – it's a practice that helps people navigate uncertainty, spark curiosity, and take action with intention. In the next chapter, we'll turn the focus to you: how Life Design can matter in your own life, and how its building blocks can help you shape a future that feels truly yours.

CHAPTER 3

Why Life Design Matters

We are living longer, working differently, and navigating more transitions than any generation before us. The old model of life – education, career, retirement – no longer fits the dynamic reality we face. In its place, a multi-stage life is emerging: one filled with career shifts, hustles, sabbaticals, caregiving roles, setbacks, side projects, and reinventions. This unfolding future is rich with possibility – but also filled with complexity. And while longevity is a gift, it raises a critical question: "How do we prepare for a life full of change?"

This is where Life Design comes in. As an interdisciplinary, science-based approach, Life Design offers not only tools, but also a new mindset to navigate transitions with agency, clarity, and confidence. It helps us make sense of the past, appreciate the present, and proactively shape the future – even in a world marked by uncertainty and disruption. In this chapter, you'll discover why Life Design is increasingly recognized as an essential transition competence – for individuals, organizations, and society as a whole.

Agency: Reclaiming Authorship of Our Life

We live in turbulent times. The so-called VUCA world – marked by volatility, uncertainty, complexity, and ambiguity – is no longer a distant theory; it's our daily reality. From geopolitical conflicts to climate-related disasters, much of what surrounds us feels unstable and beyond our control. And while emerging technologies like AI hold promise, they also contribute to our growing sense of distraction and self-doubt. With endless feeds, reels, and notifications, we're constantly nudged to consume – making it harder to pause, reflect, and engage with what truly matters.

In the midst of this crisis and noise, Life Design offers a quiet, powerful alternative. It invites us to step out of our default mode and reclaim

RECLAIM AUTHORSHIP OF YOUR LIFE!

authorship of our lives – not through grand revolutions but through small, intentional steps. It starts where we are, focusing on what's within our control: our routines, our mindset, our choices. And from there, it expands – helping us shape our careers, explore new possibilities, and move closer to the dreams we've put on hold.

Life Design connects past, present, and future. Tools like the portfolio approach or "three good things" help us recognize what is already working, uncover hidden strengths, and spark ideas for change At its core is self-efficacy – the belief that we can influence our own lives. This shift, from feeling like a victim of circumstances to becoming an active agent of change, is what gives Life Design its transformative power. It enables individuals, organizations, and even societies to navigate uncertainty, regain a sense of direction, and turn the seemingly impossible into something possible.

HOW LIFE DESIGN INTEGRATES PAST, PRESENT AND FUTURE

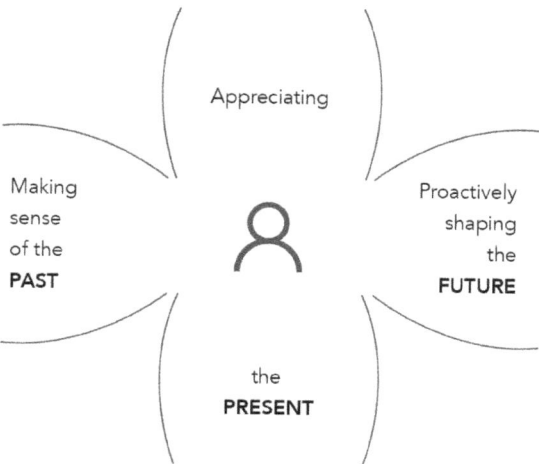

Figure 3.1 Life Design integrates past, present, and future.

How does this work? In the next section, we'll explore the unique, multidisciplinary approach behind Life Design

Science-Backed: Applying Proven Multidisciplines

Life Design combines scientific grounding with hands-on experimentation and deep human insight. As a result, Life Design is a method that is not only intellectually sound but also actionable and personally meaningful. Let's take a closer look at the key components that make this approach so distinctive.

As a science-based approach to navigating change and shaping the future, Life Design is built on a powerful and unique combination of four complementary disciplines.

(1) Design thinking brings creativity and curiosity, and legitimizes experimentation. It is a human-centered problem-solving approach that values empathy, iterative learning, and practical action. Instead of starting with the perfect answer, it begins with deep listening, embraces ambiguity, and advances through rapid prototyping.

Design thinking encourages us to treat problems as opportunities for discovery rather than puzzles to solve.
(2) Positive psychology focuses on strengths, well-being, and mental health. It shifts the focus from what's wrong with people to what helps them flourish. Drawing on empirical research, it explores concepts like optimism, resilience, flow, and meaning. Rather than being prescriptive, it offers tools and insights that help individuals and communities cultivate lives that are not just bearable, but deeply fulfilling.
(3) Behavioral economics helps us understand and improve how we make decisions by working with – rather than against – our human nature. It combines insights from psychology and economics to show that our choices are shaped by cognitive biases, social norms, and context. Rather than assuming perfect rationality, it embraces the quirks and shortcuts of real-world behavior. This opens the door to designing environments and systems that better support thoughtful, consistent, and beneficial decisions.
(4) Knowledge visualization allows us to think more clearly and communicate more effectively, both with ourselves and with others. By turning abstract concepts into visual formats – such as diagrams, maps, or visual metaphors – it makes complexity more accessible and ideas more tangible. It supports deeper understanding, shared meaning, and collaborative problem-solving. In a world saturated with information, visualization becomes a powerful tool for focus, insight, and connection.

You may have already encountered these disciplines on their own, but in Life Design they converge into something new – a holistic method for making meaningful change. They help us translate knowledge into movement. For example, visualizing your personal strengths portfolio can spark appreciation for what's already working, reveal untapped potential, and inspire fresh ideas for prototyping your next steps. Once we've seen ourselves and our options more clearly, the next step is to try them out – safely, playfully, and with purpose.

Rather than prescribing a rigid path, Life Design mirrors the realities of human behavior – and offers tools to work with, not against, our natural rhythms and emotions. It's this combination of scientific grounding, practical experimentation, and human insight that makes Life Design such a relevant and empowering approach – especially in times of transition, complexity, and reinvention.

LIFE DESIGN IS A MULTI-DISCIPLINARY APPROACH

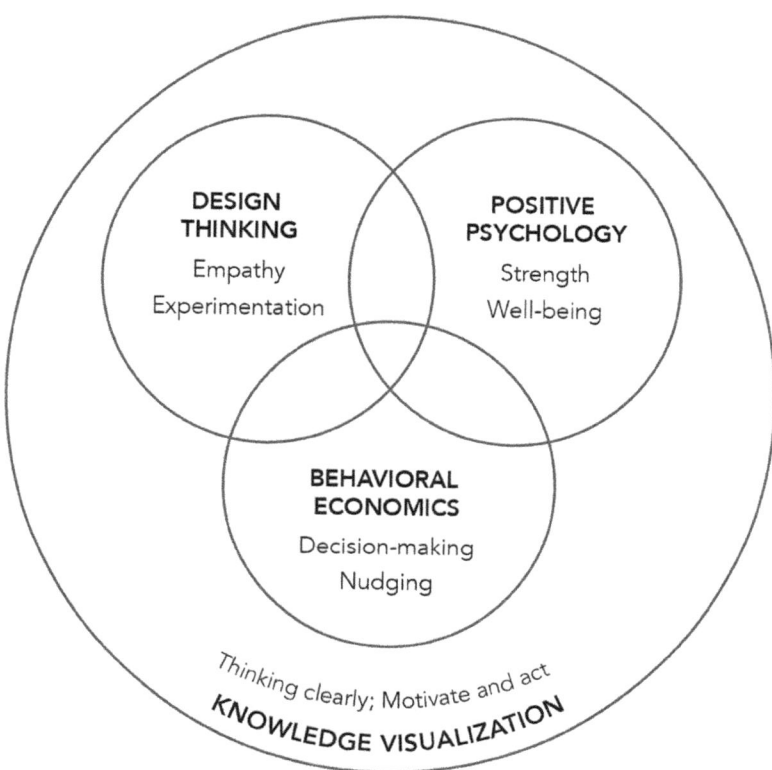

Figure 3.2 Life Design as interdisciplinary, science-based approach.

This is why Life Design is increasingly recognized as a key transition competence in the global longevity debate. In the next section, we'll explore what that means – and how Life Design can help individuals, organizations, and societies thrive in an evolving world.

Transition Competence: Navigating Uncertainty

When reading *The 100-Year Life* by Lynda Gratton and Andrew Scott, one could easily think they had Life Design in mind. They describe a future shaped by longer lifespans and increased transitions – and call for new ways to navigate life and work. But while they make a compelling case for change, they don't explain *how* to manage it. That's where Life Design comes in.

Demographic data are clear: if you're under twenty-five today, you have more than a 50-percent chance of living past a hundred. When we ask students if they're ready for that, many respond, "I don't even know what I'm doing next summer." In contrast, in our executive education programs, some participants want to design their future to become 120 or older.

The real shift isn't just in longevity – it's in the structure of life itself. We're moving from a three-stage life (education–work–retirement) to a multistage life that includes multiple careers, sabbaticals, caregiving, entrepreneurship, and new forms of contribution well into our seventies and beyond. Countries like Denmark and Sweden are already linking retirement age to life expectancy. This means more transitions – and a greater need to manage them well. As Stanford longevity expert Laura Carstensen emphasizes, transitions should no longer be seen as bugs in the system – gaps, mistakes, or failures – but as features of modern life. They need to be normalized, supported, and, most of all, designed.

Longevity demands more than just living longer – it requires a new skillset. We call it "transition competence": the ability to anticipate, navigate, and grow through life transitions with clarity, emotional stability, and confidence. Life Design builds that competence by developing a sense of agency through increased psychological capital, by allowing for portfolio thinking and by fostering resilient practice.

IMPLICATIONS OF LONGER LIVES

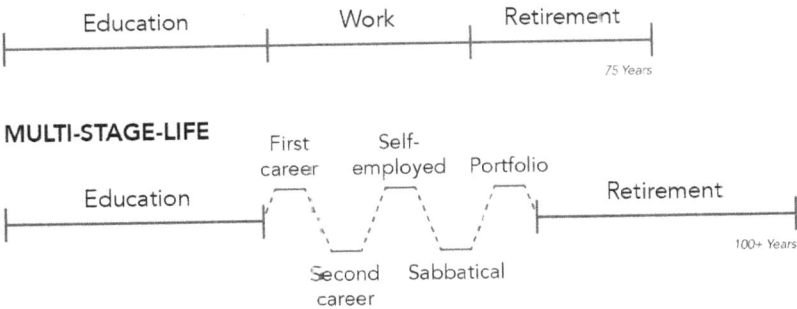

Figure 3.3 Implications of longevity: from three-stage-life to multistage-life.

> **Box 3.1 Life Transitions as Catalysts for Redesign**
>
> In navigating life's inevitable transitions, we encounter moments of profound disruption – and unparalleled opportunity. Drawing from the work of Pasqualina Perrig-Chiello, a leading scholar on biographical transitions, we see that both *normative* (e.g., retirement, parenthood) and *non-normative* (e.g., job loss, divorce) transitions require us to reorganize our lives, redefine roles, and ultimately reshape our identity. These transitions are no longer neatly age-standardized or ritualized as they once were. Instead, in our increasingly complex and destandardized world, transitions have become more frequent, individualized, and demanding of personal agency.
>
> Life Design offers a response to these challenges by providing tools and mindsets to approach transitions not as threats, but as design opportunities. Just as Perrig-Chiello emphasizes the importance of self-efficacy, self-responsibility, and character strengths in mastering transitions, Life Design invites us to not be "lost in transition" but to prototype our way forward, experiment with future selves, and build psychological capital (hope, optimism, resilience, and self-efficacy) along the way.
>
> Importantly, transitions and life design act as powerful identity laboratories. They bring to the surface latent dreams, unresolved questions, and hidden potential. As Perrig-Chiello puts it, these "grace points of zero" offer us the chance to pause, reflect, and reinvent ourselves. Life Design methods together with the Life Design framework and abilities help individuals structure this reflection and move into action, turning crisis into creative momentum.
>
> Key insight: transitions are identity catalysts – design them intentionally.
>
> - Combine inner reflection (values, strengths, dreams) with outward experimentation (prototyping, reframing).
> - Build psychological capital and leverage character strengths to foster resilience.
> - Transitions and Life Design act as Powerful Identity Learning Laboratories (PILLs).

Sense of Agency

Research on career transitions by Pasqualina Perrig-Chiello and Herminia Ibarra shows that those who navigate transitions more successfully see themselves not as victims of change, but as agents of their lives. This sense of agency through self-efficacy develops through Life Design interventions. In fact, participants in our Life Design seminars have shown measurable increases in psychological capital, consisting of self-efficacy, hope, optimism, and resilience.

3 Why Life Design Matters

Life Design empowers people to move beyond linear career paths and think in terms of adaptability, learning, and experimentation. Thus, transitions become opportunities to prototype new roles, ideas, and directions – without the pressure of immediate, irreversible decisions. Whether anticipating change, navigating it in real time, or reflecting afterward, Life Design helps people develop the tools and mindsets needed to stay emotionally resilient and open to growth.

Portfolio Thinking

A foundational mindset and tool of Life Design is portfolio thinking. Instead of expecting one job to fulfill all desires – money, meaning, fun, growth, friendships – Life Designers learn to see their lives as a portfolio of activities. Some generate income, others provide connection, learning, or purpose. This reframing is especially powerful for students and professionals who feel stuck in either-or thinking. A portfolio approach creates space, flexibility, and peace of mind. It normalizes to be in transition as it incorporates the opposite of a linear career path, embracing instead a dynamic mix of roles and experiences that evolve over time.

Emotional Stability Despite Uncertainty

When we go through transitions, we need strategies or practices to stay patient, healthy and sane. Transitions take time and instead of rushing to what's next, we need to make the process of getting to something new worthwhile and enjoyable.

In our research on practices to stay emotionally stable in transitions presented at the Academy of Management annual conference, we have identified three particular practices that those people used who went through transitions more positively than others.

(1) Self-compassion and curiosity. Those who approach others with empathy and appreciation often extend the same attitude to themselves.
(2) Empowering language. Naming their experience with terms like "portfolio" or "prototype" helps people make sense of uncertainty and gives legitimacy to experimentation. As one former NFL player told us, "Now I know what to say when people ask what I do – I have a portfolio of meaningful activities."

(3) Visual thinking. Visual tools support both reflection and communication. Like Darwin or Freud, Life Designers use visuals to think with themselves (intrapersonal communication) and with others (interpersonal communication). These visuals invite feedback, spark ideas, and create shared understanding.

Box 3.2 What Is Unexpected About Career Transitions?

Career transitions are one of those life moments that feel super personal, but are full of surprising, often counterintuitive dynamics. Here are a few unexpected truths about them.

(1) They often start with identity shifts, not job shifts. Most people think a career change begins when they update their LinkedIn or apply for something new. But in reality, it usually begins internally, with a sense that "This isn't me anymore," "I want something different," or "I didn't know what I wanted, I just knew I didn't want this anymore." The actual job change is often the last step. Often, people don't need a new job right away – they need a new narrative about who they are becoming.

(2) Clarity comes after action – not before. This one's big. People wait to act until they feel certain. But career transitions rarely work that way. You gain clarity by experimenting, prototyping, and talking to others: action → insight → new action. It's iterative, not linear. Waiting for certainty delays the very experiences that would generate it.

(3) Tiny experiments are more powerful than big leaps. We romanticize quitting everything to follow a dream – but in reality, low-risk experiments (side projects, shadowing, interviews, sabbaticals) are way more effective in creating sustainable transitions. Most successful switchers "test-drive" first. Small experiments reduce fear and build confidence through lived feedback, not imagined outcomes.

(4) Your "dream job" is usually based on outdated data. Many people chase jobs they used to want or that they think they should want – based on who they were years ago. But people grow. A big part of career transition is shedding these old narratives and rewriting what "success" means now. Without reflection, we risk designing our future using templates from our past.

(5) You're not choosing a job – you're choosing a life story. What makes a transition satisfying isn't just a title or salary – it's how well the new path fits into your life story. Does it make sense with who you want to become? Can you explain it in a way that excites you? A meaningful transition adds coherence to your personal narrative – and energy to your next chapter.

(6) "Lost time" is often where the magic is. The messy in-between phase – when nothing's clear and everything feels awkward – is not wasted time. That liminal space is where most personal growth, reorientation, and insight happens. It's uncomfortable and essential. The foggy middle is not a detour – it's the core of your transformation.

Table 3.1 *Myth versus reality of career transitions – and how Life Design helps*

Myth	Reality	Life design insight
"I need to be 100-percent clear before making a move."	You get clarity by moving. Action leads to insight.	Life Design prototypes help you learn by doing – not waiting.
"I'm choosing a job."	You're rewriting your life story. Purpose, identity, and fit matter more than job titles.	Life Design connects actions to your evolving identity and story.
"Big, bold leaps are what successful people do."	Tiny safe-to-fail experiments work better and lower the fear.	Life Design encourages low-risk experiments that build momentum.
"This is a waste of time – I'm lost."	The liminal space is where growth, redefinition, and real transformation happen.	Life Design reframes confusion as fertile ground for insight.
"Once I make the change, I'll be set."	Career design is continuous. It's not a one-time pivot but an ongoing process.	Life Design supports lifelong loops of reflection and redesign.
"My past defines what I'm allowed to do next."	Your past is raw material, not a constraint. Meaning is made looking forward.	Life Design helps you reframe your past into assets for the future.

Box 3.3 Reflection Prompt

Here are some Life Design mini-prompts to help you reflect on your transition from "drift to design."

- What are you currently tolerating? What in your current career/life feels like a slow leak of energy?
- What's your outdated story? What belief about success, identity, or your path might no longer fit?
- What tiny experiment could you run next month? A coffee chat with someone in a new field? A one-day job shadow? Starting a side project?
- What's emerging in your identity right now? If you weren't afraid of judgment, what would you say you're becoming?
- Where are you in the transition cycle? Ending: letting go of something; neutral zone: in-between, messy middle; new beginning: something is starting to take shape.

These tools not only help individuals stay emotionally centered – they also create momentum. They make it easier to move from a small personal experiment to a larger career pivot, and eventually to long-held dreams that once felt too far away.

These unexpected truths reveal that career transitions are less about one-time decisions and more about evolving identities, iterative action, and meaning-making. Life Design offers both the mindset and the toolkit to navigate this messy, beautiful process with more clarity, courage, and creativity. It doesn't promise instant answers – but it helps you ask better questions and take smarter next steps.

Potential: Inspiring Systemic Change

Life Design isn't just a personal toolset. It's increasingly recognized as a strategic resource for organizations and society. We've integrated Life Design into onboarding programs for young professionals at Credit Suisse, leadership development tracks at the Swiss stock exchange SIX, and post-MBA transition support at several universities, for example, the University of St. Gallen and Stellenbosch University. At the University of St. Gallen, we launched NEXT, Europe's first midlife transition program for accomplished professionals aged fifty and over, and collaborate with the Stanford DCI and the Nexel Collaborative to seed similar initiatives globally.

On the societal level, we've partnered with the UN Goals House at the World Economic Forum to spotlight the link between career transitions and SDG #3: Good Health and Well-Being. At the World Demographic Forum, Life Design was proposed as a key strategy for turning longevity into opportunity. We're also co-authoring a Global Report on Transition Programs to inspire governments, universities, and employers to build better support structures for adults in transition – from returnships at BP to New York City's re-entry programs for retirees.

Why is this needed? Because adults are too often left to navigate life transitions alone. We offer internships to young people – but what about their parents? Who legitimizes trying things out in midlife? Life Design does. It provides not just tools, but permission – to prototype, to reflect, to evolve. By fostering better alignment between people's strengths and emerging opportunities, Life Design becomes a bridge between potential and purpose – between what we bring to the planet and where we add most value.

PART II

Life Design Building Blocks

In this part, we present to you the main buildings blocks of the Life Design approach. It consists of five Life Design abilities, the Life Loops Framework with five key phases rooted in the infinity model of innovation by IBM, and two underlying principles – consisting of different levels of application in life and the logic from small to large loop – which show why this approach is so powerful in driving proactive behavior change.

CHAPTER 4

Life Design Abilities

Before diving into the Life Design process, it helps to understand how Life Designers think and act in practice – so-called Life Design abilities. They are foundational skills that help you navigate change and shape your future with intention. This chapter introduces you to the five core Life Design abilities. You'll first find a (visual) overview of these abilities, followed by a deep-dive on each ability and real-life stories providing psychological and practical insights.

Overview

A Life Design ability can best be understood as a way to approach yourself, others, and the world around you. They are both an attitude and a skill that Life Designers use to support their Life Design process and also use independently. For example, cultivating curiosity by simply asking someone to "Tell me more" signals appreciation, curiosity, and empathy – and often leads to more meaningful conversations.

These small shifts create space for deeper connection and creative collaboration. These abilities present an alternative to default human behavior, which the following overviews summarizes. Life Designers engage with both their dreams and challenges – as well as those of others – by following a distinct yet intuitive sequence.

Cultivating Curiosity, Appreciation, and Empathy

Life Designers begin by approaching situations with openness and interest. Instead of being overly negative or critical, they ask questions like "Can you tell me more?" or "What's behind that?" to signal curiosity and care – creating space for trust and deeper understanding.

Co-Creating through a "Yes, and..." Mindset

Instead of defaulting to "Yes, but...," Life Designers build on each other's ideas with a "Yes, and..." approach. This small linguistic shift encourages creativity, mutual support, and forward momentum.

Prototyping Low-Risk Experiences

Rather than overthinking or relying on assumptions, Life Designers test ideas through real-world experiments. Whether it's a small project, a trial run, or just a conversation, the key question is: "How might I (or we) turn this idea into a low-risk experience?" Decisions become clearer when based on experience, not guesswork.

Applying a Growth Mindset

When testing ideas, Life Designers ask, "What can I learn here?" This mindset encourages exploration over evaluation – helping to move beyond rigid either-or thinking (e.g., "Is it good or bad?") and instead focusing on learning and growth.

Thinking in Multiple Options

When procrastination or inertia hits, Life Designers don't just ask, "Can I do this or not?" Instead, they explore what's behind their resistance – and create multiple ways to move forward. Understanding the block becomes the key to unlocking momentum.

Five Life Design Principles to Proactively Shape the Future

Together, these abilities guide you from reflection to action – helping you to grow in confidence, clarify what matters, and build momentum even amid uncertainty. Each small experiment reveals new insights and helps shape a more aligned, energized future. That's how you bring more of yourself into the future.

The following illustration maps the five Life Design abilities in a simple "from–to" structure. It shows what Life Designers move away from – and what they intentionally move toward. Each ability is paired with a key phrase or question that captures its essence and invites action.

4 *Life Design Abilities*

LIFE DESIGN ABILITIES

ABILITY TO...	MINDSET SHIFT		PROMPT
	From	**To**	
1 EMPATHISE	Skepticism Negativity Rejection	Curiosity Appreciation Empathy	Tell me more
2 IDEATE	**From** Yes, BUT this will not work	**To** Yes, AND this could be possible	Yes, and ...
3 PROTOTYPE	**From** Over-thinking and assuming	**To** Low-risk prototyping and action	How might we create a low-risk prototype?
4 LEARN	**From** Fixed mindset winning or loosing	**To** Growth mindset focus on learning	What can I / we learn here?
5 PERSEVERE	**From** Stuck in either-or dichotomous thinking	**To** Flow with multi-optional differentiated thinking	What is behind it?

Figure 4.1 Life Design abilities.

Ability 1 Cultivating Curiosity, Appreciation, and Empathy

Curiosity is a powerful catalyst for shifting from negativity and paralysis to positive, proactive energy. It drives exploration and learning and, as Larry Senn describes in *The Mood Elevator*, transforms how we encounter challenges: with curiosity, difficulties become opportunities for growth rather than threats. Approaching personal or professional obstacles with curiosity opens a broader horizon of possibilities and initiates self-motivation for change.

Alongside curiosity, appreciation and empathy deepen this positive shift. Rooted in appreciative inquiry, focusing on strengths rather than problems fosters innovation, resilience, and engagement. Empathy – the ability to understand and share another's emotional experience – is equally vital. It builds trust, promotes collaboration, and enhances psychological well-being. In Life Design, empathy is applied not just toward others, but inwardly as self-empathy, creating a foundation of self-compassion critical for navigating transitions.

In Life Design, we nurture curiosity, appreciation, and empathy by exploring what truly matters – both by sharing our own stories and by listening deeply to others. We invite our peers to open up about their challenges, hopes, and dreams through thoughtful questions, and we support them by offering our full, attentive presence. Active listening is essential to empathy. It means being fully present and helping others articulate their dreams and challenges. But be careful not to confuse empathy with sympathy. For example, when a friend says, "I was in the mountains on Sunday and it was wonderful," a sympathetic response might be: "That sounds great! I was in the mountains recently too..." While this shows you relate, it shifts the focus to you. A more empathetic response would echo the Life Design principle: "That sounds wonderful – tell me more... what made it so special?" Using the other person's exact words keeps the focus on their experience, deepening insight and connection. If someone says the mountains were "adventurous," don't reframe it as "exciting" – ask instead what "adventurous" means to them. This precise mirroring fosters trust and allows for meaningful reflection. It also aligns with nonviolent communication – communication free from judgment, grounded in understanding and openness.

A Life Designer cultivates curiosity, appreciation, and empathy through small but powerful conversational tools, such as asking someone to "Tell me more" or probing deeper with, "What makes this meaningful for you?" Such questions – especially when echoing the other person's own words – help

three
magic words
for empathy and
meaningful conversations:

TELL
ME
MORE

surface underlying values, beliefs, and aspirations. In doing so, Life Design transforms superficial conversations into rich explorations of meaning, building the emotional clarity needed to design a thriving future.

Ability 2 Co-Creating through a "Yes, and..." Mindset

Most of us have experienced the frustration of sharing an idea only to be met with eye-rolls and responses like, "Yes, but we tried that before," or "Yes, but we're not Google." These "Yes, but..." reactions shut down creativity before it even starts. In contrast, the phrase "Yes, and..." opens the door to possibility. Borrowed from improvisational theatre and backed by research on creative collaboration, this simple shift creates a supportive environment where ideas can grow rather than be dismissed.

A Life Designer is a "Yes, and..." person. He or she knows that ideation thrives when we build on each other's contributions – treating every idea as a starting point rather than a finished product. By suspending early judgment and adding new layers – "What if money didn't matter?" or "What if we made this fun?" – we generate more original, feasible ideas. "Yes, and..." signals value, invites co-creation, and helps turn early sparks into breakthrough solutions.

Ability 3 Prototyping Low-Risk Experiences

Why is it so important to test our assumptions with real experiences? Because research consistently shows how often we get it wrong – especially when it comes to planning our future. Many of our assumptions aren't just inaccurate; they can act as self-sabotaging narratives that block meaningful change before it begins. Common cognitive biases like overgeneralization, confirmation bias (seeking only confirming evidence), and the sunk cost fallacy (holding on too long) distort our thinking. We might assume we're not cut out for entrepreneurship because we once disliked accounting or continue investing in a failing project just because we've already put time into it. Add to that our tendency toward catastrophic thinking – imagining everything that could go wrong – and it's no wonder we often feel stuck.

The good news is that there's a way out: start small. Research by the Heath brothers suggests that change becomes more doable when we "shrink the change." Instead of leaping into an all-or-nothing plan, take a small, low-risk step – like learning a language on an app, talking to someone in your dream job, or testing a new idea through a short, contained project. This approach reflects the psychological principle of embodied cognition: our actions shape our thoughts. When you move, act, and engage physically with an idea, your mindset shifts. Change doesn't start in your head – it starts with your feet, your hands, your body in motion.

A Life Designer understands the pitfalls of assumptions and embraces experience as a learning tool. Instead of waiting for the perfect time, a sabbatical, or a major life overhaul, Life Designers ask: "What could I do with just 10 minutes? What could I learn with 100 Euros? Who could I talk to who's done this before?" Whether you call it an experience, an experiment, or a prototype – the goal is the same: test assumptions, gain insights, and build a stronger foundation for decision-making. After all, the best decisions come not from speculation, but from lived experience.

Ability 4 Applying a Growth Mindset

Stanford professor Carol Dweck has shown that one of the most powerful beliefs we hold is how we view our own potential. A fixed mindset sees traits like intelligence or creativity as static – something you're either born with or not. In this view, success confirms your worth, and failure threatens it. In contrast, a growth mindset views abilities as evolving through effort, curiosity, and learning. It embraces challenges, sees setbacks as part of the process, and treats mistakes as valuable data for development. These mindsets shape how we learn, how we relate to success and failure, and ultimately how we experience motivation, confidence, and joy.

A Life Designer actively practices the growth mindset – especially when prototyping. Instead of asking "Did it work or not?" he or she asks, "What can I (or we) learn from this?" This mindset helps shift away from judgment and toward iteration. Of course, in moments of stress or fatigue, we may slip into fixed thinking and label a prototype a failure. When that happens, it's helpful to pause, reset, or seek out someone energizing – then return with curiosity. Every experiment contains a lesson, and with each learning comes progress, momentum, and the chance to grow.

Ability 5 Thinking in Multiple Options

We often fall into the trap of either-or thinking – believing we must choose between two opposing paths: stay in our job or start a business, take a sabbatical or commit fully to work, stay in corporate or go independent. While some decisions do require clear choices, this polarized mindset can limit creativity and fuel unnecessary pressure. Psychologist Aaron Beck called this dichotomous thinking, a cognitive distortion that becomes especially common in emotionally charged situations. The antidote lies in slowing down, unpacking the challenge, and asking: "What's really behind this dilemma?" Often, the answer isn't "either-or" – it's "both-and," or something entirely new that hasn't been considered yet.

A Life Designer is trained to look beneath the surface – whether it's a dream, a challenge, or even procrastination. By asking "What's behind it?", he or she uncovers the real motivations or fears driving their indecision. For instance, behind a desire to travel might be a need for freedom or inspiration, behind procrastination, a fear of failure or perfectionism. With this insight, Life Designers develop strategies that support forward movement – from naming a task the "first shitty version" to ease pressure, to seeking energizing conversations, to using first-principles thinking to reframe the entire situation. It's not about whether you can or can't act – it's about which small, creative strategies might help you take the next step.

Example: Stories Bringing the Abilities Alive

The five Life Design abilities will guide you through the chapters ahead – and you may find they are valuable far beyond the context of Life Design itself. A famous creative agency, for example, adopted "Tell me more" as a core company principle, using it to cultivate curiosity and appreciation in everyday conversations. Who knows – perhaps one or more of these abilities will support you in other areas of your life as well.

When it comes to designing our futures, many of us fall into the trap of all-or-nothing thinking: "Should I quit or stay? Should I follow my passion or play it safe?" These kinds of binary questions can leave us stuck, overwhelmed, or rushing into major changes without understanding what truly matters. But Life Design offers another path – one that's more curious, more creative, and more human.

To make the Life Design abilities more tangible and memorable, this section illustrates them in action through three Life Designer anecdotes. The three stories show what happens when people slow down, ask better questions, and experiment with small steps instead of chasing big, dramatic shifts. You'll meet:

(1) Steven, who learned that passion alone doesn't guarantee fulfillment;
(2) Reka, who discovered how to bring her vision to life through joyful, low-risk experiments; and

(3) Sebastian, who found surprising energy and playfulness by integrating hidden passions into his everyday rhythm.

Along the way, you'll see the core abilities of a Life Designer in action: empathizing with your own desires, ideating new possibilities, prototyping without pressure, learning through feedback, and moving beyond either-or thinking. These stories are more than inspiring – they're blueprints for building a future that reflects more of who you really are.

Story 1 Why Big Leaps Can Lead to Big Regrets

Steven had mentally quit his job at the bank long before he handed in his resignation. Restless and frustrated, he was stuck in a cycle of either-or thinking: "Should I stay or should I go? Should I follow my passion or stay safe?" One day, inspired by a glossy magazine article urging readers to "follow your passion," Steven made a bold decision. He loved dogs – always had. Growing up, they were part of the family. Now, with two of his own, the path seemed obvious: turn passion into a profession.

Without testing the waters, Steven quit his job, poured his savings into a dog trainer certification, leased an old dog school, repainted it, hired trainers, and hosted a grand opening party. Friends gathered, balloons floated, the sun shone.

But in the middle of the celebration, a quiet unease crept in: "This isn't what I imagined." Steven's dream had been clear – but his assumptions hadn't been tested. He discovered that running a business brought pressure he didn't enjoy. Training dogs professionally was different from playing with his own. The passion was real – the fit wasn't.

The Illusion: What They Don't Tell You About Following Your Passion
Steven's story begins with a common illusion: that following your passion automatically leads to fulfillment. Without testing the waters, he quit his banking job and dove headfirst into a romanticized dream of working with dogs. But what he discovered was that the reality of running a dog training business didn't align with what truly gave him energy.

The Misconception: The Myth of Overnight Reinvention and Drastic Change
Steven's story reflects a common trap: skipping the small steps in pursuit of a big dream. The leap felt courageous – but it was based more on escape than insight. What was missing? Experiments. Clarity. Curiosity. Instead of diving in headfirst, Life Designers take a different path. They don't just

chase the dream – they explore what's behind it. They ask: "What is it about this dream that really matters to me?" Then, they test that insight in small ways – before betting everything on it.

A Better Way: Discovery Over Drama and Learning from Small Prototypes
The Life Design journey begins with the ability to empathize – not just with others, but with yourself. Steven skipped this step and fell into a trap of assumptions. Life Designers learn to move from skepticism, pressure, or self-judgment to curiosity, appreciation, and empathy for their own longings. They ask: "What do I really need? What's behind this dream?" If Steven had paused to explore what truly mattered, he may have discovered a different – and more sustainable – way to connect with his love for animals. What if Steven had started smaller? He might have volunteered at a dog training center. Shadowed a trainer for a week. Hosted a few community classes in the park. These prototypes would have revealed something essential: he didn't need to own a dog school to feel connected to dogs – or to feel fulfilled.

The Lesson
Life Design doesn't require a dramatic career change or a leap into the new. It's about getting curious, starting small, and staying honest. You build momentum through joyful, low-risk experiments – not pressure-filled reinventions. Before chasing a shiny vision, pause and ask, "What is this longing really about?" Try it in a small, meaningful way. See what fits. And remember: the smartest path forward is often not the loudest – but the most aligned.

We want to show you that there is another way. The next two stories are positive examples. See how differentiated instead of dichotomous thinking can help you discover what is really behind your vision and your challenges and how you can integrate new insights into your career and life with small experiences and little experiments – and without high risk and a lot of drama.

Story 2 From Wishful Thinking to Purposeful Action

For years, Reka had been running at full speed through the corporate world. A successful management consultant on the outside, she felt stuck and restless inside. Secretly, she dreamed of trading boardrooms for yoga mats – but the idea seemed impossible, risky – even a little naive.

Tell Me More: The Power of Being Heard

One sunny Sunday, over coffee and cheesecake, Reka confessed her thoughts to her friend Tanja, a trained Life Designer. Instead of dismissing the idea or rushing to advise, Tanja simply smiled and said, "Tell me more." And Reka did. She spoke about the relentless rat race, about friends who shrugged off exhaustion as normal, and about how yoga gave her rare moments of peace. What she craved wasn't just a career change – she wanted to share the calm she had found.

Low-Risk Experiments: Putting Romanticized Ideas to the Test

Together, they designed a small, safe experiment: Reka would rent a space and teach a single "Yoga for Friends" class. No quitting her job. No radical leap. Just one simple step to see how it felt. Three weeks later, Reka stood in front of twelve friends and led her first class. It went well. But the next day, she burst into laughter: "God, I would never want to be a full-time yoga teacher!"

Growth Mindset: Learning from Testing the Waters

Teaching had been fun – but exhausting. Setting up the space, managing the energy, keeping everyone engaged, even marketing the class – it was far more work than her peaceful Instagram vision had suggested. But instead of crushing her dream, the experience helped her refine it. She still wanted to teach yoga – just not as her full-time profession, and preferably within the support system of an existing studio.

Over the following months, Reka kept experimenting. She taught a few more community classes, then joined a local studio where she led one session a week. Eventually, she realized what she missed: the closeness and warmth of teaching friends. So, she revived her original idea – once a month, she hosted her own "Yoga for Friends" class again. This time, she had the support of both worlds: the structure of the studio and the intimacy of her own circle.

What started as a vague dream became a real, joyful part of her life. One small experiment at a time, Reka didn't just redesign her career – she redesigned her rhythm. Today, she's left consulting behind and runs her own business, a future she wouldn't have dared to imagine – if she hadn't started with that one simple conversation on a Sunday afternoon.

The Lesson

Reka didn't leap. She started with a conversation – a vulnerable moment shared with a friend, and a response that opened the door: "Tell me more."

From there, she moved into a series of joyful, low-risk experiments that helped her refine what she really wanted: not to become a full-time yoga teacher, but to integrate the peace and connection she felt into her life in a sustainable way.

As a Life Designer, you can focus on your career, but at the same time, life has much more to offer than just work. That is why the third story shows how someone can use surprising connections, rhythm, and graffiti to bring more of themselves into the future.

Story 3 Bringing More of Oneself into the Future

A few years ago, a professor called Sebastian, known for his structured mind and academic rigor, gave himself permission to imagine three different futures: one likely, one fallback, and one wild card. To his surprise, the wild card sparkled with hip-hop. He pictured himself opening a hip-hop café – DJs spinning beats, MCs freestyling, walls lined with graffiti, and deep conversations about rhythm and philosophy. The image made him laugh – but it also lit something up inside him.

The Beauty of Life Design: When Others Take Your Dream Seriously
Instead of brushing it off, his Life Design team leaned in. "What exactly about hip-hop speaks to you?" they asked. As Sebastian reflected, it became clear – it wasn't just the music. It was the creativity, the culture, the raw energy. It was rhythm-and-poetry, breakdancing, graffiti, flow. But above all, it was playfulness – something he realized he'd lost touch with since stepping into the role of a professor.

Unexpected Insights: When Small Prototypes Become the Future
His team encouraged him to prototype. The first step? Not a café or a concert. Just a symbolic, almost silly change: swap dress shirts and leather shoes for T-shirts and sneakers during class. At his next lecture, a student mistook him for a fellow classmate. He laughed – and, more importantly, felt *comfortable, alive, and more himself* than he had in years. That moment cracked something open: he could bring hip-hop energy into his daily life, without blowing everything up.

From there, the experiments continued. A graffiti workshop in Paris. A hip-hop history tour in Harlem. Freestyle sessions with friends. An old-school playlist to start the day. It was never about changing careers. It was about integrating his passions into the life he already had – and letting them reshape it from within.

Today, Sebastian is still remixing. Still experimenting. Still finding rhythm, poetry, and presence in unexpected places. His T-shirt might not say much – but to him, it's a quiet revolution. A reminder that your life doesn't need to follow one beat. Because sometimes, the best way to find your groove... is to start dancing in your own shoes.

The Lesson

Sebastian's story shows what it looks like when you give yourself permission to explore a dream that feels completely outside the box – in his case, a wild-card vision involving hip-hop, graffiti, and breakbeats. He didn't start with a plan to open a café. He started with a playful shift: teaching in sneakers and a T-shirt. What followed were a series of mini-prototypes that helped him bring rhythm and play back into his life – not by changing careers, but by reintegrating lost parts of himself into his everyday world.

This story brings together several Life Design abilities:

- the ability to prototype joyfully and with low risk
- the ability to learn from experience instead of just thinking
- the ability to overcome procrastination by moving beyond rigid, either-or thinking

Sebastian's path reminds us: you don't have to "blow up" your life to feel more like yourself. You can start where you are – with a playlist, a new outfit, or a creative experiment. The goal isn't to become someone else. It's to bring more of yourself into your future.

Box 4.1 Reflection Prompt

From insight to action, now it's your turn! As you read these stories, ask yourself the following questions.

- What's a dream I've romanticized, and what might be behind it?
- Where am I stuck in either-or thinking, and what new options might be possible?
- What small experiment could I try to explore a passion or idea?
- How might I learn something meaningful – even from a "failed" attempt?

CHAPTER 5

Life Loops Framework

This chapter introduces the Life Loops framework – a dynamic, iterative process for applying Life Design in everyday life. We'll begin with a brief overview of the framework and its five phases, then walk through each of its five phases using a simple example: redesigning your morning routine. This quick application example will help you get familiar with the Life Design process on a small but meaningful part of your life. From there, we'll explore additional methods and tips for each phase in the following part of the book, equipping you to take on bigger challenges – so you can ultimately bring more fulfillment, meaning, and alignment into your life.

Overview

The Life Loops framework shows that Life Design is not a one-time fix, but an ongoing process that expands over time. Inspired by IBM's infinity framework of innovation, we've adapted it for human development – helping individuals reflect, take action, and grow.

There are many frameworks in creativity and innovation we could have chosen but the infinity logic that we have incorporated into the Life Loops framework unites three distinctive features that makes the framework unique for Life Design.

(1) Nonlinear design. Unlike traditional linear change or innovation frameworks, the infinity loop reflects the true nature of personal growth – nonlinear, iterative, and often messy. It mirrors real life, where progress rarely happens in a straight line.

(2) From small loops to big changes. The underpinning logic of the loop approach allows you to begin with low-risk, manageable loops – redesigning a habit, a moment, or a daily routine. As your confidence and self-efficacy grow, so does your capacity to take on larger loops – like shaping your career, building a portfolio of meaningful activities,

5 Life Loops Framework

or pursuing long-held dreams. This aligns with Harvard professor Teresa Amabile's "Progress Principle," which shows that small, meaningful steps forward create momentum and fulfillment.

(3) Integration of procrastination. Unlike most change or innovation frameworks that ignore it, the Life Loops framework embraces procrastination as a natural part of the process – both when getting started and when to keep going. Instead of seeing it as a failure, we treat it as a source of insight. In line with the mantra of philosopher Marcus Aurelius, "What gets in the way becomes the way," we learn to work with resistance – not against it.

In short, the Life Loops framework meets you where you are – whether you're redesigning a small habit or reimagining your entire future – and gives you a structured yet flexible way to move forward, one loop at a time.

Life Designers live in loops and navigate this framework by cycling through five key phases. The left side of the loop focuses on introspection and ideation: understanding your dreams or challenges and building ideas. The right side is about action, experimentation, and learning: creating new realities and building momentum. The following is an overview of the five phases.

Empathy

The loop usually begins with empathy – looking beneath the surface of your goals, challenges, or habits. Life Designers ask themselves and also

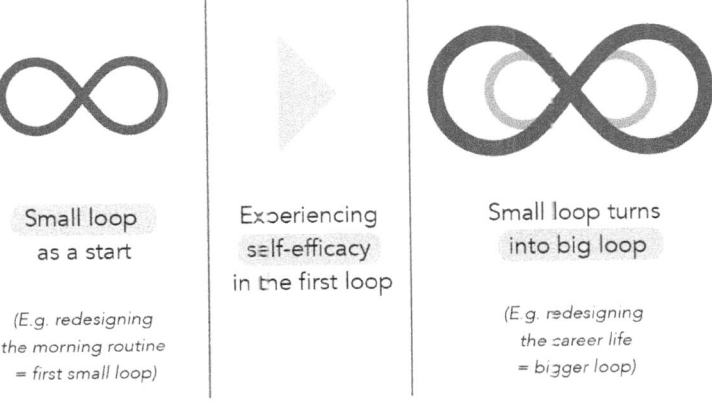

Figure 5.1 From small loop to big loop: self-efficacy through Life Design.

others: "What matters to you?" or "What's really going on here?" If this question is addressed to yourself, it opens the door to meaningful insight and compassionate self-connection. If it is addressed to others, you can create meaningful interactions and support each other to find out what is behind your dreams and challenges. You finish this phase with an opportunity statement helping you to focus on what you wish to change.

Ideation

This phase is all about finding ways to build ideas. Once you understand what matters, the next step is to generate possibilities. Life Designers ask, "What else might be possible?" to spark new ideas, perspectives, and creative options – without needing to decide yet.

Prototyping

Rather than waiting for perfect answers, Life Designers test their ideas through small, safe experiments. A question like "What's a tiny step I could try this week?" brings clarity and builds confidence through doing, not just thinking.

Learning

Every experiment becomes a source of insight. Life Designers pause to ask, "What did I notice, and what does that teach me?" Reflection turns experiences into growth and prepares the ground for the next loop.

Perseverance

At the centre of every loop is the challenge of starting and sustaining. Resistance is normal – but Life Designers learn to navigate it with gentleness and creativity. They ask: "What's one small way I can move forward today?"

***

Together, these five phases form a dynamic, looping process that turns reflection into action – and action into learning. Life Designers live in loops, moving with intention through uncertainty. Each time they

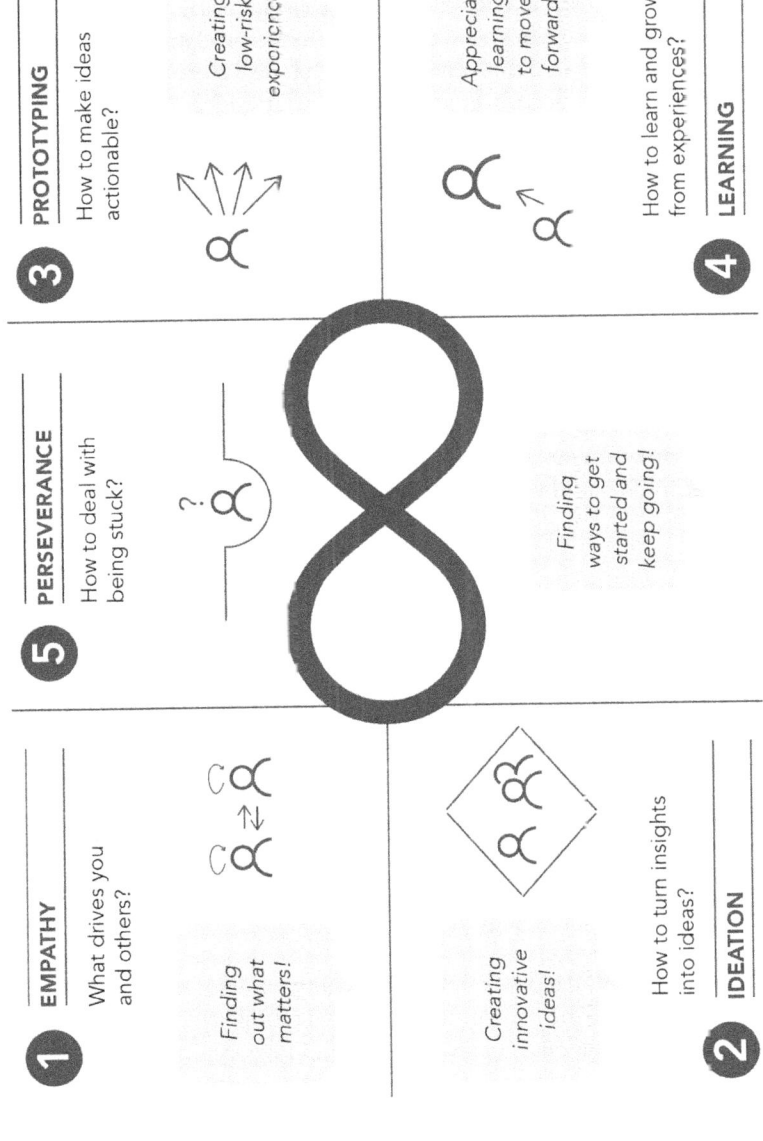

Figure 5.2 Life Loops framework.

complete a loop, they bring more clarity, energy, and alignment into their lives – one meaningful step at a time.

The illustration offers a visual overview of the Life Loops framework. It maps each of the five phases – empathy, ideation, prototyping, learning, and perseverance – across the reflective and active sides of the loop. The diagram shows how Life Designers move between reflection and action, and how each phase supports forward movement. Each phase is paired with a guiding question to spark momentum and support continuous growth.

Choosing a Metaphor: How Do You See Your Life Loop?

The Life Loops framework is not just a process – it's a way of moving through life. And like all meaningful frameworks, it becomes more powerful when it resonates personally. Having applied the Life Loops framework with thousands of people around the world, many have also adapted the approach into a new metaphor. Some have treated Life Design as dancing, some as a compass, as a map, or even as a mountain, bridge, or sailing metaphor. To help you connect with it in a way that feels natural, the following three metaphors each offer a different perspective on how Life Design unfolds – and how you might engage with it.

Life Design as a Dance

Life isn't linear – and neither is growth. Think of Life Design as a dance: a rhythm of reflection and action, of stepping forward and spinning back. Empathy and ideation invite inward movement, while prototyping and learning call you outward. And procrastination? It's the pause before the music picks up again – a beat of hesitation that, when embraced, becomes part of the choreography. Life Designers don't wait for perfect moves; they learn by dancing. With each loop, your movement becomes more fluid, more grounded, more joyful.

Life Design as a Compass

Life Design can also feel like holding a compass – something that doesn't prescribe a path but helps you orient yourself. Empathy tunes your internal sensors. Ideation reveals possible directions. Prototyping is the step into unknown terrain. Learning brings clarity. And procrastination? That's the fog. But the compass still works. A Life Designer trusts small steps and regular

5 Life Loops Framework

> **Box 5.1 Reflection Prompt**
> Which Life Design metaphor speaks to you right now? There's no right answer. In fact, your metaphor may change depending on the day, the challenge, or the dream. That's the beauty of Life Design – it moves with you.

check-ins over perfect plans – always adjusting course with awareness, intention, and curiosity.

Life Design as a Map

Or perhaps Life Design is your personal map – one you draw as you go. Each phase is a territory: empathy uncovers your inner landscape, ideation sketches new trails, prototyping lets you test the ground, and learning updates the route. Procrastination isn't a detour – it's part of the terrain, offering insights into where resistance lives. With each loop, your map grows – from redesigning your day to reimagining your future. You're both the traveler and the cartographer.

Phase 1 Empathy

Main Focus: Discovering What Is Behind Your Longings or Frustrations to Uncover the Real Problem

The empathy phase in Life Design has two central goals: first, to approach problems, challenges, hopes, and visions – both your own and those of others – with curiosity and appreciation, so you can uncover what truly lies beneath them; second, to use that deeper understanding to formulate a focused problem or opportunity statement ("How might I...") that prepares you for the next phase of ideation.

The corresponding Life Design ability is to replace negativity, skepticism, and judgment with curiosity, appreciation, and empathy – often through the simple invitation: "Tell me more." For instance, if a manager shares a passion for comics, don't dismiss it – lean in. That passion could be a gateway to meaningful insight and change.

Why Empathy?

Empathy – and self-empathy – is the starting point for self-discovery in Life Design. It's about understanding what drives you, what matters to

Be proactive.
Build self-efficacy.
Realize your potential.

**ONE
LOOP
AT
A
TIME**

you, and where your strengths lie. It is actually way beyond understanding. According to research by Harvard professor Helen Riess, empathy unfolds in three dimensions: (1) emotional empathy – you feel it, your body resonates with someone else's experience; (2) cognitive empathy: you understand it, your brain connects the feeling to context, and why it matters; and (3) behavioral empathy: you respond, and the empathy becomes visible through care, action, or support. By applying these layers of empathy and learning to see yourself and others from multiple perspectives, you build a stronger foundation for bringing more of your authentic self into the future.

In Life Design, empathy helps expand your understanding of a problem or vision – whether you're engaging with others or practicing self-empathy. With this broader view, you can generate more creative options. Instead of clinging to a single idea, you can explore meaningful alternatives. Take, for example, a manager in South Africa who dreamed of skydiving. Through deeper reflection, she realized that her desire wasn't about jumping from a plane – it was about freedom, facing fears, and courage. From that insight, she uncovered other satisfying options: paragliding, bungee jumping, or even something as simple as jumping off a table. Another example is depicted in Figure 5.3. A problem like unfulfilling networking can have multiple underlying causes. Once you understand these, a range of new options or opportunities opens up. This prevents binary, either-or thinking like "Networking doesn't work for me" and encourages thoughtful, tailored experimentation.

Key Takeaway
Don't rush from problem to solution. Stay with the problem. Expand your understanding of it, and your solution space will grow.

Phase 2 Ideation

Main Focus: Creating Ideas, Building on Each Other, and Selecting

The ideation phase in Life Design is about expanding the solution space. Its goal is to strengthen your capacity to generate a wide range of ideas – individually and collaboratively – so that you can move from insight to action with creativity and confidence. You begin with the opportunity statement developed during the empathy phase ("How might I...") From here, you apply two key thinking modes: divergent thinking, to generate as many ideas as possible, and convergent thinking, to narrow those ideas

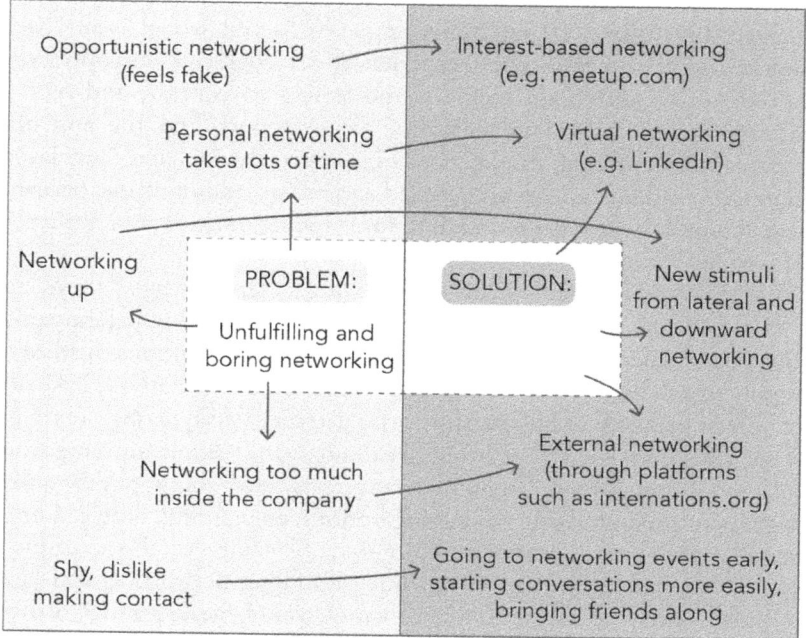

Figure 5.3 Expand problem space to increase solution space.

down to the most promising ones. The process typically unfolds in five steps: (1) clarifying your design challenge; (2) creatively warming up to loosen mental constraints; (3) generating first ideas; (4) developing ideas through collaboration; and finally, (5) selecting which ideas to prototype.

The corresponding Life Design ability is co-creating through a "Yes, and..." mindset to embrace radical collaboration and bias to action. Rather than waiting for the perfect idea, you build on imperfect ones – "Yes, and " instead of "No, but..." Creative confidence grows as you realize that ideas don't have to be original to be useful; often, it's the combination or evolution of ideas that unlocks real value.

Why Ideation?
Ideation unlocks possibility. It frees you from binary thinking – such as "This is the only path" or "That idea won't work" – and invites exploration. You create options, rather than waiting for the "right" one to appear.

Ideation also reduces the risk of failure: instead of overinvesting in a single idea, you hold ideas lightly and test them through prototyping. The process supports both creativity and practicality, helping you move forward with ideas that are meaningful and viable.

Key Takeaway
Don't wait for the perfect idea. Generate many, build on what emerges, and trust the process. The more ideas you create, the more likely you are to discover something worth acting on.

Phase 3 Prototyping

Main Focus: Trying Things and Running (Small) Experiments

Prototyping is how you bring ideas to life. After using empathy to uncover insights, framing a meaningful "How might I..." question, and generating ideas through ideation, it's time to act. In Life Design, prototyping means running small, low-risk experiments that help you test assumptions, explore possibilities, and gather real-world feedback. A prototype is not a final answer. It's a draft, a test, a quick dip into a new experience. The idea comes from product and service design – like a mock-up of a chair or a concept car, built not to be perfect, but to explore and spark feedback. You can prototype conversations (e.g., an informational interview), activities (e.g., volunteering), or environments (e.g., coworking in a new field). In Life Design, you apply this prototype approach to your habits, projects, career paths, or even dreams.

The corresponding Life Design ability is prototyping low-risk experiments. To build effective prototypes the experiment should be (1) low in emotional, time, and financial investment. Crucially, it should be (2) permission-free: you don't need anyone's approval to try it. It should also be designed to be (3) action-oriented, pulling ideas out of your head and into the real world.

Why Prototype?
Because action reveals what thinking can't. As educational pioneer Johann Pestalozzi might say, it's about integrating head, heart, and hand – thinking, feeling, and doing – so you can move forward with insight and confidence. Instead of getting stuck in overthinking, you simply try something – then reflect and learn. Prototypes test whether your ideas resonate not just in theory, but in real life. One participant dreamed of

becoming a flight attendant, but a single conversation with someone in the industry revealed a mismatch between fantasy and reality. That short interaction was a prototype – and it saved her from heading down the wrong path. Prototyping isn't about perfect planning. It's about learning quickly and safely.

Key Takeaway

Don't wait until you're sure. Build small experiences to explore your options. Prototypes are your way of thinking through doing – and they progress your path forward, one experiment at a time.

Phase 4 Learning

Main Focus: Reflecting and Taking It Further

Learning is what transforms experience into progress. Once you've run a prototype – whether a quick conversation, a trial activity, or a side project – it's time to pause and reflect. Without this step, you risk missing the insights that matter most. Learning in Life Design means resisting the urge to label things as "successes" or "failures" and instead to ask: "What went well? What was difficult? What surprised me? What might I do differently next time?" This reflective lens helps you move beyond binary thinking and turn every action into data for your next iteration. Thus, language matters: in Life Design, we talk about learning opportunities, not mistakes. Remember the story about Reka? When she taught her first yoga class, she loved the teaching but struggled with logistics. In her next step, she joined a studio – simplifying the setup but losing the close-knit community she enjoyed. Eventually, she found balance by combining both. Each step taught her something. No step was wasted.

The corresponding Life Design ability is applying a growth mindset – the perspective of embracing change, seeing potential as something to be developed, and treating every experience as a chance to grow. Life Designers don't run prototypes to prove whether something is "right." They do it to discover what's meaningful, viable, and energizing. Like the woman who dreamed of becoming a flight attendant, only to realize after one honest conversation that her dream was based on a romanticized image. That five-minute chat was a prototype – and a powerful learning opportunity that saved her time, energy, and likely some disappointment.

Why Learning?
Because reflection makes the difference between movement and growth. Prototyping alone isn't enough – what you take from it shapes what you do next. That's why many organizations are embracing failure as part of the process. Spotify's public "failure board," Princeton's "CV of Failures," and global "F*ckup Nights" all send the same message: learning from what didn't work is not a weakness – it's a superpower. The same goes for individuals. Sharing and reflecting on your own missteps fosters self-compassion, insight, and resilience. According to Bradley Staats at the University of North Carolina, learning from mistakes is essential for staying adaptable, creative, and successful over time.

Key Takeaway
There are no mistakes – only learning opportunities. If you reflect on each prototype with curiosity rather than judgment, every experience becomes a stepping stone to something more aligned, more informed, and more fulfilling.

Phase 5 Perseverance

Main Focus: Overcoming Blocks

Procrastination is not a flaw – it's part of the process. In Life Design, feeling stuck or hesitant is both natural and expected. It shows up at key transition points in the Life Loops framework: when moving from ideation to prototyping (getting started) and again after learning (keeping momentum going). You might have a brilliant idea or meaningful insight – but still find yourself avoiding action. Why? Because knowing what to do doesn't guarantee we'll do it. This is what behavioral science calls the intention–action gap. Think of New Year's resolutions: full of clarity and energy in January, abandoned by February. The walk you planned, the conversation you meant to have, the email you drafted but never sent – these are all moments where procrastination quietly steps in.

The corresponding Life Design ability is moving to multioptional thinking. When we procrastinate, it's often because we're unknowingly trapped in either-or thinking: "I must do this perfectly or not at all; I act now, or I've failed." This kind of rigidity fuels pressure and paralysis. Life Designers are trained to pause and ask, "What's behind this hesitation?" – not to shame it, but to understand it. Sometimes it's fear of failure. Sometimes perfectionism. Sometimes a hidden need – like freedom, clarity, or connection – that's not being met. With this awareness, they shift into small, creative strategies: renaming the task as a "first shitty version," designing a lighter first step, or reframing the goal entirely. The goal isn't forcing action. It's designing motion that fits your energy, mindset, and values.

Why Perseverance?
Because progress rarely follows a straight line. The power lies in iteration, not intensity. And usually, procrastination is also a form of feedback: In *The War of Art*, Steven Pressfield writes that "Resistance will tell you anything to keep you from doing your work." And yet, he reminds us: the more important a call or action is to our soul's evolution, the more resistance we will feel toward pursuing it. Life Design helps you meet resistance not with brute force, but with compassionate structure. You move forward by expanding your options, reframing your inner narratives, and returning to what matters – even imperfectly.

Key Takeaway
Procrastination doesn't mean you're lazy – it means there's something worth listening to. Life Designers respond not with pressure, but with perspective. They move from stuckness to movement by expanding their

---

Box 5.2 Regulating Affect with Life Design

One of the key challenges in Life Design is not just thinking or planning – it's acting. Bridging the gap between intention and action often comes down to one important factor: affect regulation – our ability to manage emotional states.

Affect refers to short-term emotional reactions – like joy, frustration, or disappointment – that arise from external events or internal thoughts. Unlike moods, affects are brief but powerful. According to Personality Systems Interaction (PSI) theory by psychologist Julius Kuhl, affect regulation plays a critical role in translating our thoughts and goals into action.

Our research shows that engaging with Life Design can help regulate affect in two key ways.

(1) Downregulating negative affect: finding access to the self. Negative emotions like fear, self-doubt, or shame can block us from accessing our deeper

> **Box 5.2 (cont.)**
>
> motivations or taking the first step. Life Design reduces this blockage by creating safe, appreciative environments – especially through Life Design Teams. Practicing empathy, kindness, and curiosity toward others during the empathy phase fosters the same attitude toward ourselves. This process strengthens self-compassion, allowing us to reconnect with what really matters and articulate goals that feel authentic and energizing. Visualization also helps – mapping your inner world makes the invisible visible. It helps you see options, regain perspective, and activate more future-oriented thinking.
>
> (2) Upregulating positive affect: building momentum. Positive affect helps us stay motivated, resilient, and creative – especially when prototyping. The playful, low-risk nature of prototyping in loops supports learning through small wins. This fosters a sense of accomplishment and reinforces positive emotion. In our studies, Life Designers reported that deliberately scheduling microrewards – like going for a bike ride, cooking a favorite meal, or catching up with friends – helped them stay on track and made the process feel enjoyable and sustainable.
>
> **KEY INSIGHT: EMOTIONAL SHIFTS DRIVE ACTION**
>
> When you regulate your affect, you don't just feel better – you act differently. Whether it's creating space for self-compassion, designing your physical and emotional "crime scene," or tricking your subconscious with playful nudges, Life Design gives you tools to manage your internal state and move forward with confidence.

thinking, adjusting their approach, and designing their next step – no matter how small.

Example: A Quick Tour of the Life Loops Approach

The simplest way to explain the five phases of the Life Loops approach is through the example of a morning routine. Research shows that a consistent routine not only boosts productivity but also improves sleep quality. We've used this example with thousands of participants across workshops and seminars – and found it to be one of the most effective ways to help people grasp and apply the Life Design Loop. From spending a night without their phone to using playful prompts for getting dressed or integrating a glass of water with intention, participants discover how even small changes can spark meaningful shifts.

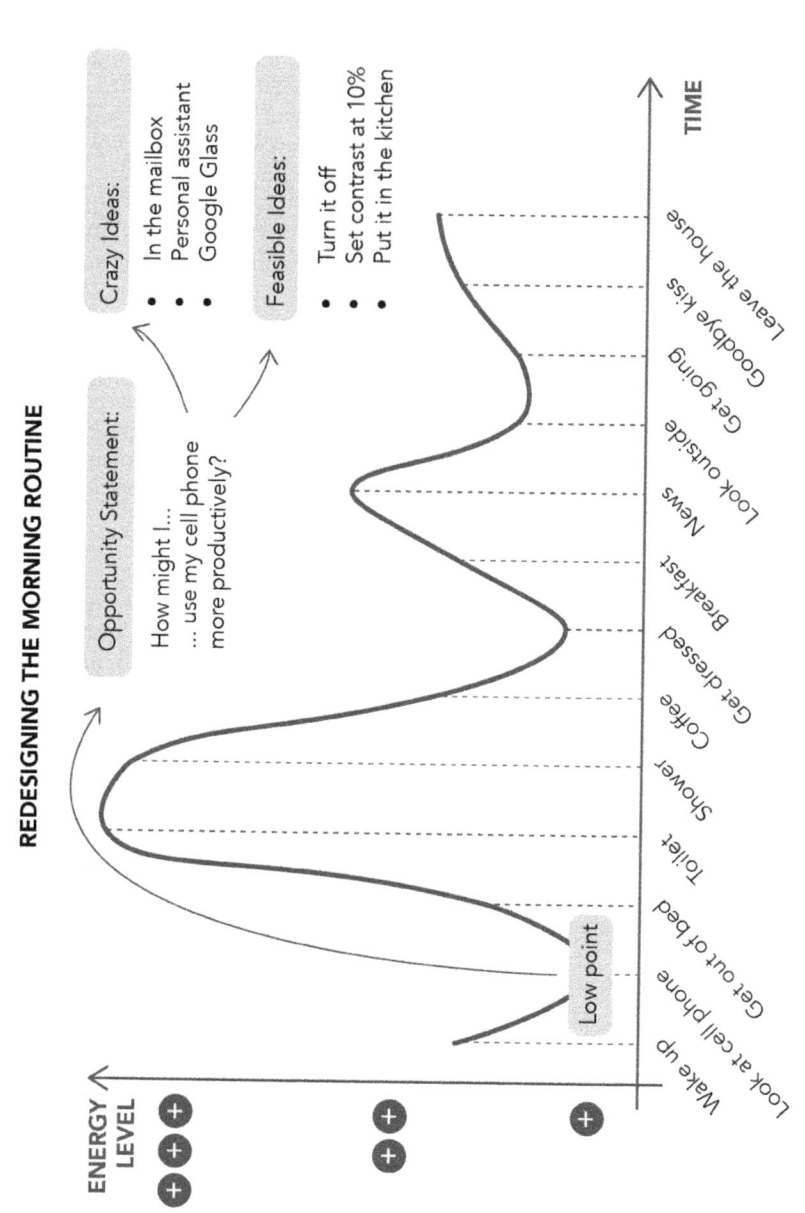

Figure 5.4 Redesigning the morning routine.

Table 5.1 *Life Design approach with morning routine example*

Example: Redesigning your morning routine with five phases of the Life Loops approach		Real-life story: Better dealing with your cell phone in the morning
(1) Empathy	Empathy has two parts: first, we open up to understand the situation more deeply; then, we focus on what we'd like to redesign. To explore our morning routine, we approach ourselves with curiosity and ask others about their mornings: "Tell me more..." We observe what happens between waking up and leaving the house, noting each moment and the energy it evokes. From this empathic lens, we identify one or two experiences we'd like to shift. For each, we craft an opportunity statement beginning with "How might I..." For instance: 'How might I better deal with my phone?" or "How might I make getting dressed more interesting and fun?"	This exercise often sparks powerful insights. One MBA student realized that her day began with checking her phone – even before getting out of bed – and that it continued to distract her throughout the morning, leaving her feeling unsettled. She framed her challenge as: "How might I better deal with my distracting phone in the morning?"
(2) Ideation	With imagination, we generate a range of ideas – some simple and practical, others bold or seemingly impossible. We then share our challenge with someone else and invite them to build on our ideas using the phrase "Yes, and..." From this exchange, we choose one easy-to-implement idea and one wild idea – with the clear intention to try at least one.	The simple idea was to charge her phone overnight in the kitchen. The wild one was to leave it in the mailbox, connected to a power bank, before entering her apartment – and retrieve it only the next morning when leaving. She chose the wild idea.

Table 5.1 (*cont.*)

Example: Redesigning your morning routine with five phases of the Life Loops approach		Real-life story: Better dealing with your cell phone in the morning
(3) Prototyping	Treat your idea as a low-risk experiment – something quick, simple, and inexpensive in terms of time, money, and emotion. Ask yourself: "How might I try this with minimal effort?" You shouldn't need anyone's permission. The smaller and easier the prototype, the more likely you are to follow through. Especially for everyday habits like your morning routine, it helps to frame it as a one-time trial – just to see what you can learn.	It may sound extreme, but the MBA student went through with it – she spent one night without her phone. She chose an evening with no urgent communication needs and plans to watch her favorite show with a friend. No permission needed, no big risks. Framing it as a one-time experiment made it easy enough to try – and she did.
(4) Learning	Approach every experiment with the goal of learning – not proving success or failure. This step is about structured reflection. Instead of a fixed mindset, adopt a growth mindset and ask: "What can I (or we) learn from this?" This opens the door to richer insights: "What worked? What was hard? What was surprising?" As MIT's Edgar Schein often asked when exploring new territory: "What else was going on?"	After the experiment, we asked her, "So, how did it go? What did you learn?" She laughed and said, "First, I realized I don't even own a clock – I always used my phone to check the time." And with that came the insight: every glance at the time pulled her into a spiral of notifications, messages, and endless scrolling. She also discovered that a night without her phone felt incredibly freeing. What began as fear of missing out (FOMO) transformed into joy of missing out (JOMO) – being fully present with herself and her friend, uninterrupted. That one experiment led her to buy an analog wristwatch, reducing her reliance on her phone. While she never repeated the mailbox trick, it sparked a shift. She now has "cell phone hours" in the evening and sets her phone aside

Table 5.1 (cont.)

Example: Redesigning your morning routine with five phases of the Life Loops approach		Real-life story: Better dealing with your cell phone in the morning
		outside those windows. She's even testing playful rules with her partner – like no phones after 9 pm or before 9 am – creating space for more learning along the way.
(5) Perseverance	This phase has two challenges: getting started and keeping momentum. When you're stuck at the start – moving from idea to action – ask whether your prototype is small enough to feel doable. Notice which inner voices (like fear of failure or perfectionism) might be holding you back, and how to gently quiet them. When you're trying to keep going – looping your learning into the next cycle – sustaining change becomes the focus. This is key to long-term transformation through Life Loops In both cases, beware of either-or thinking: "Can I do this or not?" As a Life Designer, you look deeper and ask: "What's behind this procrastination?" That's where new options begin.	At first, the idea of spending a night without her phone felt overwhelming – she nearly backed out. But framing it as a one-time experiment made it manageable. She now applies the same mindset to other areas, like exploring a healthier diet. Instead of overhauling everything, she gets curious, runs a single test, and sees what she can learn. That shift – "Just once, just to learn" – was a game-changer.

> **Box 5.3 Action Prompt**
>
> How could you redesign your morning routine? Your morning is more than just a start to the day – it's a powerful playground for change.
>
> Use your own morning routine to apply the five phases of the Life Loops approach. Approach it with curiosity, playfulness, and a willingness to learn – not to be perfect. Here's how.
>
> (1) Empathy. Observe your current morning habits with fresh eyes. What actually happens from the moment you wake up to when you head out (or start work)? What energizes you? What drains you? Ask: "How might I. . .?" (e.g., "How might I start my day without immediately checking my phone?").
>
> (2) Ideation. Brainstorm ideas – some simple, some bold. Share your "How might I. . ." question with someone and build ideas together using "Yes, and. . .". Pick one idea that feels easy and one that feels a little wild. Try at least one.
>
> (3) Prototyping. Treat your idea as a one-time experiment. Keep it low-risk, low-effort, and just for learning. Ask: "What's the easiest way I could try this once?"
>
> (4) Learning. After your experiment, reflect. Ask: "What went well? What was difficult? What was surprising?"
>
> (5) Perseverance. If you're stuck, shrink the experiment. If you're losing momentum, return to curiosity. Ask: "What's behind my hesitation – and what's one small way forward?"
>
> Remember: you only need to do it once. Focus on what you can learn from it. This mindset – "Just once, just to learn" – can be surprisingly liberating.

The following section provides an overview of the five phases of the Life Loops approach, each illustrated with a brief explanation using the morning routine as an example – along with a real-life story from an MBA student in our course to show how it works in practice.

Incidentally, the MBA student in our example told us afterwards that she would recommend the experiment of spending a night without a cell phone to everyone to see how it affects them. Let's see – maybe you want to do the exact same experiment or your own prototype. The following action prompt will guide you through the process. Do no forget, a game-changer for changing small things could be to "Do it once and focus on what you can learn from it."

The Life Loops framework shows that Life Design is not a one-time solution, but a dynamic, iterative process that helps you move forward with clarity, confidence, and compassion – one small, meaningful step at a time. By cycling through empathy, ideation, prototyping, learning, and perseverance, you build the mindset and momentum to navigate change with curiosity and creativity. In the next chapter, we'll explore how you can apply these loops at different levels – from redesigning daily routines to shaping your portfolio of activities and even bringing your biggest dreams to life.

CHAPTER 6

Life Design Levels

Life Design adapts to where you are and can be applied to different levels of your everyday life. This chapter introduces the three levels of Life Design: daily habits and routines (Level 1), portfolio activities such as jobs, side projects, or volunteering (Level 2), and aspirations or big life dreams (Level 3). You'll first find a visual overview, followed by a deep-dive into each level with practical entry points and reflection prompts. To make the levels more tangible, the chapter closes with four real-life stories showing how people have applied Life Design – either at a single level or across all three.

Overview

The beauty of Life Design is that you can apply it in small, low-risk, and immediate ways to directly impact your future, starting today, but you might also use Life Design to finally realize the big dreams that have always been waiting quietly in the background – ready to be reawakened and brought to life, one step at a time.

A Life Designer knows that immediate impact comes from the things we can control and not from the things we cannot. Therefore, we apply Life Design on different levels of application in career and life. The level of application suggests that you can apply Life Design for (1) small daily habits and practices that allow you to create changes immediately, create low-risk prototypes, and get the life loop started. Another larger level could be the (2) portfolio of activities you do in life, consisting of your job and further activities such as side hustles, hobbies, or volunteering. A third application level could be (3) aspirations and big dreams, things you always wanted to do but for which you never found the time or energy.

The typical Life Design journey starts with a redesign on Level 1 and then using the self-efficacy to continue the journey on Levels 2 and 3 and create more loops. This is the "small-to-big loop" development: a natural

LIFE DESIGN LEVELS

Figure 6.1 Applying Life Design on different levels of life.

unfolding that begins with one simple change and gradually opens space for larger shifts in direction, identity, and purpose.

However, it is important to notice that not all Life Designers follow this process. Some may also go straight into working on their portfolios or immediately using methods like the Magic Circle to follow their dreams. So, be flexible with where you wish to start and see where it takes you.

Level 1 Habits and Practices

At Level 1, we focus on redesigning what's already within reach – your habits, your energy rhythms, your mindset. You don't need a sabbatical or a career coach to begin; you need curiosity and a willingness to experiment. This level is about taking action where you have the most control: your everyday life. It's the entry point into Life Design – deceptively simple, yet deeply powerful. When we change the way we start our mornings, reflect on our day, or manage our energy, we change the way we experience ourselves and the world. Tiny shifts, repeated with intention, create momentum.

Why This Level Matters

In times of transition or uncertainty, big decisions can feel overwhelming. That's why Life Design starts small – with everyday actions that are safe to try, quick to test, and easy to learn from. These micro-experiments build your self-efficacy – the belief that you can influence your own life. As Harvard's Teresa Amabile reminds us, "small wins" are the engine of inner progress. When you succeed at something small, you're more likely to try something bigger.

Instead of getting stuck in overthinking or analysis paralysis, you move into a mindset of playful action. That's what Level 1 offers: a low-risk, high-learning way to get unstuck, re-energize, and start shaping your future today.

Why Start Here

Level 1 teaches you that you don't need permission to begin. You don't need to figure everything out. You just need to move – gently, playfully, and with curiosity. When you change your day, you change your direction. And when you change your direction, you start redesigning your life. From our experience, this level often becomes an important entry point for Life Design processes on Levels 2 and 3. While there is certainly no obligation to start a design process on Level 1, you'll profit from more self-awareness, tuning into your energy, and cultivating a bias toward action. You'll set yourself up for bigger shifts – with far less risk and far more confidence. Because the future isn't designed in one big leap. It's shaped in the small steps you take today.

Ways to Get Started

If you wish to start with a routine or practice, you can go for the morning routine or any other routine you want to redesign, for example, the evening routine or getting out of the afternoon lows. In addition, you can use the "Three Good Things" method or focus on your energy competence with the "Energy Curve" and "Energy Map."

Box 6.1 Reflection Prompt

How could a life design process starting with your habits and routines be beneficial for you? At this point, you might want to ask yourself the following questions.

- What is one part of your day that consistently drains you? How might you redesign it?
- When in your week do you feel most alive, focused, or calm? How can you protect or expand that time?
- What experiment could you run this week to test a better rhythm, habit, or routine?

Level 2 Portfolio Activities

At Level 2, we focus on mapping what already works – your strengths, your patterns, your hidden resources – and exploring new options with curiosity to extend your portfolio of activities on these drivers. You don't need to reinvent yourself to move forward; you need to look at yourself with fresh eyes and explore creatively what's possible. This level is about combining self-awareness with ideation. It helps you step back from daily routines to recognize patterns, name your unique assets, and generate opportunities beyond binary choices. Life Design at this level means thinking in portfolios – not one perfect role, but a set of meaningful activities that reflect your evolving identity.

Why This Level Matters

Many people get stuck in either-or thinking: "Should I stay or go?", "Corporate or creative?", "Stability or freedom?" Level 2 helps you move beyond these false dilemmas. By focusing on your signature strengths and generating a broad set of options, you learn to see that your life doesn't need to be defined by a single job or linear path. Here, you begin to design a portfolio of meaningful roles and projects that balance income, meaning, joy, and growth. This perspective lowers the pressure on any one decision and creates space for exploration, learning, and playful ambition. Life Designers at Level 2 stop asking, "What should I do?" and start asking, "What else is possible?"

Why Start Here

Level 2 teaches you that you are already more resourceful and multidimensional than you think. Your strengths are not just what you're good at – they're what energize you. And opportunities are not only found – they can be designed. You don't have to leave your job to try something new. You can start with a side project, a volunteer gig, a conversation, or a thirty-day experiment.

Ways to Get Started

To begin, try mapping your "Strengths Portfolio" across personal and professional domains. You can take a Values in Action character strengths test to identify your signature strengths – and redesign your activities to activate them more often. Or try "Opportunity Bingo" to creatively expand your option space and spark new directions.

> **Box 6.2 Reflection Prompt**
>
> How could a life design process starting with your portfolio activities be beneficial for you? At this point, you might want to ask yourself the following questions.
>
> - What strengths do others consistently see in you? Where do you feel most energized and at your best?
> - What opportunities have you overlooked because they didn't fit the "official plan"?
> - What small experiment could combine something you're good at with something you've always wanted to try?

Level 3 Aspiration and Big Dreams

At Level 3, we focus on turning long-held dreams into prototypes. This is where you stop postponing what matters and start putting your big ideas into motion – not through leaps of faith, but through joyful, structured steps. This level is about exploring your deeper aspirations – the things you rarely say out loud, the ideas that make your heart beat faster. It invites you to dream boldly but act lightly. Using the tools of Life Design, you break down the seemingly impossible into doable experiments that feel safe, fun, and meaningful.

Why This Level Matters

Most of us carry dormant dreams – to write a book, start something of our own, make a bold career shift, or move toward a different way of living. These dreams often feel too big or too late. But what if they're not? What if the real problem isn't the size of the dream, but the lack of a stairway to get there? Level 3 helps you design that stairway. It offers methods to clarify what your dream is really about, and then create a path that brings it to life – one step at a time. Even if you never fully "arrive," the journey changes you. It reintroduces agency, energy, and meaning.

Why Start Here

Level 3 teaches you that your boldest visions are not unrealistic – they are undertested. You don't need to risk everything to explore a big idea. You just need to prototype the essence of it – a weekend version, a symbolic act, a small pilot. And in doing so, you'll often discover that your dream is more

> **Box 6.3 Reflection Prompt**
>
> How could a life design process starting with your aspirations and big dreams be beneficial for you? At this point, you might want to ask yourself the following questions.
>
> - What's a dream you've been carrying for years – and what might be behind it?
> - If you could test one part of that dream in the next month, what would it look like?
> - What would be your very first step if you weren't trying to get it perfect?

flexible, and more accessible, than you thought. Because your dream isn't waiting for the perfect moment. It's waiting for your first playful step.

Ways to Get Started

Use the "Magic Circle" method to surface a bold dream by combining your values, energy sources, and longings. Then use the "Stairway to Heaven" to break that dream into tangible microsteps. Start with the smallest joyful prototype that captures the essence of what you want – without risk or pressure.

Example: Stories of Life Design at Different Levels

Life Design can be applied at different levels of life – from your daily routines to your work portfolio to your boldest dreams. While some people start small and stay there for now, others use the method to build toward something much bigger. There's no wrong place to begin.

The four stories that follow show what Life Design looks like in real life. The first three focus on people who applied it at just one level – redesigning an everyday habit (Level 1, Amir), exploring new roles (Level 2, Monica), or prototyping a long-held dream (Level 3, Jonas). The fourth story illustrates how powerful a Life Design journey can become when it evolves across all three levels – from small tweaks to a fully reimagined life direction (Levels 1–3, Elena). You'll meet:

- Amir, who shifted his energy and mindset by redesigning how he ends his day;
- Monica, who turned her stable job into a richer portfolio of meaningful activities;

FROM
coffee routines

↓

TO
calling dreams

- Jonas, who brought a long-held creative dream to life one gentle step at a time; and
- Elena, who began with one small change and gradually reimagined her whole path – from routine to dream.

Together, these stories show that transformation doesn't have to start big – it just has to start. Whether you redesign your day or reawaken your vision, Life Design can meet you where you are.

Story 1 Redesigning the End of the Day

Amir, a twenty-eight-year-old junior architect, often found himself wide awake at midnight, mindlessly scrolling through his phone or jumping between tabs on his laptop. His evenings bled into the nights, and he'd fall asleep wired and restless, waking up groggy and behind. He knew he needed more rest, but the real issue wasn't sleep – it was the lack of a rhythm to wind down. Instead of trying to fix everything at once, Amir applied Life Design to his evenings. He began by noticing what happened between dinner and bedtime. He kept a short log for a week and identified a pattern: unstructured digital drift from 9:30 pm onward. That time wasn't relaxing – it was numbing.

So he ran a small experiment. One night, he set a gentle "evening bell" at 9:15 pm – a signal to unplug. He swapped screens for a short walk and a shower, followed by light journaling with the "Three Good Things" exercise. He didn't aim to be perfect – just curious. Over time, this became a ritual. He also used the "Energy-Tension Matrix" and saw that his late-night habits were high in tension and low in true energy. So, he added low-tension, high-energy elements to his wind-down: quiet music, sketching ideas in a notebook, and reading for pleasure.

After two weeks, the effects showed up not only in how he slept, but in how he felt the next morning: more rested, more alert, and – most importantly – more in control of his time. Evenings, once a messy endnote, became a source of calm. Amir hasn't changed jobs or goals. But by redesigning how his day ends, he has unlocked a better version of how it begins. Level 1 gave him back his evenings – and with them, his energy.

Story 2 From Role to Portfolio

Monica, a forty-one-year-old finance team leader, was good at her job. She had a stable role at a mid-sized company and managed a competent team.

But she felt boxed in. "Is this really it?" she often wondered during her lunch breaks. The job paid well, but the days felt flat. She wasn't burnt out – just underinspired.

Rather than seek dramatic change, Monica began mapping her "Strengths Portfolio." She reflected on where she felt energized – and where she didn't. She realized her signature strengths lay in mentoring, simplifying complexity, and hosting engaging workshops. With this insight, Monica began assembling a portfolio of activities that extended beyond her core job. She offered to mentor junior colleagues from other departments. She started facilitating internal lunch-and-learns. She even tested an idea to co-host a budgeting workshop for freelancers on the side.

Monica isn't planning to leave her job. But she's redesigning the composition of her work life. She's no longer stuck in the question, "Should I stay or should I go?" Now she asks, "What else can I add?" Level 2 helped her shift from role identity to role plurality – without any high-stakes leap.

Story 3 Dream in Progress

Jonas, a fifty-six-year-old head of logistics, had spent thirty years climbing the ranks of the same logistics company. He had security, a pension on the horizon, and a reputation for getting things done. But beneath the surface, something stirred. For years, he'd harbored a quiet dream: to write and illustrate a graphic novel about his childhood growing up in East Germany. It wasn't something he spoke about. It felt personal, almost sacred – and wildly unrelated to his career. But after attending a Life Design workshop hosted by a friend, he was struck by the invitation to surface long-held dreams.

He used the "Magic Circle" method to connect the dots: his love for storytelling, his sketchbooks from the 1980s, his values around memory, resistance, and humor. With the "Stairway to Heaven," he mapped a gentle path forward: digitize his old drawings, sign up for a local comic workshop, and schedule one artist date a week – just for himself.

Jonas hasn't shared this project at work. He's not starting a business. He's not retiring early. But something has shifted. He's in motion. And that motion is meaningful. Level 3 reminded him: the dream matters, even if no one else sees it – yet.

Story 4 From Small to Big Loop

Elena, thirty-five years old, was doing everything right – she was a respected marketing manager in a stable company, with good performance reviews and a steady rhythm of life. But beneath the surface, she felt stuck: stretched thin during the day, low on energy, and unsure how (or whether) to reconnect with what really mattered to her.

Level 1 Habits and Practices
She was especially used to dreading Monday mornings. She'd hit snooze three times, scroll through emails in bed, and arrive at work already depleted. The rest of her week followed suit: reactive, rushed, and quietly frustrating. Her energy dipped mid-afternoon, and she noticed a growing disconnect between her professional success and personal fulfilment.

One Friday evening, after venting to a friend over drinks, that friend suggested something different – not quitting her job, but redesigning her mornings. Skeptical but curious, Elena decided to try it. The next Monday, instead of checking her phone, she began with a ten-minute walk and a cup of coffee outside. On Tuesday, she added a short journal prompt: "What would make today meaningful?" By Friday, something had shifted – not the world, but her mindset.

Inspired, she tracked her energy curve and realized she had her clearest focus between 9 and 11 am. So, she blocked that time for meaningful work. Emails and meetings were moved to afternoons. Small wins added up: she had more clarity, a better mood, and the sense that she was back in charge of her days. Level 1 gave her traction. And with traction came courage.

Level 2 Portfolio Activities
With more energy in her day, Elena began to reflect on a deeper unease: while she was good at her job, it didn't fully engage her. In a Life Design session, she mapped her "Strengths Portfolio" and saw clear patterns. She lit up when brainstorming, mentoring junior colleagues, and telling stories – not when managing spreadsheets or pushing performance decks.

She ran the Ideation method "Opportunity Bingo" and surprised herself: one square read "teach a storytelling class," another "launch a podcast," and another "mentor students." These weren't new dreams – they were buried ones.

Instead of quitting her job, she prototyped around the edges. She volunteered to mentor interns at her company. She offered a free storytelling workshop at a local coworking space. Then, she co-created a podcast pilot with a friend. Each step made her feel more alive. Elena had unknowingly begun designing a portfolio of meaningful work – one that blended structure and creativity, stability and experimentation.

Level 3 Aspirations and Big Dreams
While reflecting with her Life Design team, Elena used the "Magic Circle" method. What truly energized her was not just content creation – it was helping people tell their own stories. A long-dormant dream resurfaced: launching a retreat centre for women in transition, where story, reflection, and design thinking could come together. Ten years ago, this would have felt like a midlife crisis, a fantasy. Now, it felt like a question of *how*, not *if*.

Using the prototyping method "Stairway to Heaven," she mapped the first tiny steps: interviewing three people who ran similar initiatives, co-hosting a weekend retreat with a coach friend, sketching a simple landing page. She didn't quit her job. But she started spending Fridays on this vision, using her vacation days to test ideas. The goal wasn't to build the retreat center tomorrow. It was to put the dream in motion. To test it joyfully, without pressure. And in doing so, she discovered what it was truly about: creating space for others – and for herself – to feel seen, heard, and redesigned.

What Changed?
Elena didn't blow up her life. She didn't have to. She began with one morning. Then followed the energy. Then built a bridge from what *was* to what *could be*. Through Level 1, she reclaimed her rhythm. Through Level 2, she reimagined her roles. Through Level 3, she reactivated her dream. That's the beauty of Life Design: it meets you where you are – and moves with you as you grow.

PART III

Life Design Toolbox

You've explored the five core phases of Life Design: empathy, ideation, prototyping, learning, and perseverance. Now it's time to move from understanding the process to applying it – step by step. In this section, we offer practical methods to help you bring each phase to life. In short: this section is your toolbox. Turn to it when you're ready to act, reflect, shift perspective – or start again. First, you'll find a dedicated chapter for each phase featuring three methods:

- one key method that captures the essence of the phase and is especially helpful for getting started, since it begins by designing a small aspect of life. If you follow each key method, it will take you once through the entire Life Loop (known as the "Core Toolbox");
- two additional methods that offer deeper or alternative ways to work with the same phase, with a potential focus on careers, your portfolio or big life dreams, depending on your context, energy, or personal preference. (known as the "Extended Toolbox").

You don't need to use all the methods – pick what fits. Some readers choose to focus on the key method for each phase; others mix and match based on their current challenge. Overall, we have picked only methods that are effective, with a proven effect, and that have become quite popular with the people and organizations, at all ages and stages, with whom we work. For example, the Strengths Portfolio is very popular among MBA students, the Magic Circle and Stairway to Heaven have become favorites among Stanford DCI fellows, and the Core of Creativity has become part of company manifestos and symbolic anchors within teams and departments.

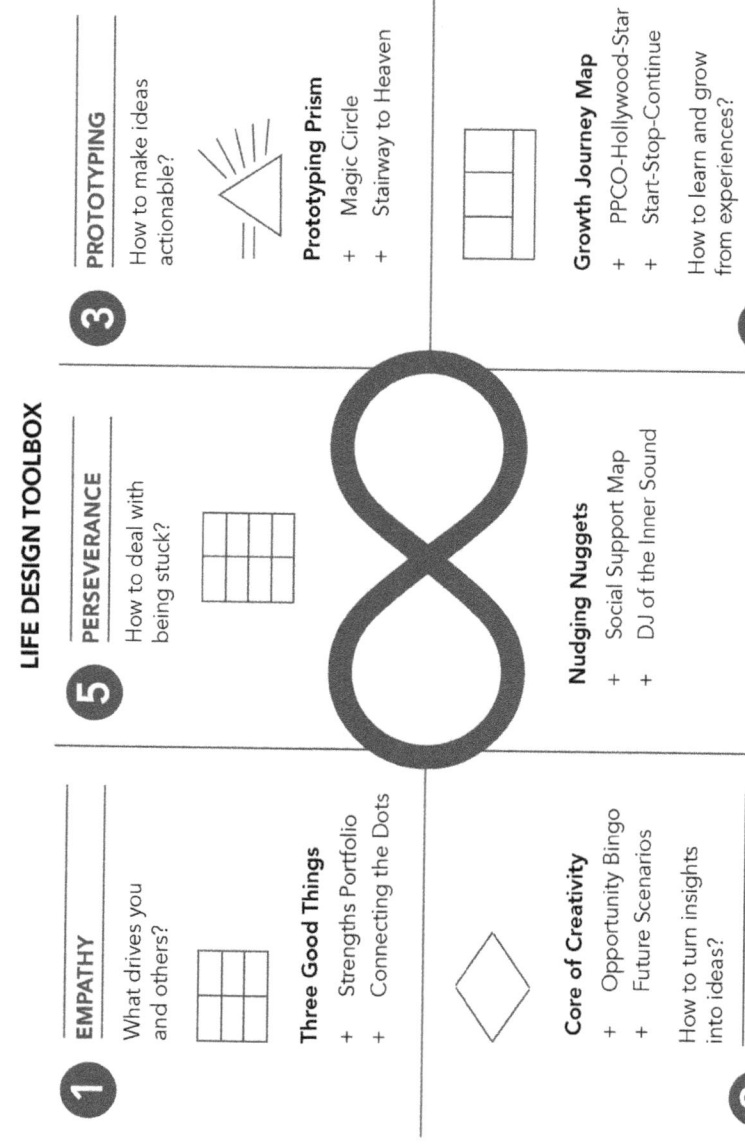

Figure P.1 Methods per phase (Core and Extended Toolboxes).

CHAPTER 7

Methods

Empathy is often where the Life Design journey begins. Before making any big decisions or plans, it's essential to understand what truly matters to you – how you feel, what energizes you, and what gives your life meaning. Empathy in this context means paying close attention to your own experiences and emotions as valid sources of insight. It's the foundation for designing a future that feels aligned, not just strategic. This chapter introduces three methods that help you cultivate awareness, self-understanding, and personal insight.

We start with the Core Method.

- Three Good Things is a simple but powerful daily practice that builds emotional clarity and helps you notice what truly matters to you. Eventually, it allows you to define your own opportunity statement ("How might I...").

From there, you may choose to go further with two Optional Methods.

- The Strengths Portfolio supports you in identifying and applying your personal strengths, drawing from research in positive psychology.
- Connecting the Dots guides you in reflecting on meaningful life experiences and uncovering the patterns that can inform your next steps.

Whether you choose to focus on the Core Method alone or explore the Optional Methods too, this chapter is designed to help you start the Life Design process with deeper self-empathy and insight.

Three Good Things

This method is one of the best-known interventions in positive psychology. Its positive effects – significantly increasing well-being and reducing depressive symptoms – have been scientifically proven multiple times.

THREE GOOD THINGS

	TITLE / HEADLINE	SMILING STRANGER, CONTAGIOUS SMILE, FEELING CONNECTED WITH THE WORLD
①	What happened?	Walk along the street, bus passes by, stranger smiles at me, I had to smile too :)
②	How did it make you feel?	Weird at first, but then great, kind of warm and nice
③	Why did it make you feel this way?	I felt connected with this guy, and also with the world somehow

Figure 7.1 Three Good Things.

The idea is simple: each evening, take a few minutes to write down three things that went well during your day. In the spirit of the Stoic philosopher Seneca, the goal is not to live a long life, but a wide and deliberate one. This method helps you become more aware of the good things already happening around you – many of which you might otherwise miss.

Among all positive psychology interventions, this one offers the best return on investment (ROI). If you take ten minutes a day for just seven days, you'll experience six months of increased well-being and reduced depressive symptoms – an effect that has been confirmed in several studies. Looking back, it's striking that after just one week, you'll have documented twenty-one positive experiences, and after two months, around sixty. This practice helps you live more consciously, slow down, and notice the good – especially valuable during challenging times. The following steps will guide you through writing down your Three Good Things.

Procedure and Steps

At the end of each day, take about ten minutes to write down three things that went well that day, for example, exchanging a quick smile with a stranger on the bus, a message you received, a flower you saw, or meeting your team for a beer after work. Follow these steps so you can enjoy greater well-being.

(1) What happened?
   Describe each event in detail. What did you see, hear, feel, smell, or taste? Try to engage your senses. For example, "I was walking along the sidewalk, a bus passed by, and a stranger smiled at me. I smiled back – it felt unexpectedly nice."

(2) How did it make you feel?
   Identify the emotions you experienced. For example, "It made me feel warm and happy – like a quiet connection with someone I didn't even know."

(3) Why did it make you feel this way?
   Reflect on what made the moment meaningful to you. For example: "The smile was contagious. It reminded me that the world can be kind and connected, even in small moments."

(4) Add a title.
   Give each moment a short, memorable headline – something that helps you recall it at a glance. For example: "Stranger on the Bus: Contagious Smile, Feeling Connected."

(5) Repeat for two more things.
   They don't have to be big. A cold drink, fresh air through a window, a favorite song – small moments count.

(6) After seven days, reflect.
   Review your twenty-one entries. Notice how many good things you've experienced. Let the memory of these moments sink in – you might even catch yourself smiling. Share a few with someone else, if you like. And don't forget to ask them: "Tell me more."

(7) Look for patterns (optional).
   Review your list to spot recurring themes. Do many good moments involve nature, people, or quiet time? These patterns can inform your Life Design process by highlighting what energizes and fulfills you – and they may become the starting point for your next prototype.

Tips and Tricks

- Try the Three Good Things exercise at least once.
  Ten minutes may feel like a lot – or like nothing. Just try it one evening. Then take it one day at a time. A full seven-day period offers the full benefit, but even one entry can shift your perspective.
- Focus on the small stuff.
  It's tempting to look for big events, but the real magic often lies in everyday moments. A kind word, a quiet moment, a deep breath – these are worth noticing.
- Create a "Shower of Good Things."
  Write the titles of your positive moments on slips of paper and collect them in a jar. On tough days, pick one out to lift your spirits – or pour them all out and let the good memories rain down on you.

From Insights to Opportunity: Creating Your Opportunity Statement

After completing the Three Good Things exercise and gaining a deeper understanding of what energizes and matters to you, it's important to focus your insights. The second part of empathy helps you avoid getting overwhelmed by details and instead define what lies at the heart of your emerging vision or challenge – by formulating an opportunity statement.

Good opportunity statements often begin with "How might I..." or "How might we..." and are formulated in a positive and open way, where you wish to find an answer. This approach helps you discover what you truly want – and opens up a wide range of potential solutions. Expect your first version to be a draft, not the final product. Learning and iterating are part of the process.

Procedure and Steps

The following step-by-step process will support you in becoming skilled at opportunity statement formulation, especially useful when faced with too many insights or ideas. It will help you overcome the paradox of choice by giving you a clear, attractive, and actionable focus.

(1) Capture your most interesting empathy-based insights.
  Start by writing down the most important insights you've gained – particularly those that spark curiosity, energy, or a sense of "I want more of this!"

7 Methods

Every day is filled with many experiences.

Capturing three good things of the day.

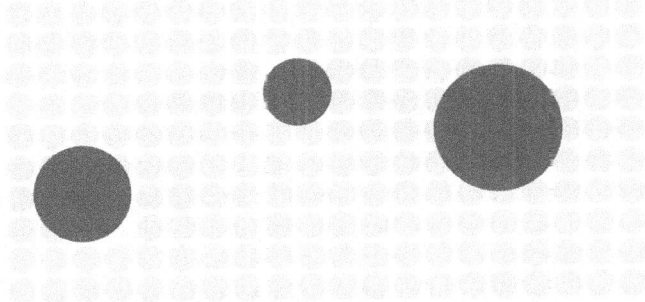

Increases your well-being and reduces depressive symptoms.

From the Three Good Things exercise this might include experiences related to social connections, appreciating beauty, or enjoying time alone.

If you end up with a focus on negative things, for example, making your morning less stressful, reframe it to something positive, for example, making your morning enjoyable or relaxing.

Think about where your patterns lie and what themes you notice emerging.

(2) Draft initial opportunity statements.

Write down two or three rough opportunity statements, starting with "How might I..." (for individuals) or "How might we..." (for teams). For example, "How might I create more meaningful social connections in my daily life?"; "How might I carve out more quality time for myself?"; "How might I bring more beauty and inspiration into my everyday environment?"

At this stage, don't worry about perfection – the goal is simply to get started.

(3) Refine: make it positive, open, and attractive.

Review your statements. Are they phrased positively? Are they open enough to invite a range of creative ideas? Are they attractive to you – would you be excited to explore solutions?

For example, instead of "How might I be less lonely?", try, "How might I create more meaningful connections?" Instead of "How might I have more time on Tuesday at 8 pm?", try, "How might I create more space for myself in ways I enjoy?" Instead of "How might I have more beauty in my life?", try, "How might I bring beauty into my life to feel more alive?"

(4) Advance your statement with "despite" (optional).

Adding "despite" can acknowledge real-life constraints while keeping your statement empowering. For example, "How might I bring more beauty into my life despite my busy schedule?"; "How might I enjoy peaceful mornings despite the chaos of family life?"

This is optional but can make your opportunity statement even more grounded and realistic.

5 Select a statement to work with.

Choose the statement that feels most energizing and relevant to you right now. This will be your working focus for the next phase: ideation. And remember: your statement is not set in stone. It can – and often will – evolve as you move through the design process.

For example, a manager at the International Red Cross started with, "How might I do more sports in the morning?" but, through the ideation phase, realized that fun was the missing ingredient. Her evolved statement became: "How might I do more sports in the morning – and make it fun?" Iteration is not a failure – it's a natural and healthy part of Life Design.

Tips and Tricks

- Do it once – and iterate. Allow yourself to draft multiple versions. You might discover that your first insights weren't the most decisive ones – and that's okay. Flexibility is key.
- Discuss with others. Saying your opportunity statement out loud or discussing it with someone else often helps sharpen it. Feedback can reveal whether it truly gets to the heart of what matters.
- Choose excitement and inspiration. Move forward only with an opportunity statement that genuinely excites you and sparks ideas. Life Design is all about energy – follow what feels alive.

The Strengths Portfolio

The Strengths Portfolio exercise brings together two powerful elements: who you are (your strengths) and what you do (your activities). It helps you connect your personal drivers – like your values, motivations, and especially your signature strengths – with the everyday activities and relationships that shape your life and work.

The process begins with identifying your character strengths, which you'll then narrow down to your three to seven signature strengths – the ones you use naturally and joyfully, even when you're tired. These are the qualities that energize you, spark learning, and can transform your career and life from "just fine" to deeply fulfilling.

Research in positive psychology shows that using four or more of your signature strengths regularly can transform how you experience your career – shifting it from "just a job" toward a true calling. This work is grounded in science, and the VIA Institute on Character is

Table 7.1 *Classification of twenty-four character strengths and virtues*

Virtues	Strength type	Character strengths
Wisdom	Cognitive strength	Creativity, curiosity, judgment, love of learning, perspective
Courage	Emotional strength	Bravery, perseverance, honesty, zest/enthusiasm
Humanity	Interpersonal strength	Love, kindness, social intelligence
Justice	Leadership strength	Teamwork, fairness, leadership
Temperance	Mental strength	Forgiveness, humility, prudence, self-regulation
Transcendence	Spiritual strength	Gratitude, hope, humor, spirituality, appreciation of beauty and excellence

a trusted source. You can take the free VIA Character Strengths Survey in about ten minutes at www.viacharacter.org. If you're short on time or energy, you can also get a quick overview of the full list of twenty-four character strengths at www.viacharacter.org/character-strengths.

Once you've identified your signature strengths (see instructions below), the portfolio approach helps you map them onto your current life – your projects, responsibilities, relationships, and routines. Traditionally used in finance or career strategy, the portfolio concept here takes on a broader meaning. The word "portfolio" is often associated with finance a portfolio of stocks, investments, or assets. But the concept has long been used beyond that context. Management thinker Charles Handy popularized the idea of the "portfolio life," and today, with careers becoming more fluid and nonlinear, the term "portfolio career" is gaining traction. Here, the portfolio approach invites you to map your personal "assets" – your strengths, values, and motivations – against your current life and work. What are you already doing that aligns with your drivers? Where might there be untapped potential?

By making these patterns visible, the Strengths Portfolio supports you in shaping a more intentional future – one that plays to your strengths and feels both meaningful and motivating. Let's begin by discovering your signature strengths and then use the portfolio approach to put them to work in your life.

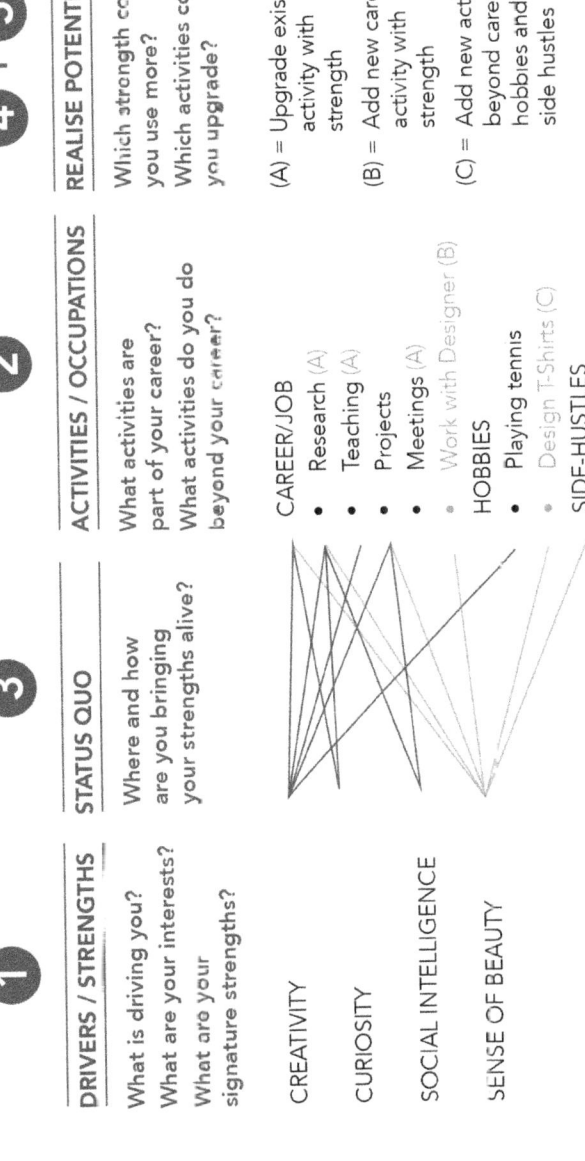

Figure 7.2 The Strengths Portfolio.

Procedure and Steps

The Strengths Portfolio is a powerful and versatile tool that is built in two parts.

- Part I: signature strengths. Identify your core personal "superpowers" using research-based methods from positive psychology.
- Part II: life portfolio. Map these strengths to your professional and personal activities to see what's already working, where you might want change, and how to prototype meaningful new directions.

Part I: Signature Strengths

(1) Take the test.
   Visit the multilingual website of the Via Institute on Character (www.viacharacter.org) and take the free Character Strengths Survey. It takes just ten to twelve minutes and provides a personalized ranking of your twenty-four character strengths. Alternatively, you can have a look at the descriptions of the twenty-four character strengths at www.viacharacter.org/character-strengths and go straight to Step (3).

(2) View your strengths ranking.
   After completing the test, download your personal ranking as a PDF. The order gives you an initial sense of how strongly each strength shows up for you. But don't overinterpret the results. If a strength you value deeply appears in seventh or even ninth place, that's still meaningful. In positive psychology, we don't speak in terms of strengths versus weaknesses – only more natural and less natural strengths.

(3) Identify your signature strengths.
   Now, from the list of twenty-four, identify your signature strengths – usually three to seven in total. These are the strengths that feel most "you." Use these five criteria to guide your selection: you're intrinsically motivated to use them; you have a strong learning curve when using them; they energize you more than they drain you; they feel authentic ("This is who I am"); you use them so naturally that you almost can't help it.
   A helpful test is to imagine yourself in a difficult situation. If you still find yourself expressing the strength – like brainstorming ideas even with a fever (creativity) or admiring artwork after a long day (appreciation of beauty) – you've likely found a signature strength.

Go through your list, read the brief descriptions, and choose the strengths that resonate most intuitively. Don't overthink it – signature strengths usually come top-of-mind. If you have to debate for too long, it's probably not one. Imagine your photo on a wall – what strengths would belong next to your name? Write them down on a separate sheet. These are your personal superpowers.

(4) Activate and expand your use of signature strengths.

Knowing your signature strengths is a treasure. You can now integrate them across many Life Design methods, for example, add them to your morning routine to start your day with energy, link them with insights from Three Good Things to discover deeper patterns, or use them as a springboard in ideation methods like Opportunity Bingo.

The following two-step mini-exercise will help you activate and expand your use of signature strengths and prepare you for the portfolio approach.

- Watering the plant.
  Where and how are you already using these strengths? Choose one or two of your signature strengths and write down how you're already using them in work and life. You can reflect privately or exchange ideas with a partner or Life Design team. The more you notice and "water" your strengths, the more they grow. This is in line with the famous saying: "The grass is always greener... where you water it!"
- Signature strength in a new way.
  Where could you use them more – or for the first time? Choose one signature strength and brainstorm new ways to use it – personally and professionally. To frame your exploration, create an opportunity statement like: "How might I bring more creativity into my career?" or "How might I express kindness in my leadership style?" Trying a strength in a fresh context often leads to surprising insights and renewed energy.

Part II: Life Portfolio

(1) Drivers. What drives you?

On the left side of your portfolio, list what drives you – your needs, values, and especially your signature strengths. Start with two or three and gradually add more (seven are usually enough). In our example, we'll use four signature strengths (creativity, curiosity, social intelligence, and appreciation of beauty), but keep in mind that even focusing on one strength can be a powerful starting point.

(2) Activities. What are you doing?

On the right side, list your current activities. These can include your job (with main tasks or responsibilities); hobbies and leisure activities; and side hustles or personal projects – even ideas you're not yet working on. In our example, the portfolio includes "Job: science manager (research, teaching, project management, meetings)"; "Hobby: playing tennis"; "Side hustle: not yet defined." You can start with five to seven core activities per area and go deeper later if needed.

(3) Analyze the status quo. How are you already using your strengths?

Now connect the left side (drivers) with the right side (activities) by drawing lines between strengths and the activities where you currently use them. You can go left-to-right or right-to-left – whichever feels more natural. You'll quickly start to see patterns.

On the left: which strengths are you already using frequently?

On the right: which activities tap into multiple strengths?

In our example, creativity and curiosity show strong overlap with several activities, and teaching connects with three strengths – explaining why it feels fulfilling. This part often leads to "aha!" moments. People who initially say, "My job is terrible," may realize that it's not the entire job, but specific parts that lack alignment – while other parts are surprisingly energizing.

(4) Realize your strengths potential. How could you use your strengths more?

Now look at strengths with few or no connections. These reveal untapped potential. In our example, social intelligence is underused, and appreciation of beauty isn't used at all. Use opportunity statements like, "How might I bring more appreciation of beauty into my work or life?" You can explore three levels.

Enrich existing activities. Can you add this strength to something you already do? For example, redesign your meeting slides to be more visually appealing.

Add a new activity. Create a new work-related task or project. For example, collaborate with a designer to make reports more engaging.

Go beyond your job. Use the strength in hobbies or side hustles. For example, design t-shirts or start a local creative project.

One factory worker discovered his unused social intelligence and created a peer-led training session – something he never imagined doing in his assembly line role.

(5) Realize your activity potential. How can you upgrade existing activities?
Now look at activities where you're not using many strengths. Ask yourself, "How might I energize this activity using my strengths?" For example, to make meetings more engaging, add curiosity by experimenting with new formats or running your own meeting stats; add creativity through warm-ups like, "What would Federer do?" or quirky icebreakers; add social intelligence with formats like brainwriting, where each person first writes down ideas individually, then shares them in a group discussion.[1]

(6) Use the Portfolio in Different Ways (Optional).
The Portfolio is a flexible tool that can be expanded and adapted for a variety of life and career decisions. Here are three powerful ways to take it further.

> Compare career options. Use the portfolio to evaluate different job opportunities. On the left side, list your strengths, values, and key needs. On the right side, map out the main activities of two or more job options you're considering. Now, draw connections between the two sides to assess how well each job aligns with your drivers. This approach helps you compare roles based on more than just job titles or salaries – it shows you which job allows you to express your strengths and meet your deeper needs.
>
> Add a well-being layer. You can integrate a third column to represent well-being, using the PERMA framework from positive psychology: P for "positive emotions," E for "engagement," R for "relationships," M for "meaning," and A for "accomplishment." For each activity on the right side, indicate which aspect(s) of PERMA it supports. This gives you a holistic view of how your activities contribute to your overall well-being – not just your productivity.
>
> Map your needs. Another way to expand the portfolio is to add a third pillar using Maslow's "hierarchy of needs": physiological, safety, belonging, esteem, and self-actualization. This can help you understand which activities fulfill which needs. For

---

[1] Need more ideas? Check out our award-winning book *Meet Up! Better Meetings through Nudging* at www.meetup-book.com.

example, some activities may secure income and stability (physiological and safety). Others may fulfill purpose, mastery, or creative expression (esteem and self-actualization). This insight can be liberating. It may lead you to balance one job that "pays the bills" with another role or side hustle that feeds your growth and purpose – without pressure to monetize it immediately. This is how many sidepreneurs begin: testing ideas in a low-risk environment before deciding whether to scale or keep them as a meaningful complement to their main work.

Tips and Tricks

- Start small. Avoid overwhelming yourself at the beginning. Start with two or three signature strengths, five to seven core job activities, one or two hobbies or personal interests. Once you're in the flow, you can add complexity where it feels meaningful – by expanding job-related tasks, adding more strengths, or exploring life beyond work through hobbies, volunteering, or side hustles.
- Make it visual – without aiming for perfection. Some people hesitate to create visuals that feel messy or unfinished. But your portfolio doesn't need to be "clean" or "beautiful." Think of it as a sketch-in-progress. Rough visuals often invite more reflection, more engagement, and better conversations – both with yourself and with others.
- Use it as a conversation starter. Start your portfolio on your own, but don't keep it to yourself. Sharing your visual with a colleague, coach, or friend helps you articulate your thoughts more clearly. It invites others to understand you better – and often leads to new insights, encouragement, or helpful ideas just by pointing to something on the page.

Connecting the Dots

Sometimes the best way to move forward is to look back. Connecting the Dots is a reflective method that helps you uncover direction, patterns, and purpose from meaningful past experiences. Inspired by Steve Jobs' famous Stanford commencement speech – "You can't connect the dots looking forward; you can only connect them looking backward" – and Søren Kierkegaard's insight that "life can only be understood backwards," this tool invites you to explore your personal timeline – not for nostalgia, but for guidance.

Rather than focusing on achievements or milestones, you'll zoom in on moments when you felt truly alive – times when you were energized, authentic, and at your best. These memories are more than highlights; they are signals. When examined with care, they reveal your core values, strengths, and sources of joy – all of which can help shape more aligned choices in the present and future.

This method has become a favorite in Life Design workshops, coaching, and leadership training because it combines the power of storytelling with the structure of positive psychology. It also includes a technique called Me at My Best, which allows others to help reflect your strengths back to you in a supportive, deeply empathetic way.

In the next steps, you'll become a time traveller – mapping, sharing, and making sense of key life experiences. With the help of your Life Design team, you'll connect past energy to future possibilities. Let's begin.

Procedure and Steps

This method unfolds in two parts: first on your own, then with others. You'll begin by mapping meaningful moments from your past – times when you felt truly alive, authentic, and energized. Once you've captured these stories, you'll share one with your Life Design team. It works best in groups of three or four people, creating a safe, focused space to surface meaningful insights and build emotional connection. They'll help reflect your strengths and values back to you using a structured, empathetic process. The following steps will guide you through this journey, from solo reflection to shared insight.

(1) Prepare your space.
   Draw a simple visual timeline: let the X-axis represent your energy level – from slightly positive to highly energized; the Y-axis represents time, with you standing at the bottom right, looking back.
(2) Map your "Me at my Best" stories.
   Recall between one and five moments when you truly felt at your best – full of energy, deeply yourself, and joyful just thinking about it. We're focusing here on positive moments – times you felt energized, authentic, and truly alive. (You could also include challenging moments for resilience insights, but for this method, we stay in the positive space.) These experiences can come from any point in your life – last week, last year, a decade ago, or even your childhood. Map them on the visual timeline.

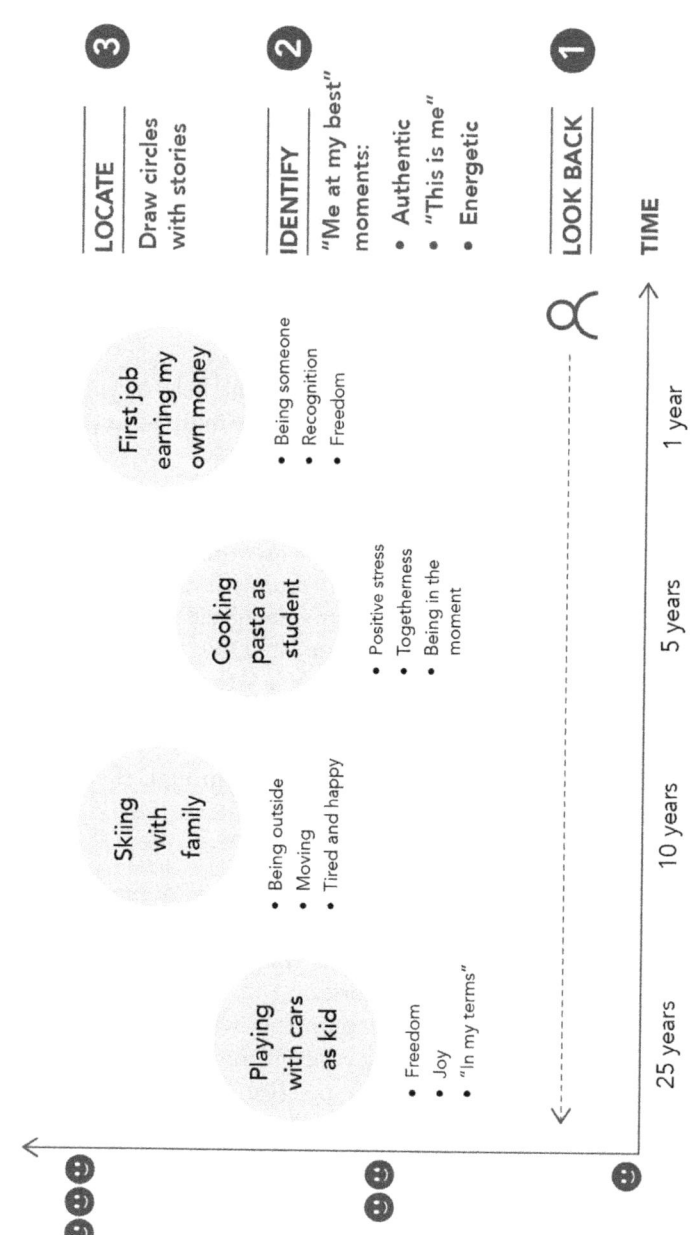

Figure 7.3 Connecting the Dots.

Draw a circle for each moment on your timeline.
Give each story a title or use keywords to describe it.
Optionally, add one or two short sentences below to describe what made that moment so special.

These don't have to be grand achievements – they're about aliveness, not success.

(3) Share a story and bring your team into the moment.
Share one of your stories with your Life Design team. Take about seven minutes, and focus on bringing the moment to life.
Use sensory detail. What did you see, hear, feel, or even smell?
Speak in the first person, not as an outside observer. For example, "It was a student event – I was cooking pasta, the room was hot, I was sweaty, people were shouting for food, the line was long... and I loved it. I felt alive, connected, part of something." Don't worry about structure – just let the memory unfold naturally.

(4) Your team members become strengths detectives.
While you speak, your partners act as strengths detectives. Their job is to listen attentively, take notes using a visual template (tracking your interests, skills, values, and other clues), and ask only empathetic questions, such as: "Tell me more about that moment...", "What was it that energized you most?", and "Why was that meaningful for you?"
Your team members should not offer interpretations or advice – only presence and curiosity. This process is grounded in the positive

OBSERVATION SHEET

INTERESTS	SKILLS
VALUES	WHAT ELSE?

Figure 7.4 Observation sheet for Connecting the Dots.

psychology method Me at My Best, which helps uncover often-unspoken inner truths through storytelling.

(5) Receive feedback.

After your story, your strengths detectives share what they heard – highlighting recurring themes, strengths, and insights they picked up. As the storyteller: listen quietly – there is no need to respond, explain, or debate; take notes on a separate sheet – jot down what resonates, and even what doesn't (you can reflect later); and just let it in – you'll be surprised what others notice that you may have missed.

(6) Show gratitude.

If not all feedback is spoken, feel free to collect your teammates' notes. Express your appreciation for their listening and insights. You can end the round with a shared gesture – a high-five, a thank-you, or a smile – and then move on to the next person.

Tips and Tricks

- Fewer stories, more depth: cultivate empathy. Aim to focus on one story during the seven minutes – occasionally two, but never more. If you finish early, your teammates can help by asking empathetic follow-up questions like, "Tell me more..." or "What made that moment so meaningful?" It's far more powerful to dive deeply into one vivid story than to skim the surface of three. The goal is emotional resonance and self-discovery – not coverage.
- Reconnect with your childhood. If you're struggling to think of times when you felt at your best, try going all the way back to your early memories. Ask yourself: "What did I love doing when I was five?" or "What made me feel alive at age ten or fifteen?" These moments often reveal early sources of joy, energy, and authenticity – clues that are still relevant today.
- Link insights to other methods. Don't let your insights end with the story – bring them forward into other Life Design tools, for example, add relevant interests, strengths, or values to the left side of your Strengths Portfolio, and use them as inspiration in Opportunity Bingo. You may also want to reflect with three guiding questions: "What do I want to keep?", "What do I want to reduce or eliminate?", and "What do I want to increase or add?" These simple prompts can help you translate insights into action – both in small daily choices and big life shifts.

CHAPTER 8

Ideation Methods

The second phase of Life Design – ideation – centers on the ability to generate ideas and, just as important, to build on each other's ideas using the spirit of "Yes, and..." This chapter invites you to explore both divergent and convergent thinking to create and refine meaningful possibilities for your life, work, and beyond. Rather than trying to get it "right," the goal here is to think broadly, curiously, and creatively.

We start with the Core Method.

- The Core of Creativity is a foundational framework that helps you balance divergent thinking (opening up possibilities) with convergent thinking (focusing your energy) to access your creative potential.

From there, you may choose to go further with two Optional Methods.

- Opportunity Bingo is a fun and structured tool for generating fresh ideas by recombining your interests, strengths, and values.
- Future Scenarios encourages you to imagine vivid versions of your life in the years ahead – expanding your view of what could be.

Whether you stick with the Core Method or explore all three, this chapter supports you in imagining new possibilities – and building the creative momentum to move toward them.

The Core of Creativity

Creative thinking doesn't require genius – just the right conditions. That's exactly what this method provides. The Core of Creativity method helps you move from "I feel uninspired" to "I have more ideas than I expected," by guiding you through a structured ideation flow of five steps. It encourages you to go wide before narrowing in – to explore both realistic and wild ideas before selecting a few promising ones to prototype.

It's time to remix your possibilities!

Remember the morning routine example with the MBA student who explored two ideas. Her feasible idea for reducing phone distractions was to leave her phone charging in the kitchen overnight. Her wild idea? To place it in her mailbox in the evening and not retrieve it until the next morning. In the end, she chose the wild one – and spent a night and morning without her phone. What seemed extreme at first turned out to be entirely doable.

The method draws from research in creativity, improvisation, and design thinking, balancing divergent and convergent thinking. You'll start with a playful creative warm-up to break habitual thought patterns, then work through idea generation, collaboration, and selection. Whether your starting point is deeply personal or professionally focused, this method helps you turn insight into inspiration – and prepares you to turn inspiration into action.

Procedure and Steps

You can begin this process on your own or with others, but it's most effective when shared. You'll first warm up your creative muscles, then generate and expand ideas – individually and as a team (divergent thinking). Finally, you'll narrow in on those ideas with the most energy, excitement, or potential to try out in real life (convergent thinking). Let's walk through it step by step.

(1) Start with a clear opportunity statement.
Use the opportunity statement you crafted in the previous phase as your starting point for ideation. For example, "How might I find more time for myself despite the busyness of life?"

(2) Warm up your creative mind.
Begin with a short creative warm-up to help break free from conventional thinking patterns. Use the Alternative Uses Test (AUT) to boost cognitive flexibility. This popular method requires you to think of alternative uses for a regular object, for example, a paper clip, a fruit, a book, and so on. Ask playful questions such as: "What else can you do with a paperclip besides holding paper together?"; "What can you do with a brick besides building walls?"; "How could you earn money from a cow, aside from using its milk or meat?"; "How could you smuggle a gorilla into the office?" Give yourself and your team 90–120 seconds to write down as many ideas as possible.

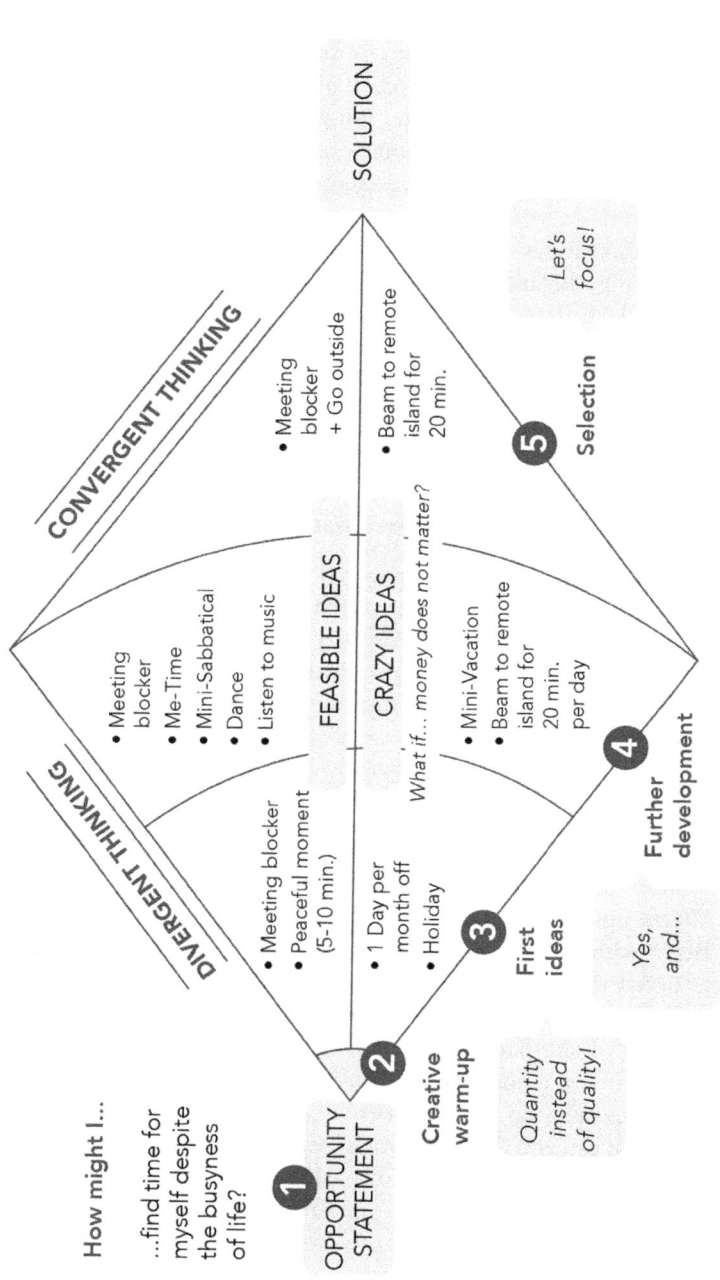

Figure 8.1 The Core of Creativity.

This primes your brain for divergent thinking – encouraging quantity over quality and delaying judgment.

(3) Generate first ideas individually.

Next, respond to your opportunity statement with as many ideas as possible – on your own. Use the mindset of the warm-up: suspend judgment, embrace playfulness, and go for volume. Distinguish between feasible ideas – practical and implementable solutions – and original or "crazy" ideas – which are imaginative, bold, or seemingly unrealistic. This distinction helps prevent early filtering and encourages more creative thinking. Use prompts like, "What if money didn't matter?"; "What if I had only twenty-four hours?"; and "What if I had to make it more fun or more social?"

For example, block your calendar for "me-time"; take a monthly day off; create a daily ten-minute moment of peace; go on a mini-sabbatical; or imagine teleporting to a remote island for twenty minutes.

Write everything down – don't evaluate yet.

(4) Build on ideas together.

Now it's time to share and co-create. Present your ideas to others and use the "Yes, and..." technique (from improvisational theater) to build on each other's ideas.

For example, "Yes, and you could step outside during your me-time"; "Yes, and add music or dancing to make it joyful"; "Yes, and give it a fun label like 'mini-vacation.'"

Focus on expanding, not judging. Keep all ideas visible – write them on post-its, a whiteboard, or a shared document. This encourages idea scaffolding, group flow, and synergy. Even moments of silence are valuable. Creativity often lives in those quiet, in-between spaces – embrace the awkwardness.

(5) Select ideas to prototype.

Move into convergent thinking. Choose one or two feasible ideas and one or two original ideas to take forward into the next phase: prototyping. Choose ideas based on: excitement, if they put a smile on your face; or curiosity about how they might work.

You can also define your own criteria: can it be done in under ten minutes? Does it involve someone else? Does it cost nothing?

This phase is about ideation and then focus – narrowing down to the ideas with the most energy and potential.

Tips and Tricks

- Visualize. Write everything down, even ideas you're unsure about. It clears your mind and allows unexpected connections to emerge.
- Embrace awkwardness. Silence and uncertainty are part of the creative process. Trust the process – not every moment needs to be exciting.
- Revisit and revise. Creativity is iterative. Come back to your ideas later – what seemed wild before might now spark something brilliant.

Opportunity Bingo

If the Core of Creativity method is about generating wild, blue-sky ideas without constraint, then Opportunity Bingo is where imagination meets intention. This method is less about limitless possibilities and more about purposeful play – using what you already know about yourself to explore what might come next. Here, you're not just dreaming big; you're remixing the raw ingredients of your life – your interests, skills, values, and environments – to spark ideas that could actually work.

What's at stake in Opportunity Bingo is you. Your real life. Your energy, your time, your future. The goal isn't to invent something totally new, but to notice surprising patterns and possibilities hiding in plain sight. It's a chance to ask, "What if I gave myself permission to bring more of what matters into my everyday life?" And then, to see where that leads.

Whether you're playing solo or with a team, the structured randomness of the game helps you generate ideas that are both grounded and expansive. It's a space to imagine real opportunities – some small, some bold – that align with who you are and where you want to grow.

Procedure and Steps

To make the most of Opportunity Bingo, it helps to follow a simple but structured process. As a starting point, we recommend keeping your opportunity statement intentionally open to invite as many ideas as possible, for example, "How might I bring more of myself into my life?" The following steps guide you through setting up your Opportunity Bingo sheet, working creatively with others, and selecting ideas that could shape your next experiments in life design. Whether you're doing this solo or with a group, the method works best when approached with openness, curiosity, and a willingness to explore the unconventional.

8 Ideation Methods   97

OPPORTUNITY BINGO

INTERESTS	SKILLS	VALUES	WHO	WHERE	WHEN
Design	Writing	Freedom	Girl friend	In bed	9am
Mountains	Presenting	Fun	Children	Online	Tomorrow
Color Pink	Explaining	Togetherness	Alone	Moon	When it rains
Cancer detection	Creating a good atmosphere	Fair	People at the beach	Home Office	27 September 2044

Figure 8.2 Opportunity Bingo sheet.

(1) Create your Opportunity Bingo sheet.
On a large sheet (A3, poster-sized, or a digital tablet), draw six columns, titled, "Interests," "Skills," "Values," "Who With?," "Where?," and "When?" Add six rows under each column.

(2) Fill in what you want more of.
Populate each column with six elements you'd like more of in your life. For the first three columns, "Interests," "Skills," and "Values," draw from previous empathy methods (Three Good Things, Signature Strengths, Connecting the Dots) and add anything else that feels important. The last three columns represent environmental factors. Use the following examples for inspiration.

Who: partner, work colleagues, kids, strangers on a train, neighbors, new friends.

Where: Zurich, forest, in bed, online, Cape Town, in the kitchen, on a plane, on the moon.

When: 9 am, on vacation, this week, in 2027, during lunch, once a week, when it rains.

Fill in the columns freely – there's no need for logic or alignment. If you're working in a group, feel free to get inspired by others' ideas too.

(3) Warm up as a team.

Get into a creative mindset with a quick warm-up. In a group of three to five people, try something like the Alternative Use Test (AUT). An example prompt is, "How could you earn money from a cow, aside from using its milk or meat?" Each person has two minutes to write down as many ideas as possible. Then briefly share your favorites.

(4) Set up for your creativity session.

Choose one person to start. Hang their Opportunity Bingo sheet where everyone can see it (e.g., on a wall or flipchart). Give each team member a pen and a pad of post-its. Set the mood with an energizing playlist – a favorite track is "The Less I Know the Better" by Tame Impala.

(5) Play round one.

A team member (not the author) randomly selects one item from each of the six columns. This combination becomes your creative prompt. Now, generate ideas by combining two or three elements from the selection; write each idea on a post-it, read it aloud, and stick it near the Opportunity Bingo sheet; other members can extend ideas using "Yes, and. . ." or add their own.

(6) Play rounds two and three.

After two or three minutes, make a new random selection. This time, the author of the Opportunity Bingo sheet picks their favorite items – quickly and intuitively. Repeat the creative process, generating and extending ideas on post-its. You can do a third round if energy is high, but limit the session to eight to ten minutes in total.

(7) Close the session for one person.

The author should thank their team with a two-handed high-five (make it loud – it's a fun, physical energy release). Then move on to the next person's Opportunity Bingo sheet and repeat the process.

(8) Sort and select ideas.

Once everyone has had their turn, review the post-its around your Opportunity Bingo sheet. Sort them into three categories: "feasible," "wild," and "not for me." From there, select one or two feasible ideas and one or two wild ideas that you're excited to bring into your life – through small steps, experiments, or future planning.

Tips and Tricks

- Make it about your whole life. When filling out your Opportunity Bingo sheet, remember that this is about bringing more of yourself into your life – not just your job. Feel free to include both realistic and seemingly impossible things that matter to you. One manager at the Swiss Stock Exchange later reflected, "I wish I had made my matrix more personal and less business-focused – the ideas would've been even more exciting." Let that be your invitation to go big and be bold.
- Do a brain dump first. Before refining your ideas, let them flow freely. Too often, we censor ourselves before we even get started. Instead, write down everything that comes to mind – without judgment. At Stanford, our students call this a brain dump: a total release of raw ideas onto paper or post-its. It's a great way to get unstuck and discover unexpected directions.
- Create a Life Design Space. If you're feeling stuck between empathy and ideation – or want to work more visually and intuitively – build yourself a Life Design Space. Here's how. Post up the results from previous methods (e.g., Three Good Things, Strengths Portfolio, Connecting the Dots). Write key interests, skills, values, and ideas on individual post-its. Use colored tape to define zones or give your space a title. Let it grow over time – like a living collage of what matters to you. This visual, ever-present setup not only makes your ideas more tangible, but also taps into the research-backed benefit of permanent visibility: it reduces cognitive overload, enhances focus, and helps you see new connections as you step back and take it all in.

Future Scenarios

The Future Scenarios method invites you to stretch your imagination and explore your future through multiple scenarios. It encourages you to think beyond the obvious, consider alternative paths, and discover creative ways to integrate insights from different possible worlds.

The idea behind Future Scenarios is to stretch your thinking beyond the familiar and move past binary, either-or decisions such as "Can I do this or not?" and instead embrace multi-optional thinking. This method challenges you to imagine different versions of your future and pushes you beyond the obvious and your comfort zone.

The concept draws on scenario thinking, a strategic planning approach used by companies, militaries, and other organizations to explore multiple possible futures. By combining trends, uncertainties, and aspirations, scenario thinking helps people and systems make more informed decisions in the face of unpredictability. It's also a powerful tool for breaking free from mental ruts by surfacing hidden assumptions and imagining alternative paths.

In Life Design, we apply this principle on a personal level – inviting you to explore several distinct future scenarios for your own life. The process that follows will help you step into these different futures, explore them creatively, and reflect on what they might reveal about who you are and what you truly want.

Procedure and Steps

To stretch your thinking and embrace multiple versions of your life through the Future Scenarios method, the following steps will guide you through building those futures. Each scenario invites you to shift perspective: from the predictable path to unexpected detours, to uninhibited dreams. This process is not about picking the "right" future – it's about surfacing insights from each, noticing what energizes you, and clarifying what truly matters. Use this as a chance to imagine freely, reflect deeply, and begin shaping a future that feels more fully yours. Let's start.

(1) Scenario A. What is most likely to happen?
   Start with the most realistic scenario – your current three-year plan based on what you expect will happen. What's already in motion in your work and personal life? What kind of lifestyle are you aiming for? What kind of job or career path might support that lifestyle?
   Write it out clearly and give this scenario a title that captures its essence.

(2) Scenario B. What if you had to completely switch careers?

8 Ideation Methods

FUTURE SCENARIOS

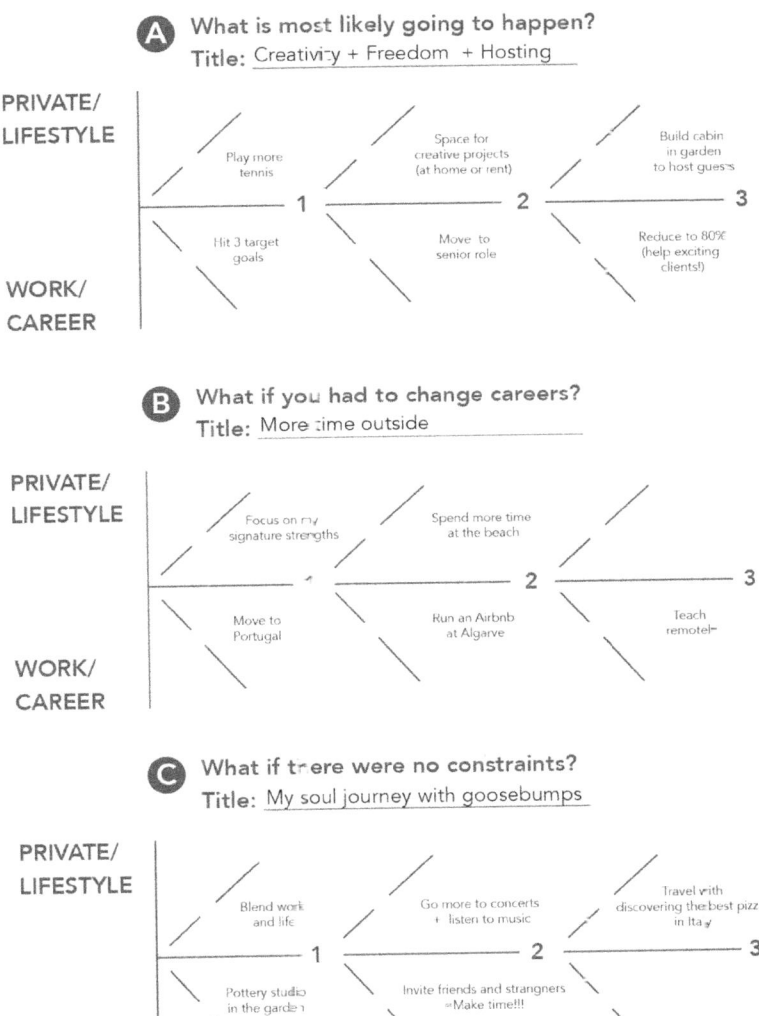

Figure 8.3 Future Scenarios.

Imagine your current job or profession no longer exists or holds no value – what would you do instead? Assume you still need to earn a living, and explore both work and private-life possibilities.

If this feels too abstract, choose from alternative prompts, like: "What if I could only live on 1,000 USD/EUR/CHF per month?"; "What if I had to move to a new country?"; What if I had only three years to live?"

Write down your thoughts and give this scenario a title.

(3) Scenario C. What if there were no constraints?

Now dream without limits. Forget money, status, or practical concerns, imagine your costs are covered or you have all the resources you need, and focus on passion, purpose, and what matters most to you.

What would your life look like? What would you do and why? Once again, give this vision a title that reflects its spirit.

(4) Share your scenarios.

In groups or pairs, take ten to fifteen minutes per person to share and reflect. You can focus on just one plan or discuss all three. This is not about impressing each other – it's about inviting curiosity and clarity. And you can, of course, always use the three magic words of empathy: "Tell me more…"

Use these guiding questions: "What themes or contrasts do you notice across your scenarios?"; "What surprised you?"; "Which ideas felt particularly energizing or meaningful?"; "Are there insights you'd like to carry forward?"

(5) Capture your key insights.

After the conversation, take a moment to reflect and write down: patterns, trends, or recurring themes you noticed; anything that felt close to your heart; two or three key ideas or elements you'd like to integrate into your near future.

These ideas can feed directly into the next phase: prototyping.

Tips and Tricks

- Go visual. It's easy to fill your scenarios with text, but adding symbols or simple sketches will make them more memorable and inviting to revisit. Visuals help your brain connect emotionally with the content and make sharing easier. Need inspiration? Check out free icon libraries like www.TheNounProject.com or www.Icons8.com to spark ideas for what to draw.

- Create a Scenario D. Go big. Once you've explored the first three scenarios, consider crafting a fourth one: a scenario that blends your favorite elements from A, B, and C, or one that goes beyond all three – your boldest, most expansive vision yet. Use a fresh sheet of paper (A3, poster-sized, or a digital tablet) and add post-its, drawings, or color codes to give your future the space and respect it deserves. Let this be your vision board in motion.
- Make time for rich conversation. This method often sparks deep reflection and lively conversation. In our workshops, participants sometimes spent thirty to sixty minutes per person sharing and exploring their scenarios. So, if you're meeting in groups of three or four, don't rush it. One evening might be just enough to talk through your future plans together. The richness lies in the exchange.

CHAPTER 9

Prototyping Methods

Prototyping is what turns ideas into movement. Instead of waiting for the perfect plan, you take small, low-risk steps that allow you to explore, learn, and adapt. Whether you're testing a new habit, a side project, or a bigger life transition, prototyping helps you move forward through action – not overthinking. This chapter introduces three practical methods to help you design and carry out meaningful experiments in your life.

We begin with the Core Method.

- The Prototyping Prism is a structured tool that helps you shape an idea into an experiment by looking at it from multiple angles – such as time, energy, support, and emotional risk. It offers a flexible yet focused way to move from possibility to action.

From there, you may choose to explore two Optional Methods.

- The Magic Circle is a creative one-page canvas for mapping and launching your next experiment. It's supported by Ten Ways of Prototyping, a framework that expands how you might try something out – through shadowing, storytelling, time-boxed trials, and more.
- The Stairway to Heaven supports you in breaking down ambitious ideas into smaller, energizing steps, so you can move toward big dreams without feeling overwhelmed.

This chapter focuses on prototyping methods that can be applied to habits and routines, career shifts, personal projects, or even lifestyle redesigns. Whether you're starting small or dreaming big, these tools are here to help you move forward – creatively, confidently, and on your own terms.

The Prototyping Prism

When it comes to turning ideas into action, perfection is the enemy of progress. The Prototyping Prism offers a flexible yet focused way to test

What if TRYING SOMETHING ONCE changed everything?

Part III Life Design Toolbox

PROTOTYPING PRISM

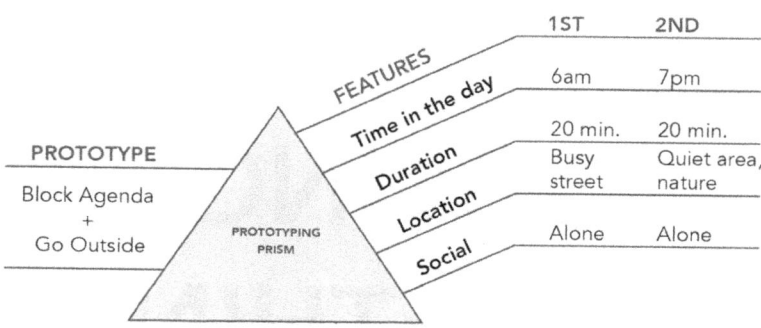

Figure 9.1 The Prototyping Prism.

your ideas – both practical and wildly ambitious – through small, learnable experiments. This method helps you move from "someday" to "let's try it once," breaking down the fear of commitment and replacing it with curiosity, adaptability, and momentum.

What makes the Prototyping Prism unique is its dual approach: one strategy is for making feasible ideas happen now, and another is for bringing even your most imaginative, out-there ideas to life in grounded ways. Just like turning a real prism, each small adjustment reveals a new pattern – a new possibility. The goal isn't to get it perfect – it's to get moving.

Procedure and Steps

The steps that follow walk you through two clear strategies for prototyping: one for ideas that already feel doable (Strategy 1), and one for ideas that feel far-fetched but meaningful (Strategy 2). Each strategy is grounded in action, not overthinking, and offers you concrete tools for experimenting with time, place, energy, and intention.

Strategy 1 Bringing Feasible Ideas to Life
Some ideas already feel possible, but they often stay stuck in our heads. This strategy helps you take that first step by testing a realistic idea in a small, low-risk way.

(1) Let go of "forever" thinking.
Don't fall into the trap of thinking your idea has to become a permanent habit right away. That mindset – common in New Year's Resolutions – creates pressure and unrealistic expectations. Research shows that only 8 percent of Resolutions stick. Instead, give yourself permission to try it once.

(2) Just do it once – and learn from it.
Instead of aiming to create a routine, simply try the idea once. This first version is your prototype. For example, block thirty minutes in your calendar and go outside. Whether it works perfectly or not is secondary – the real question is: "What did I learn?" This insight becomes the basis for the next iteration.

(3) Think in features and dimensions.
Every experience has multiple features you can adjust: time of day (morning versus evening); duration (ten minutes versus thirty minutes); location (city street versus nature); social setting (alone or with someone). By viewing your prototype as a bundle of adjustable dimensions, you can redesign and experiment without starting from scratch.

(4) Iterate toward better fit.
Based on your reflections, tweak one or more features in the next round. For example, if your first walk was at 6 am on a noisy street, try 7 pm in a quiet park. Maybe you invite a friend next time, or add music. Each version brings the idea closer to what fits your life.

Strategy 2 Making Crazy Ideas Real
Some ideas feel exciting but impossible – like "Beam me to a remote island for twenty minutes a day." This strategy helps you bring the essence of such ideas into reality.

(1) Uncover the need behind the idea.
Ask yourself: "What's behind this idea? What is it really about?" The "beaming" example might point to a need for separation, physical activity, playfulness, or joy.

(2) Create new options based on the need.
Now develop ideas that fulfill those underlying needs. Based on the example of "separation," take a break on the balcony or go into the garden. Based on the example of "physical activity," dance, stretch, or shoot hoops. Based on the example of "joy/fun," listen to music, sing, or, again, play basketball.

(3) Combine features for powerful alternatives.

Sometimes, you'll find one activity that satisfies multiple needs, for example, listening to music while stretching on the balcony, or playing basketball – which offers separation, activity, and fun in one. These alternatives might not be as "cool" as teleportation, but they make the invisible need visible and actionable.

Tips and Tricks

- "Do it once and learn." This mantra keeps your expectations light and your mind in learning mode.
- Stick to a few features. Limit your prototype to two to five features to avoid overwhelm and increase your motivation to act.
- Use a fresh opportunity statement. When stuck, ask yourself: "How might I make this more fun?" or "How might I make it more meaningful or social?" These questions keep your energy flowing and your mindset open.

The Magic Circle (and Ten Ways of Prototyping)

The Magic Circle is a simple yet powerful method to help you turn ideas, dreams, and wishes into action. Whether your idea is crystal-clear or still a bit fuzzy, this tool helps you take the first step. It's designed to help you move forward – even if you're unsure where exactly you're headed. The process begins with a single idea, dream, or wish (the first circle), then explores the deeper motivations and values behind it (the second circle). Finally, it invites you to generate concrete, low-risk ways to bring that idea to life through prototyping (the third circle). The visual format makes it intuitive and energizing, helping you move from inspiration to implementation, one small experiment at a time.

To support your creative momentum, we also introduce the Ten Ways of Prototyping – a practical framework designed to expand your sense of what's possible. While product designers and startups prototype as second nature, adults navigating career changes, life transitions, or new creative directions often don't feel they have permission to try things out. This framework aims to change that. It offers diverse, accessible strategies for testing ideas across intensity levels – from quick, low-effort steps like desk research or observation, to deeper engagements like volunteering, shadowing, or taking a mini-sabbatical. Each way provides a legitimate path to explore, refine, and adjust your ideas in the real world – without needing to quit your job, make a big leap, or get everything figured out first.

Together, the Magic Circle and the Ten Ways of Prototyping give you a flexible and empowering toolkit to take action. You don't need to wait for clarity to begin – clarity often comes through doing.

Procedure and Steps

The process that follows is divided into two parts, designed to help you move from reflection to action.

- In Part 1, you'll work with the Magic Circle – a three-step method that helps you name an idea or wish, uncover what's truly behind it, and generate small, low-risk ways to start bringing it to life. Whether your idea is fully formed or still taking shape, the Magic Circle gives it structure, energy, and direction.
- In Part 2, you'll explore the Ten Ways of Prototyping – a set of practical strategies you can use to expand, test, or refine your ideas from Part 1. These approaches range from quick and simple to more immersive, giving you a wide range of options to suit your time, energy, and curiosity.

Together, these two parts offer a creative, flexible pathway from "I'd love to. . ." to "I'm already doing something about it." Let's get started!

Part 1 The Magic Circle

The Magic Circle unfolds in three circles: the first helps you name a dream, idea, or wish; the second invites you to explore the deeper motivations behind it; and the third guides you in designing low-risk, meaningful prototypes to bring it to life. Think of it as zooming out from a spark of inspiration, understanding what fuels it, and then zooming back in to take the first real step. Let's begin

1. Define Your Idea, Dream, or Wish: What Do You Want to Bring into Your Life?
   In the first (inner) circle of the template, write down the idea, desire, or dream you want to explore. It could be something concrete (e.g., "write a book," "start my own school," or "live in a camper van") or fuzzier (e.g., "do more with people," "connect art with research," or "live by the sea"). This is your space to think big – ambitions like

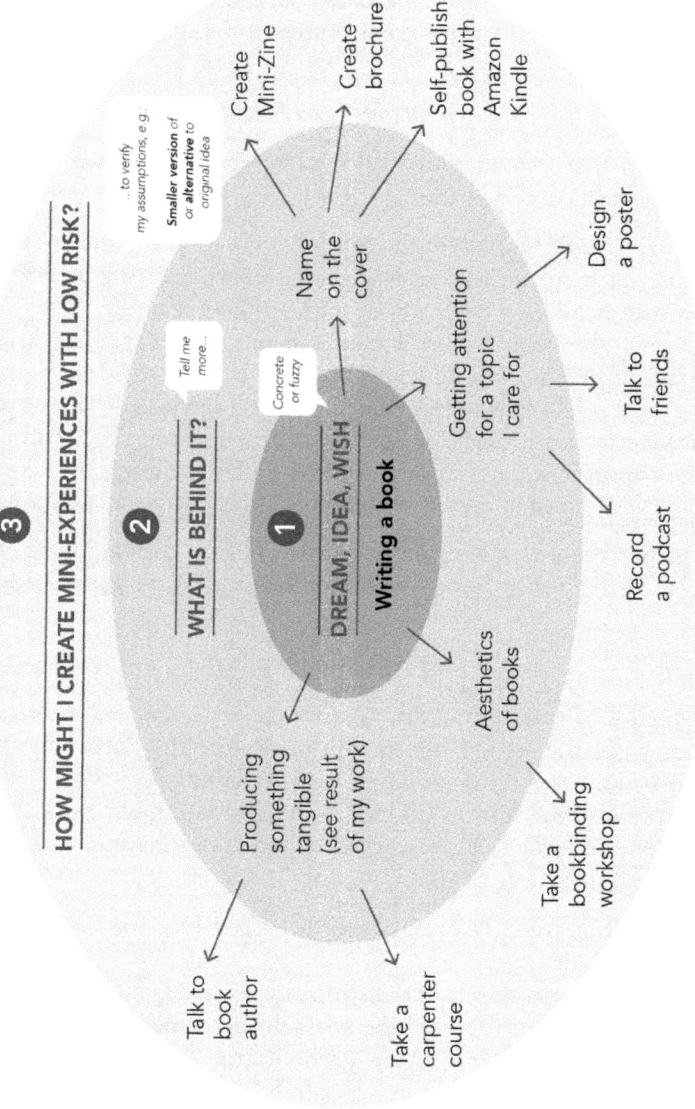

Figure 9.2 The Magic Circle.

"more peace of mind" or "more me-time" are just as welcome. In the related figure, you can follow the example of "writing a book."

2. Explore What's Behind It: Why Do You Care?
In the second circle, articulate the deeper reasons or motivations behind your idea. Imagine a close friend asking, "Tell me more..." What would you say? Be honest. The real insights often emerge when we drop the filters.

For example, someone wrote, "Hands down, I just want my name on a cover" in response to their book idea. That kind of clarity is powerful. Additional reasons might follow, like, "I want to spark a conversation" or "I want to create something lasting." In Figure 9.2, you can see the reasons: "name on the cover," "getting attention for a topic I care about," "appreciation for the aesthetics of books," and "desire to create something tangible and see the result of my work."

3. Develop Prototypes: What Small Steps Could Bring This to Life?
In the third circle, come up with low-risk, low-effort prototypes – mini-experiences that allow you to test or explore your idea. These can be a smaller version of the original idea, or an alternative expression of the intention behind it. For instance, if your goal is to write a book and your core motivation is "having my name on the cover," a first prototype might be creating a mini-zine or a mock book cover.

That's what one participant did – and in doing so, she realized the deeper desire wasn't the book itself, but "to be seen," specifically "by her home university in China." That insight redirected her toward writing an article for the alumni magazine – a completely different, yet highly meaningful, way of realizing her goal. In the related figure, you can see the prototype ideas: "create a mini-zine," "design a brochure," "self-publish a short book on Amazon Kindle," "design a poster around my topic," "talk to friends about the topic," "record a podcast episode," "take a bookbinding workshop," "join a carpentry course to explore tangibility through a different medium," or "reach out to a book author and ask about their experience." This is the beauty of Life Design: action generates insight, and sometimes that insight changes everything.

4. Lower the Threshold: How Could You Make it Even Easier?
Still in the third circle, ask yourself the following questions.

- "How can I reduce the time, money, or emotional energy this will require?"
- "What's the simplest version I could try – even today?"

We often dream big, then delay because it feels overwhelming. But you don't need a sabbatical to start prototyping. A few real-life examples include the following.

> One executive started her day with "just three deep breaths in bed."
>
> A student dreaming of solo travel took the first step by "dining out alone that evening."
>
> Another placed a glass of "water on his phone" to nudge himself to hydrate before scrolling or snoozing.

What do these examples all have in common? Small acts lead to powerful shifts.

5 Select Your Top Prototypes: Which Ones Excite You Most?

Choose two or three prototypes to try – starting with at least one you can implement within the next twenty-four to forty-eight hours. Pick something that feels energizing, not like a chore. If a prototype starts to feel heavy, give it a twist.

- "How might I make this more fun or joyful?"
- "How might I make it feasible within five to ten minutes (despite a busy life)?"
- "How might I do it with someone else?"
- "How might I connect it to something I already enjoy doing?"

The goal is not perfection – it's momentum.

Tips and Tricks

- Add a fourth circle – spark action with micro-prototypes. If you feel stuck or want to energize your process, try adding a fourth circle – or use the four corners of your page – to capture immediately feasible prototypes. Use prompts that lower the bar to action and invite playful experimentation, like: "What would I do if I had only 10 minutes?"; "What if I could only spend 10 dollars?"; "What would I recommend to a friend?"; "What could I do right here, right now?" One manager actually jumped off a table to prototype skydiving in the moment. It may sound wild, but the act sparked valuable insights and laughter all around.
- Pass it around – let others ideate for you. Another great way to build energy and perspective is to hand your Magic Circle to someone else and invite them to come up with prototypes for you. Or exchange circles with fellow Life Designers. Discuss the connection between circle one (your dream) and circle two (what's behind it) – which is especially helpful if your prototypes in circle three feel flat or

uninspired. Often, a deeper reconnection with your motivations unlocks new energy. Ask each other the classic empathy prompt: "Tell me more..." You can also explore the link between circles two and three by building on emerging ideas using the "Yes, and..." approach, while focusing on reducing risk and effort. A ten-minute conversation per person is a great starting point – but don't be surprised if these exchanges spill over into dinner. We've seen it happen!
- Normalize prototyping – especially for adults. Prototyping is second nature in product design – it's how ideas are tested and refined. But when it comes to career shifts, lifestyle changes, or side hustles, adults often feel they're not allowed to experiment. Kids and students get internships and trial phases. Grown-ups? Not so much.

Part 2 Ten Ways of Prototyping

To complement the Magic Circle, we've developed a practical framework: Ten Ways of Prototyping. It's a collection of actionable strategies designed to make life prototyping more accessible and effective for adults, especially when it comes to life design for career and work. You may go through these Ten Ways step-by-step to expand and refine the ideas in circle three of your Magic Circle and give yourself full permission to explore, test, and play.

Note: these strategies represent our current thinking on how people can prototype their way forward – whether it's for a career shift, a side hustle, or a long-held dream. If you know of additional approaches, let us know – we're constantly evolving this list. We hope it sparks inspiration for your own experiments.

1 Desk Research: Start Exploring from Where You Are
- The idea: a fifteen-minute search or online course can unlock fresh momentum – and maybe even a new direction. Sometimes, the simplest way to prototype an idea is to start by gathering information. Desk research may sound trivial, but it can open doors and spark momentum.

Take the example of a participant who dreamed of writing a book. As she explored her idea further, she realized it wasn't necessarily the writing that excited her most – it was the aesthetics of books. She began researching local bookbinding courses and soon found one in her city that aligned perfectly with her interest. Another participant, feeling uninspired by her home-office setup, searched for coworking spaces nearby to test working in a different

TEN WAYS OF PROTOTYPING

Figure 9.3 Ten Ways of Prototyping (for careers, side hustles, and big life dreams).

environment. Others wanted to combine travel and learning, so they looked into conferences like the Web Summit in Lisbon or the Inner Development Goals Summit in Stockholm – asking themselves, "Where would I go, and how could I combine it with something I care about?"

Not all exploration needs to be global. Local groups on platforms like Meetup.com, Internations.org, or A Small World offer regular opportunities to join interest-based communities. For example, in Zurich, there's a vibrant Data Storytelling Group that meets monthly to discuss trends and share projects. Why not try attending such a meetup alone or with a friend – just once? See how it feels, what the people are like, and reflect on the experience afterward. You don't need a long-term plan to give something a try.

Online courses also offer great low-risk prototypes. Coursera, edX, and Udemy host countless free or low-cost courses across every topic imaginable. You don't need to commit for months – browsing a course for thirty minutes can be enough to spark new insights. One senior researcher took a quick look at an entrepreneurship course and immediately realized he'd need to hire someone to handle operations if he pursued his idea. That one insight, gained in half an hour, saved him time, energy, and unrealistic expectations. Also, Airbnb offers plenty of virtual and in-person experiences next to renting out homes; a quick search might help you discover an experience in your hometown or somewhere where you can combine it with travelling.

In the end, even a short burst of focused research can help you move from stuck to inspired. As one participant put it: "Just taking fifteen minutes to look into something meaningful gave me a real sense of agency-and self-worth." Let curiosity lead the way. The next step might be just one search away.

2 Observation: Watch First, Then Act

- The idea: just by watching others in action, you can test assumptions and fine-tune your dreams before jumping in. Observation is a low-risk, high-reward way to start prototyping. It requires no permission, no investment – just your attention and curiosity.

At Stanford, one of our students had a deep passion for coffee and dreamed of working part-time as a barista. His first prototype? Simply observing. He spent one hour at the campus Starbucks, carefully watching what the baristas actually did. But when he returned, he looked disillusioned. "They're just running around, filling orders. There's no time to savor the craft of coffee-making," he said. For him, it was a sobering reality check.

Luckily, another student suggested he try again – this time at Philz Coffee, a beloved California chain known for its soulful coffee culture. He followed the advice and came back beaming: "That's it. That's the kind of place I want to work. One person takes care of the customer, while the others prepare coffee with care – almost like cocktail artists." The vibe, the pace, the values – it clicked.

What this story shows is the power of small, simple actions. By engaging with the world through observation, he quickly tested his assumptions and refined his dream. And sometimes, the first prototype – even if it doesn't fit – leads you to the second, more meaningful one. If he hadn't started with Starbucks, he might never have discovered Philz.

So, next time you're unsure whether something is right for you, don't jump in headfirst. Start by watching: "What do people actually do? How does it feel to be in that environment? Who's energized – and who looks drained?" And if you're ever in California, yes, Philz Coffee is absolutely worth a visit.

3 Role-Playing: Test Ideas through Perspectives

- The idea: step into different roles – dreamer, realist, critic – and gain surprising clarity without ever leaving the room. You'd be surprised how much clarity you can gain from just ten to fifteen minutes of role-playing.

One powerful approach is the Walt Disney Method: team up with three others who take on the roles of the dreamer, the critic, and the realist. We once worked with a participant who dreamed of becoming a professional storyteller for adults. The critic asked, "Who even needs that?" The dreamer encouraged, "That's amazing – what's your unique angle?" And the realist grounded the vision: "Have you done any research? What's the demand and the model?" Through these voices, he saw his idea from multiple sides – emotional, imaginative, and practical.

Another great technique is the "If I were you" variation. Present your idea to a group and have each person respond with a quick suggestion, starting with, "If I were you, I would. . ." – for example, "talk to this person," "attend this event," or "explore that website." You can jot down their inputs, ask clarifying questions, then wrap up by summarizing your key takeaways.

These simple yet powerful exercises help you uncover blind spots, challenge assumptions, and expand your perspective – without ever leaving the room.

4 Thirty-Day Challenge: A Time-Limited Path to Change

- The idea: set a thirty-day challenge and try something you've always wanted to – because the next month will pass anyway. The time limit makes change feel manageable. It isn't a forever commitment – it is "just thirty days."

Take inspiration from Matt Cutts, a Google employee who gave himself thirty days to try out new habits or routines – then decided afterward whether to continue. This time-bound experiment helped him finally get started and stick with things long enough to make an impact.

He cycled to work for thirty days, took a photo every day, and later expanded his experiments into bigger loops – like walking 10,000 steps a day for thirty days, which eventually led him to climb Mount Kilimanjaro. He wrote his first novel in just thirty days by joining National Novel Writing Month (NaNoWriMo) and hitting the goal of 1,667 words per day. He also tried a sugar-free diet for thirty days – and thoroughly enjoyed the chocolate waiting on day thirty-one. His blog (www.mattcutts.com/blog) is full of further experiments and Life Design inspiration.

So, what have you always wanted to do? The next thirty days will pass anyway. Why not try something you've been putting off? And if thirty days feels too long, start with just three. That's the power of a healthy constraint: a simple time frame can free you to take action.

5 Life Design Conversations: Learn from People Who've Lived It

- The idea: if you can't test something directly through an experiment, talk to someone who has already lived it. These conversations can give you invaluable insights into careers, life choices, or lifestyles you're curious about. A twenty-minute call with someone who's walked your imagined path can change everything.

You might ask, "What's it like to work as a product manager at L'Oréal?" or "What was it like to travel around the world in eighty days, solo?" or even "How do you balance being a parent and an entrepreneur?" These kinds of ideas often seem impossible to prototype, but what we frequently overlook is this: we can at least talk to someone who is living, or has lived, that idea in real life.

For example, Sebastian once had a Life Design conversation with David Kelley, the founder of IDEO and a pioneer of Design Thinking. David shared that he didn't see himself as an expert in any one field, but rather as a conductor – someone who brings experts together, listens deeply, and helps ideas take shape. This mindset of facilitating rather than controlling was what led him to found IDEO. Hearing this firsthand was a powerful reminder of how valuable it is to try things out – and how much more meaningful that can be than endlessly theorizing.

Life Design conversations can also happen online. A short twenty-minute call can stretch far beyond that when you show genuine interest and ask open-ended questions like "Tell me more..." People are usually glad to share their experiences if they feel truly heard. These conversations often lead naturally into the next step: shadowing someone in their environment – which we'll explore next.

Box 9.1 Inspiring Questions for Life Design Conversations

Great Life Design conversations are rooted in curiosity, humility, and empathy. Especially during the empathy phase, it's essential to stay focused on the other person – not to tell your own story, but to listen deeply to theirs. Avoid the trap of "false empathy" where attention subtly shifts back to you. Instead, hold space and let the other person lead. The right questions can help. The following sections give a curated collection of questions and sources to spark meaningful dialogue in Life Design conversations – whether with a friend, a mentor, or a stranger.

The Classics: Always a Good Start

These open-ended questions signal genuine interest and invite people to expand their story.

- "Tell me more about..."
- "What exactly interests you about...?"
- "How did that begin for you?"

Learn More about a Job or Activity

These are great for informational interviews or exploring prototypes:

- "What does a typical day look like in your role?"
- "How was your transition from one job (or life chapter) to another?"
- "What's the best – or hardest – part of this work?"
- "What skills are essential to succeed in what you do?"
- "What kind of person would struggle with your job, and why?"

The Humble Inquiry: Asking with Curiosity and Respect

Edgar Schein, MIT professor and pioneer in organizational psychology, reminds us: "Good questions are not about being clever – they are about being curious." In his model of humble inquiry, he describes three types of questions.

> Box 9.1 (cont.)
>
> - Pure humble inquiries. These keep the focus entirely on the other person's story: "And then?"; "Can you give me an example?"; "Tell me more..."
> - Diagnostic inquiries. Use these once you've built some rapport: "Why do you think that happened?"; "What were the contributing factors?"; "What were you most concerned about at the time?"
> - Confrontational inquiries. These are best used later in a conversation, and only if appropriate (they can be powerful – but only when trust is already present): "Did you consider...?"; "Why don't you try...?"
>
> *More Sources for Great Questions*
>
> **36 Questions that Lead to Connection**
> Originally developed for creating intimacy (yes, even love), the first few questions work well as *icebreakers* or *deepeners*. View the full list and an animated version at: nytimes.com/36questions. Examples include: "Given the choice of anyone in the world, who would you want as a dinner guest?"; "For what in your life do you feel most grateful?"
>
> **100 Life Coaching Questions from PositivePsychology.com**
> PositivePsychology.com has a rich collection of prompts across categories like strengths, values, and career. You can explore them at: positivepsychology.com/life-coaching-questions. Examples include: "What does success look like for you?"; "What's one thing most people don't know about your work?"; "What are the three most important things someone needs to do your job well?"
>
> **Questions for Deeper Human Connection**
> Warren Berger's book *The Book of Beautiful Questions* provides questions for deeper human connection. Examples include: "What's your passion?"; "What problem would you most like to solve?"; "When you were a kid, what did you want to be when you grew up?"

6 Shadowing: Step Into Someone Else's World

- The idea: shadowing allows you to step into someone else's world without taking an active role – just observing, listening, and soaking up the experience. It's an ethnographic method often used in research, but it's also a powerful Life Design tool. By participating in someone's daily work or life setting as authentically as possible, you can learn things no brochure or website can tell you.

At Baloise Insurance, for example, employees are encouraged to shadow colleagues in other departments for half a day before applying to a new role. This helps both sides reduce the risk of mismatched expectations. Cambridge University offers a similar program, letting staff explore other job opportunities through shadowing before making a formal switch.

Shadowing doesn't have to be a big deal. It could be as simple as joining someone for a factory visit, a team tour, or even just a casual look around their workplace. If you've already had a Life Design conversation, a natural next step could be grabbing a coffee and getting a behind-the-scenes peek at the office, studio, or field where the action happens. These small glimpses can offer big insights.

7 Volunteering: Try Before You Dive In

- The idea: volunteering lets you move beyond passive observation and take an active role – without the pressure of long-term commitment. Whether you're curious about a new job, hobby, or life direction, volunteering gives you a low-risk, hands-on way to test the waters for a few hours or days.

Take the protagonist of our anti-Life Design story: before opening a dog school, he could have simply volunteered at one – just for a day or even a couple of hours – to see what the work is really like. We've had participants volunteer at local zoos, only to discover that their dream of bonding with animals clashed with the practical realities of cleaning cages and managing feeding schedules.

There are countless opportunities to volunteer, both locally and globally. The following are a few established platforms to explore.

- Workaway connects travelers (Workawayers) with hosts worldwide for skill-based exchanges in return for accommodation and cultural immersion.
- Helpstay offers affordable travel and meaningful cultural experiences through volunteer placements.
- Stoke Festival combines volunteering with world-class music and cultural festivals, giving you a front-row seat and hands-on role.
- UN Volunteers offers opportunities to contribute skills to global development projects through the United Nations.

- Volunteer World is a global directory comparing top international volunteer programs run by NGOs and local organizations.

You can also search for local opportunities: schools, shelters, museums, events, or nonprofits often welcome short-term help. Volunteering is a powerful way to learn, grow, and test your assumptions – one experience at a time.

8 Side-Hustle: Scaling Up Your Dream (Without Quitting Your Day Job)

- The idea: once you've explored small experiments and want to go a step further, starting a side hustle can be a powerful way to continue prototyping your dreams – on a slightly bigger scale, while keeping the security of your current role. It's a way to deepen your learning, test ideas in real life, and maybe even earn money along the way (though that's not essential).

For example, one workshop participant launched an online shop for used children's clothing. In South Africa, another started a weekly reading circle in the townships to give mothers space to breathe and connect. Then there was the IT consultant – successful on paper, but deeply unfulfilled. Through Life Design, he realized his true passion had more to do with cars and helping people. He had a Life Design conversation with a driving instructor, then volunteered to sit in on lessons. Eventually, he took the exam himself. For a while, he split his time 80/20 between consulting and teaching driving – before ultimately switching careers completely. His income dropped, but his sense of purpose skyrocketed. Sebastian and his wife started their own local side hustle, creating branded merchandise to support their neighborhood. They donate 100 percent of the profits to community events like open-air cinemas and music festivals. (Curious? Take a look at wpkngn.ch.)

Side hustles aren't distractions – they're energizers. Research shows that pursuing a meaningful project outside of work can actually boost your engagement at your main job. In Germany, the platform sidepreneur.de offers hundreds of stories and honest insights into side-hustle life. A side hustle is more than a project – it's a creative space where your ideas meet the real world. It's one of the most dynamic forms of prototyping your future.

9 Internship: Rediscover the Power of Trying Things Out

- The idea: even as an adult, internships (short or long) offer a low-risk way to explore new paths. When people think of experimenting with a new direction, they often picture taking time off or doing an internship. And while the previous examples have shown that there are many ways to prototype your future, internships still offer a valuable, realistic window into new jobs, activities, or lifestyles.

The good news? Internships aren't just for students anymore. Even experienced professionals can explore short-term opportunities without embarrassment – and without needing to quit their current job. These experiences don't have to last months. Sometimes, just a few days can make a real difference.

Take inspiration from Emma Rosen, who documented her journey through twenty-five internships in a single year in her book *Radical Sabbatical*. Or look to a bank in Zurich that enables employees aged over fifty to intern at startups – while keeping their salary. The goal is simple: to return with new insights, fresh energy, and renewed purpose.

As kids or young adults, we're often encouraged to try things through one-day or one-week internships. But as adults, this permission often fades – when we need it most. That's why new formats are emerging: Boston Consulting Group now offers four-week "Intenciveships" aimed at women. The UN and other global organizations run three-day "Immersion Programs." These bite-sized experiences help professionals explore new paths with minimal risk. Internships, in all their evolving forms, remind us that it's never too late to try something new – and learn from it.

10 *Sabbatical: The Classic Reset (Big or Small)*

- The idea: take a day, a week, or a few months – intentionally stepping back could be the start of something big.

The final option is the classic sabbatical – often the first thing that comes to mind when people think about trying something new. It's the ultimate "someday" plan: "If I only had three months off, then I'd finally do all the things I've always wanted to..."

Yes, sabbaticals can be big in terms of time and planning, but they also offer powerful opportunities – whether it's traveling through Fiji for a month, walking the Way of St. James, or diving into a creative passion like pottery or writing.

But here's the thing: a sabbatical doesn't have to be grand or far away to be meaningful. Many people feel a deep longing when they hear the word – so why not use that emotional power intentionally? At our NEXT program

CHECKLIST FOR TEN WAYS OF PROTOTYPING

① DESK RESEARCH
- ☐ Research a topic, course, community, or opportunity for 15–30 minutes.
- ☐ Save 1–2 links or notes that spark your interest.

② OBSERVATION
- ☐ Pick a place or event related to your interest.
- ☐ Spend 30–60 minutes simply observing.
- ☐ Write down what surprised you.

③ ROLE-PLAYING
- ☐ Organize a quick role-play (Dreamer, Critic, Realist) with friends or colleagues.
- ☐ Alternatively, ask 3 people to complete: "If I were you, I would .."

④ 30-DAY CHALLENGE
- ☐ Choose a new habit, hobby, or experiment to try for 30 days (or 3 if needed).
- ☐ Track your progress daily with one sentence or photo.

⑤ LIFE DESIGN CONVERSATIONS
- ☐ Identify 1–2 people living your dream or doing something you're curious about.
- ☐ Request a 20-minute conversation (online or in-person).
- ☐ Ask "Tell me more..." to deepen the conversation.

⑥ SHADOWING
- ☐ Ask someone if you can shadow them for an hour, half-day, or full day.
- ☐ Take notes on what feels energizing – and what doesn't.

⑦ VOLUNTEERING
- ☐ Find 1–2 volunteering opportunities (local or international).
- ☐ Commit to a few hours to get a realistic taste of the experience.

⑧ SIDE-HUSTLE
- ☐ Start a small side project based on your interests or strengths.
- ☐ Set a simple first goal (e.g., sell your first item, organize one event).

⑨ INTERNSHIP
- ☐ Explore short-term internships, shadowing programs, or professional exchanges.
- ☐ Apply for one that fits your exploration goals.

⑩ SABBATICAL
- ☐ Plan a "mini-sabbatical" (even half a day!) dedicated to prototyping something new.
- ☐ Name it intentionally (e.g., "My Mini Sabbatical for Creativity").

Figure 9.4 Checklist for Ten Ways of Prototyping.

in Switzerland, participants often say it feels like a three-day sabbatical. Some even describe a single seminar as a "two-hour sabbatical" because it creates space to reconnect with themselves. At Swiss Re, employees take one day or even half a day off per month and treat it like a mini-sabbatical – with intention and purpose.

Never underestimate the power of language. The words we use send subconscious signals to ourselves. In one study on staycations, participants were asked to spend a week off at home. One group did so without any further guidance. The other group was simply asked to call it a "Staycation." The result? The second group felt more relaxed and refreshed. Why? Because naming it gave it meaning and meaning shaped the experience. So, whether it's a grand escape or a single day with a clear intention, consider how a "mini-sabbatical," "staycation," or "creative break" could become a prototype for something bigger. The name alone might be the nudge you need.

That's why it's time to legitimize prototyping for adults – and build institutional support for it. We're working with the World Demographic Forum on a report that highlights forward-thinking transition programs in companies, universities, and governments. These programs reduce mismatches, attract talent, and help people bring their full potential to the world.

The Stairway to Heaven

This method invites you to take any idea that energizes and prototype your way toward it, starting today. The Stairway to Heaven helps you break down your journey into manageable timeframes, guiding you from small immediate steps to longer-term milestones. It's a simple yet powerful way to move from intention to action. The method is inspired by the Ten–Ten–Ten Framework, which asks:

- what can you do in the next ten minutes?
- what can you do in the next ten days?
- what might you aim for in the next ten months?

You're welcome to stick with the Ten–Ten–Ten format, or adapt it to suit your context. You might prefer labels like "now," "soon," and "later," depending on the timeline that fits your life.

What makes this method so helpful is its focus on the very first step. In challenging moments, we often get caught in short-term emotions and fail to think beyond the next few minutes or days. The Stairway to Heaven expands your horizon, helping you create a sequence of meaningful experiments across time. It invites you to dream, test, and adjust along the way.

The visual format of the method gives you a tangible way to map your progress. You can bring in ideas from the Ten Ways of Prototyping or your own creative experiments, shaping a pathway that leads upward – with flexibility to pivot as new insights emerge.

Procedure and Steps

The following steps guide you through building your own Stairway to Heaven – starting with a dream, and breaking it down into immediate, doable actions. You'll map your next moves across time: from what you can try today, to what you might explore soon, to what could grow over months ahead. With each step, you turn intention into movement.

(1) Write down your wish: what do you want to bring into your life?
   On the far right of your Stairway to Heaven, write down one or two wishes you want to move toward. These can be concrete (e.g., "Write a book") or more open-ended (e.g., "Do something with paper"). Stick to a maximum of two wishes per template. They can relate to your personal or professional life.

(2) Identify what's driving you: why does it matter?
   Next to each wish, note the deeper motivations behind it. For instance, the desire to "write a book" might be driven by "seeing my name on the cover," "sharing my story," or "loving the aesthetics of books." If you've done the Magic Circle, you can copy two or three keywords from circle two. Otherwise, take a moment to reflect and write down two to five words that capture your personal reasons.

(3) Pull your wish into the present: what could you do today?
   Now imagine drawing that future dream toward you with a rope – bringing it into the present:
      Next ten minutes (now): what's a small step you could take right now, in the next ten minutes (or twenty-four hours, or over the next few days)?
      Next ten days (soon): what could you explore in the next ten days (or few weeks)?
      Next ten months (later): where could your prototype be in the ten months (or year) ahead?
   Place these prototyping ideas along the Stairway, from now to later. For example, someone who wanted to write a book began by researching bookbinding workshops, creating a mini-zine, joining

STAIRWAY TO HEAVEN

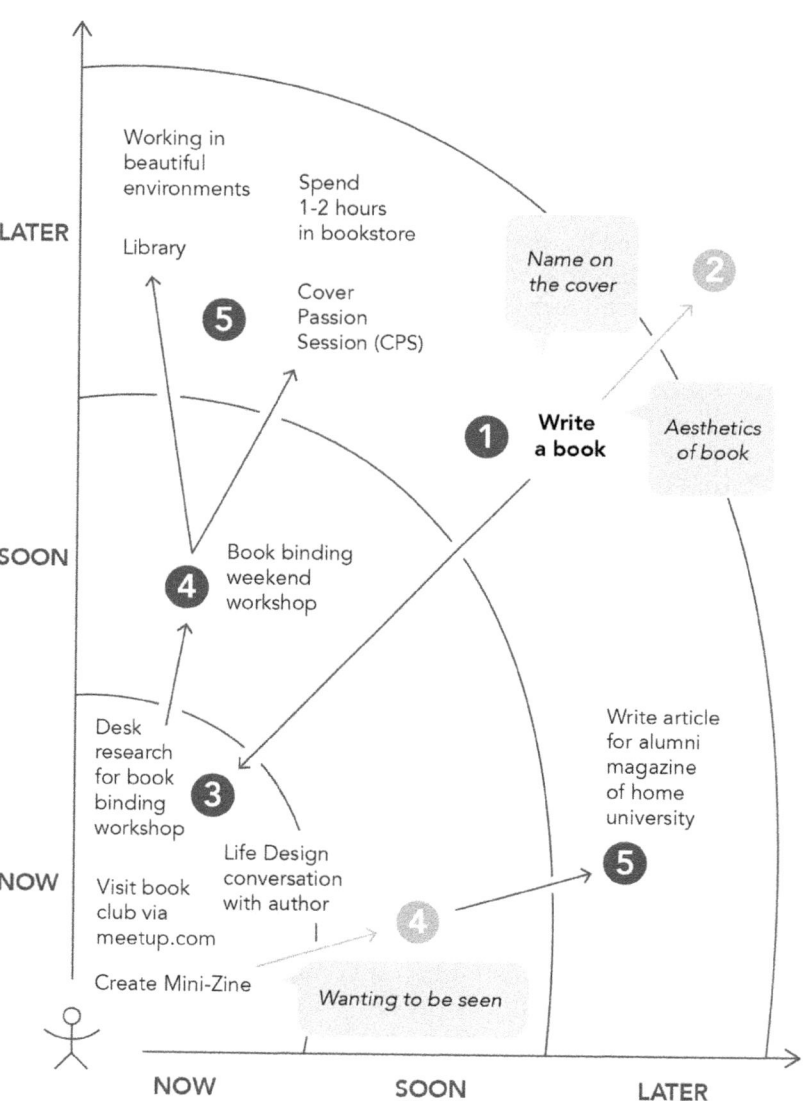

Figure 9.5 The Stairway to Heaven.

a book club via Meetup.com, and scheduling a Life Design conversation with an author.

(4) Design your way forward: what actions will you take?
With your Stairway mapped out, start putting one or two prototypes into action. In the preceding example, the participant signed up for a weekend bookbinding class and created a mini-zine with her name on the cover – a ten-minute prototype.

(5) Learn and adapt as you go: what insights are emerging?
Every prototype brings learning. The bookbinding class revealed she didn't want to bind books – but she *did* love their aesthetics. This led to a new, low-pressure prototype: visiting bookstores each Saturday just to admire cover designs – her self-declared "Cover-Passion Sessions." The mini-zine sparked another insight. After seeing her name on the cover, she thought, "That's nice, but actually I want to be seen." When her Life Design team asked, "Tell us more: by whom do you want to be seen?" she replied, "By the alumni of my Chinese university." This realization led to her writing an article for the alumni magazine, aiming to inspire young women from her home country to take bold steps abroad.

Tips and Tricks

- Follow the energy. Always write down what's *behind* your wish – what gives it energy for you? Without this clarity, participants often struggle to generate meaningful ideas or feel disconnected from the ones they do have. Take the time to articulate your motivation. It's the fuel for everything that follows.
- Take action within twenty-four hours. Filling in ideas along the stairway is great – but make sure at least one is something you can do *today* or *tomorrow*. One student who dreamed of traveling the world started by going out to dinner alone that very evening. A small step, but one that set everything in motion. That's the kind of momentum you want.
- Use it for big and small goals. The Stairway to Heaven isn't just for grand life changes like writing a book or switching careers. It's equally powerful for everyday shifts – like finding more peace of mind, building a morning routine, or testing a side hustle. In organizations, people use it for everything from planning sabbaticals to improving their listening skills. Try it across different areas of life – you'll be surprised where it takes you.

CHAPTER 10

Learning Methods

Learning is what transforms action into progress. It's not just about whether a prototype worked – it's about what you discovered in the process. The learning phase helps you reflect, adapt, and carry forward what matters most. By shifting your focus from outcomes to insights, you create momentum – even when things don't go as planned. This chapter introduces three simple but powerful methods to help you pause, reflect, and integrate your learning before you take your next steps.

We start with the Core Method.

- The Growth Journey Map is a guided reflection tool that helps you make sense of your experiences, surface key insights, and connect dots across your Life Loop. It supports you in honoring your growth – especially the parts that may not have gone according to plan.

From there, you can build on your learning with two Optional Methods.

- PPCO Hollywood Star is a playful, structured feedback technique that helps you see the value in what you've tried, while generating fresh ideas for what could come next.
- Start–Stop–Continue is a straightforward tool to clarify your next steps by identifying what to keep doing, what to let go of, and what to try anew.

Whether your last experiment felt like a success, a struggle, or something in between, these methods help you close the loop and prepare for your next iteration – with clarity, confidence, and a growth mindset.

The Growth Journey Map

After you've tried out a prototype – whether it was a bold leap or a tiny experiment – it's easy to move on without fully recognizing what just

It's not whether it works or not.

It is all about what you can learn here.

happened. But that's where much of the magic lies. The Growth Journey Map is a simple yet powerful reflection tool that helps you pause, process, and make sense of your experiences. It turns scattered impressions into meaningful insights, and helps you learn not just from what worked, but also from what felt hard, surprising, or incomplete.

This method gives structure to your reflection – so you're not just replaying what happened, but actively learning from it. Whether used individually or in conversation with others, it helps you uncover themes, clarify next steps, and deepen your personal growth journey.

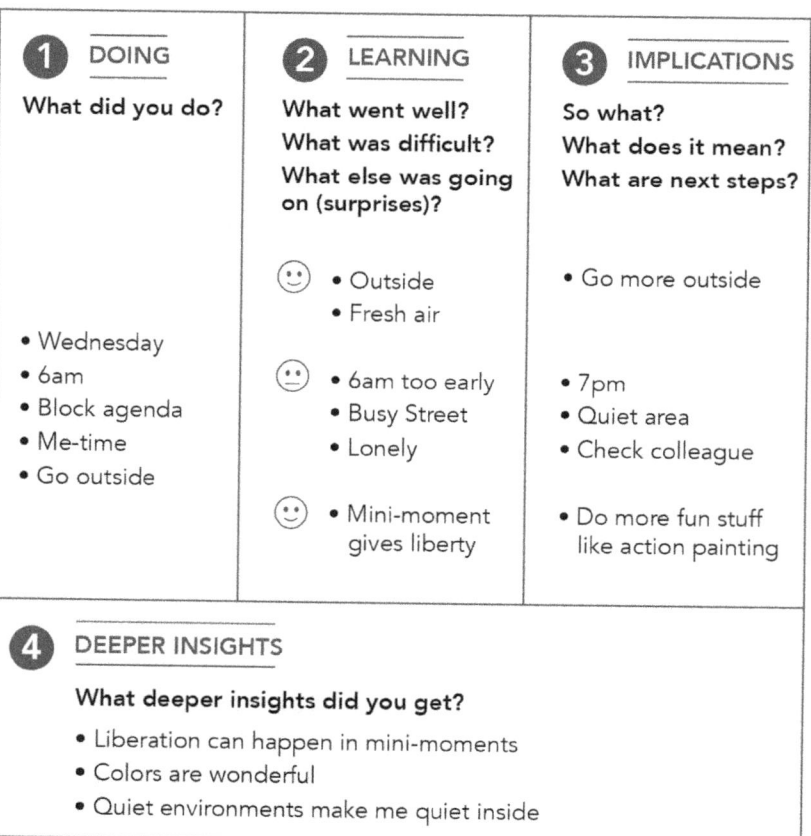

Figure 10.1 Growth Journey Map.

Procedure and Steps

Meaningful reflection doesn't happen by accident. It needs structure. The following steps guiding you through the Growth Journey Map support both individual reflection and team conversations. They help you make sense of what happened, extract insights, and prepare for your next iteration. Here's how it works.

(1) Doing: what did you do?

Write down what you did – include when, where, and with whom. Be as specific as possible. Examples might include: "Bought three interior design magazines at the Monocle store"; "Stayed in bed and took three deep breaths with my eyes closed at 8 am"; "Attended a Tuesday conference with Susan on AI and Female Leadership in San Francisco."

In our example, she wrote: "Blocked me-time in Outlook on Wednesday at 6 am and went for a walk around my neighborhood."

(2) Learning: what did you learn?

Reflect on what you learned – during the experience, shortly afterward, and now in hindsight. Ask yourself: "What went well?"; "What was difficult?"; "What surprised me?"; "What else was going on?"

You can also add your own reflection questions. In our example, for what went well, she wrote: "Going outside felt great. The fresh air really lifted my mood. Being alone was relaxing." For what was difficult: "I felt guilty for blocking the time. I immediately thought, 'What if someone sees this? What would they think?' 6 am was a bit too early, I felt a bit lonely, and parts of the walk were too busy – crossing streets, watching traffic." For what was surprising: "Giving yourself a small moment of time can feel incredibly liberating. I totally underestimated that. Even short time windows can have a big effect. Yeah!"

(3) Implications: so what?

Now connect what you did and what you learned to next steps. Ask yourself: "So what?"; "What will I do with this?"; "What might my next prototype look like?"

In our example, she checked with a colleague to see how blocked time appears in shared calendars. She also made adjustments – changing the walk to 7 pm instead of 6 am, inviting a colleague to join, and choosing a quieter route. Finally, energized by the idea that "small things can have big impact," she signed up for an action-painting class.

(4) Deeper insights: how has this affected you?
Take a step back. Has this – or a series of prototypes – revealed something deeper? A pattern? A shift? A new theme emerging? In our example, she noted: "Mini-moments of freedom feel deeply liberating. Color energizes me. Quiet outside helps me feel calm inside." These insights didn't require a plan, just awareness.

You can note down questions, themes, or new opportunity statements, such as: "How might I bring more meaningful connections into my life?"; "How might I reconnect with my love for art?"; "What environments bring me most alive?"

Tips and Tricks

- Talk to others. Filling out the Growth Journey Map on your own is powerful – but even more so when shared. If you're in a Life Design team, pair up and exchange insights. Listening to someone else's reflection – and hearing their "Tell me more..." – can deepen your own.
- Reflect – even if you think nothing happened. Don't dismiss your experience just because it felt small. Many participants say, "I didn't do much," only to realize – once they write and talk about it – that a lot actually happened. Trust the process.
- Include what you didn't do (advanced tip). Reflect on what you intended but didn't do. What held you back? What did you learn from not taking action? This normalizes inaction as part of the creative process and builds a bridge to the next chapter on procrastination, where we'll explore how to get unstuck and move forward.

PPCO Hollywood Star

There may be plenty of stars in Hollywood, but one of the brightest when it comes to feedback is the PPCO method, a go-to tool used by professional screenwriters to develop scripts for major films and hit series in Hollywood to turn actors into stars. Fun fact: the writing team behind the hit show *Dr. House* used PPCO to fine-tune episodes with constructive input that was both honest and empowering.

In Life Design, you can use this same framework to reflect on your own prototypes or to give supportive, structured feedback to others. Whether you're offering input on a new habit, a creative side hustle, or someone's bold career experiment, PPCO creates a safe and energizing space for learning. The acronym stands for: "plus" – what's working? What did you like? "Potential" – what's the opportunity here? Where could this go? "Concern" – what's missing or unclear? "Overcome" – how might the concern be addressed?

It's a method we've used to transform feedback cultures inside teams and organizations, and it works just as well one-on-one or for self-reflection. The following steps will show you how to apply PPCO to your own prototypes, so you can move from "That was interesting..." to "Here's what I'll try next."

PPCO-HOLLYWOOD-STAR

PROTOTYPE	
First conversation as a mentor	
① PLUS What was good?	**② POTENTIAL** What has more potential?
• Showed enthusiasm and interest in mentee • Mentee was motivated at the end of the conversation	• Offer more suggestions for social skills (not just technical support)
③ CONCERN What was difficult?	**④ OVERCOME** How could it be overcome?
• Added too much of my own interpretation • Mentee's moments of reflection were too long ago	• Listen more patiently • Address the mentee's statements • Phone call immediately after an important event (lightning rod)

Figure 10.2 PPCO Hollywood Star.

Procedure and Steps

Let's explore the PPCO method using a real-life example: someone testing out mentoring by having their first mentoring conversation. Mentoring today comes in many forms, from formal programs to reverse mentoring and informal mini-mentorships (inspired by the work of Bernie Roth at Stanford d.school). Here's how you can use the PPCO formula to reflect and grow from your prototype.

(1) P for "plus": what went well?
    The first "P" stands for "plus" and highlights what worked – both during the experience and in hindsight. In our example, the mentor noted she had been fully present, asked thoughtful questions, and her mentee left the conversation feeling motivated and understood.
(2) P for "potential": what could be expanded?
    The second "P" is for "potential," focusing on what went well and could be developed even further. The mentor realized she mostly offered technical advice but saw untapped potential to also support her mentee's interpersonal development in future sessions.
(3) C for "concern": what was difficult?
    The "C" stands for "concern." This is where you acknowledge challenges – not by labeling them as failures, but by neutrally identifying what felt hard. The mentor noticed she sometimes inserted her own interpretations, and that long reflection gaps made it harder for her mentee to recall key moments.
(4) O for "overcome": how can it be improved?
    Here's the heart of the method: every concern must come with at least one idea for how to "overcome" it, marked by the "O". In this case, the mentor decided to pause more often, reflect back only the mentee's own words, and offer a quick call right after important events to capture fresh impressions while they were still vivid.

Whether you're mentoring, testing a new career idea, or building a habit, PPCO helps you stay constructive, curious, and focused on learning.

Tips and Tricks

- Use it solo or in conversation. The PPCO method works beautifully both as a self-reflection tool and in dialogue with others. You can use it to analyze your own prototype experience – or explore it together with peers. As Heinrich von Kleist described in his essay "On the Gradual

Formation of Thoughts While Speaking," verbalizing your experience can surface fresh insights. If you did a prototype with someone else, take turns giving each other feedback using the PPCO structure – not just on the process, but also on subtle observations. For example: 'When you held the book in your hand, there was a glow on your face-like a quiet kind of joy." You can also use PPCO as an interview guide: when someone returns from a prototype experience like shadowing or volunteering, go beyond "How was it?" and ask, "What was a plus? Where did you see potential? Any concerns? And how might you overcome them?"

- Start with what's working. Begin with the two "Ps" – "plus" and "potential." It takes awareness and effort to notice and name what went well, rather than skipping straight to what didn't. Celebrating strengths builds momentum and helps identify what to amplify. For example, in our earlier bookbinding story, the participant recognized her joy in the aesthetics of books during a workshop – an insight that later inspired bookstore visits to admire typography and design.
- Balance critique with solutions. In Hollywood, screenwriters follow the golden rule: for every critique, offer at least one concrete idea to improve it. That's the essence of the "concern"–"overcome" combo in PPCO. Instead of just highlighting what didn't work, you're challenged to suggest a way forward. And if you're just starting out, it's okay to collect concerns first, then collaborate to find ways to overcome them. That's where the creative growth happens.

Start–Stop–Continue

Many people tell us that while prototyping is challenging, the real hurdle comes afterward: taking the time to pause and learn from the experience. That's why we created one of the shortest and most practical reflection tools: Start–Stop–Continue.

Instead of falling into black-and-white thinking – what worked versus what didn't – this method helps you reflect more constructively. It invites you to ask:

- "What do I want to continue because it worked well?"
- "What do I want to start or do more of?"
- "What do I want to stop or do less of?"

These three simple prompts make it easier to extract key insights and translate them into small adjustments or entirely new prototypes.

START-STOP-CONTINUE

PROTOTYPE Action painting		④ OK COOL, NOW WHAT?
① START ↑	Share with friends	Bring partner, bring best friend, glass of Prosecco
② STOP ↓	Pressure to perform, big size Canvas	Work with kids, reduce to postcard size
③ CONTINUE →	Letting go, celebrate celebrate	Find more opportunities to let go

Figure 10.3 Start–Stop–Continue.

Procedure and Steps

Use the following four steps to reflect on your prototype experience in a structured yet simple way. Let's follow the story of Laura, a Life Design workshop participant who explored action painting – experimenting with colors on a blank canvas in a small group setting. Here's how she reflected on it.

(1) Start: what do you want to bring in next time?

Think about what was missing and what you'd like to add. For example, in the case of Laura, she realized she would have enjoyed sharing the experience with others – so her next prototype was to bring a friend or even organize an action painting session as a team event at work.

(2) Stop: what would you change or do less of?

Reflect on anything that felt off or draining. For example, Laura noticed that her pressure to "create something beautiful" limited her joy. That changed when she painted with two children in the group – whose playful energy helped her let go. She also found the single large canvas intimidating. When she discovered smaller postcard-sized canvases and worked on three instead of one, her energy and confidence soared. A small shift made a big difference.

(3) Continue: what do you wish to keep and how?
Capture what worked well and energized you. For example, Laura loved the experience of letting go and decided she wanted more moments like that in her life. Her insight turned into a new question: "How might I create more moments of freedom and playfulness in everyday life?"

(4) Okay, cool, now what? What's your next step?
Review your Start–Stop–Continue insights and choose one idea that gives you energy. Write it down as your next prototype. This is your launchpad. You don't need to have it all figured out – just take the next small step forward. That's how real change begins.

Tips and Tricks

- Turn it into a three-by-three learning grid. Enhance the method by adding three perspectives to each of the Continue, Start, and Stop categories: "What did I learn about myself?"; "What did I learn about the situation?"; "What did I learn from others (if they were involved or observed me)?" This turns a simple reflection into a deeper learning grid, helping you gain richer insights and iterate more intentionally.
- Use it for life transitions. Although this method is designed to reflect on prototypes, it also works beautifully for life transitions – like changing careers, entering a new life chapter, or even moving into a new year. With executives, we reframe the prompts into poetic transition questions like: "What starts? What stops? What stays?" or "What comes? What goes? What remains?" These questions invite meaningful conversations – both with yourself and others – and shift your thinking from either-or decisions to more layered, future-oriented reflections. Bonus tip: add a "how" to each question for even more clarity, for example, "What stays – and how?"
- Need-to-have versus nice-to-have. In Step (4), "Okay, cool, now what?", when deciding what to do next, try sorting your ideas by priority. Which are need-to-haves – essential for your growth or well-being? And which are nice-to-haves – valuable, but not urgent? This small shift helps you focus your energy where it matters most.

CHAPTER 11

Perseverance Methods

Moving forward isn't always about motivation – it's often about strategy. Whether you're struggling to begin a new prototype or finding it hard to keep going, procrastination can quietly stall even your best intentions. But instead of treating it as a personal failure, Life Design treats procrastination as part of the human experience – and offers tools to work with it, not against it. This chapter introduces three evidence-based methods to help you bridge the gap between intention and action, no matter where you are in your Life Loop.

We begin with the Core Method.

- Nudging Nuggets is a behavioral economics approach that helps you design small cues and structures that support follow-through – without relying on willpower alone.

To go further, you can explore two Optional Methods.

- DJ of the Inner Sound is a neuroscience-informed practice to recognize and redirect unhelpful self-talk that may be getting in your way.
- The Social Support Map is a simple yet powerful way to identify and activate the kinds of relationships that energize, motivate, and hold you accountable.

These methods are part of our broader research initiative, The Science of Action, and have helped people from all walks of life take meaningful steps – even when stuck. Let's explore how you can keep moving forward, with less pressure and more momentum.

Nudging Nuggets

One effective way to overcome procrastination is through *nudging* – a concept rooted in behavioral economics. This method is part of our broader Science of Action project, which maps common reasons people

11 Perseverance Methods

What gets in the / Becomes the **WAY**

procrastinate to science-based strategies that help them take action. In this method, we focus on how nudging can support you in changing habits and routines – and even help with larger goals like career shifts, side projects, or long-held dreams.

Behavioral economics is a field that explores how people make decisions – especially how they can influence their own behavior. It goes beyond conscious, rational decision-making to examine the often-invisible power of subconscious choices. Daniel Kahneman, Nobel laureate and author of the book Thinking, Fast and Slow, describes two systems that govern how we think.

- System 1: fast, automatic, intuitive, and unconscious.
- System 2: slow, deliberate, effortful, and conscious.

Most of us assume we operate mainly in System 2, carefully weighing options and making reasoned decisions – like what to eat for dinner. But in reality, 70–80 percent of our daily decisions are driven by System 1 – without us even noticing.

This is where nudging comes in. Nudging uses the natural tendencies of System 1 – our mental shortcuts, inertia, and desire for convenience – to gently guide us toward better choices. Rather than forcing action through willpower, nudging creates conditions where the easiest choice is the right one. In other words: you can use your own laziness to your advantage.

Procedure and Steps

The following steps show you how to apply four core Nudging Nuggets to help overcome procrastination and make desired behaviors more likely. Each principle uses behavioral science not to force change, but to gently guide it – making it easier to do the things you already want to do.

These steps are flexible and personal. You can use them to support small habit shifts, creative routines, or even bigger life changes. Try them individually or combine them to create a "Nudge Stack" that works for you. The goal isn't to hack your life – it's to make taking action feel more natural, joyful, and doable. Let's look at how.

(1) The Power of default: create new standards.
  Humans are creatures of habit. We tend to stick with the default – whatever feels familiar or easiest. Use this to your advantage by establishing a new standard behavior.

NUDGING NUGGETS

IDEA / TOPIC		
What idea or topic are you procrastinating on? Going out for a walk enjoying Me-Time		
	NUDGING PRINCIPLES	**APPLICATION**
1 DEFAULT	How could you connect this to an existing standard or default behavior?	Connect with bringing out the trash.
2 SIGNALS	What kind of "signals" could you install to remind you of this behavior?	Post-it note next to screen or mirror showing "Mini-Retreat is Calling".
3 PRE-STRUCTURING	How could you pre-structure or prepare your behavior to reduce the effort in the moment?	Have jacket, shoes (and umbrella) ready to go straight into outdoor-mode.
4 FUN FACTOR	How could you make this behavior more fun?	Listen to favorite music, get an ice-cream or enjoy the view.

Figure 11.1 Nudging Nuggets to overcome procrastination.

For example, Ryan wanted more quality time with his wife in the mornings. They created a new routine: coffee in bed followed by breakfast and the radio. After a few repetitions, it became automatic – no longer something they had to decide each day.

(2) Signaling: send cues to yourself.

Use simple cues to remind yourself of your intention or desired behavior. These signals nudge you back on track without requiring active thinking.

For example, place a water bottle on your phone so you hydrate before checking it; stick a post-it note on your mirror with a phrase like "mini-retreat is calling"; or lay out running shoes and clothes the night before to increase the chance you'll go for a jog.

(3) Prestructuring: reduce effort in the moment.

Structure your environment or routine in advance to reduce decision-making later. Make your future behavior easier by preparing for it ahead of time.

For example, block time in your calendar in advance and treat it like any other meeting; prep your workspace, breakfast, or walking route the night before; or keep your jacket, shoes, and umbrella by the door so it's effortless to step outside.

(4) The fun factor: make it enjoyable.

Fun reduces resistance. When something feels joyful or rewarding, you're more likely to follow through and come back to it.

For example, Peter wanted to take afternoon walks but found them boring. When he combined them with a stop at the kiosk for his favorite drink, walking became a treat – and a habit.

Tips and Tricks

- Make it your own. You'll get advice from others about what works for them – but what works for you may be different. Be open to experimenting and adapting nudges to your needs.
- Prototype different nudges. If one doesn't work, try another. A consultant at BCG tried putting out her running clothes as a signal – but it didn't help. Then she used the default strategy and slept in her running gear. That worked.
- Nudge others. These principles work for teams, families, and organizations too. You can support others' behavior through nudging – like positioning food in the fridge, setting up defaults, or creating fun

meeting rituals. Even the European Central Bank used nudging to make meetings more effective (check out meetup-book.com for more than 100 nudges for meetings).

DJ of the Inner Sound

Your inner voices are constant companions. Most of them begin as external voices – parents, teachers, coaches, friends, even advertisements – that gradually become internalized. These voices show up every day, especially in challenging moments, and can be a powerful resource. But sometimes, they get in the way, holding us back from taking action on the things that matter most.

It's not just people close to us who shape our inner dialogue. Society, too, speaks through us. Cultural norms and deeply embedded beliefs – often dysfunctional – can take root in our minds and subtly dictate what's possible. Ideas like "first hard work, then have fun," "at your age you can't do this" (whether you're seemingly too young or too old), or "retirement means finally doing nothing" can become invisible scripts that steer us away from what we really want. These beliefs aren't facts – they're stories. And recognizing them is the first step to rewriting them.

Philosophers, athletes, and high-performing leaders all understand the power of self-talk. That's why many of them actively practice shaping their inner dialogue. In a Life Design conversation, we asked a gold-medalist from the US swim team, Breeja Larson, what helped her stay motivated, bounce back from failure, and keep going on tough mornings. Her answer? "Being my own best friend." She described a practice of speaking to herself with compassion, patience, and constructive encouragement. So, how can you become your own best ally? How can you guide your inner choir to support – not sabotage – you?

The method you're about to explore helps you map your inner voices onto specific areas in your body, making them more tangible and easier to observe. You'll identify which voices hold you back and which ones push you forward, and learn how to reshape the inner soundscape to support your ideas, decisions, and next steps. As Steve Jobs once said: "Don't let the noise of others' opinions drown out your own inner voice. And most important, have the courage to follow your heart and intuition." Let's turn down the volume on what doesn't serve you and tune into the voice that does!

Part III Life Design Toolbox

DJ OF THE INNER SOUND

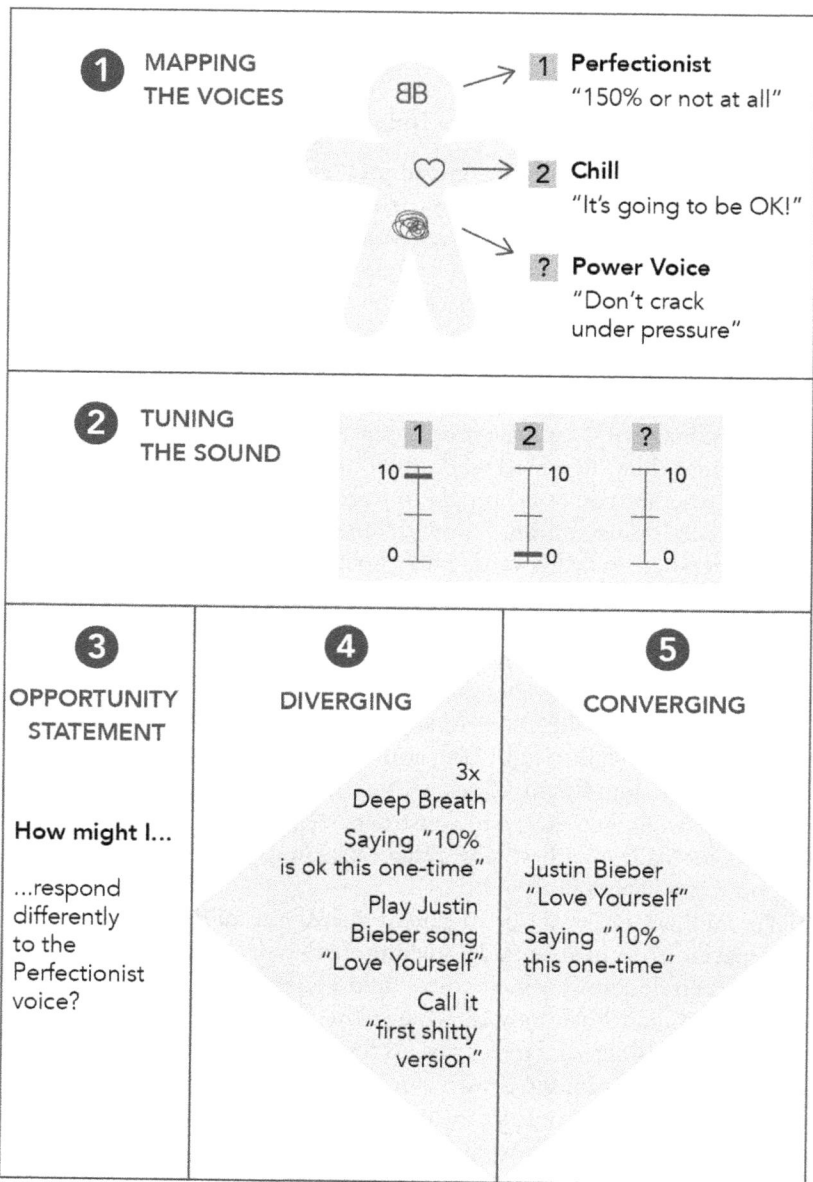

Figure 11.2 DJ of the Inner Sound.

11 Perseverance Methods

Procedure and Steps

Our inner voices are always speaking – sometimes cheering us on, sometimes holding us back. The way we respond to them can shape not only our actions, but also how we see ourselves. This method helps you bring those voices into the open so you can observe them with curiosity rather than judgment – and start to remix the soundtrack that plays in your head.

In the steps that follow, you'll map your inner voices – both distracting and supportive – onto a simple body outline to make them more tangible. This visualization helps create a healthy distance from automatic thoughts, making it easier to shift from self-sabotage to self-support. You'll then use a DJ-style mental "mixer" to adjust the volume on key voices and explore creative ways to amplify the ones that move you forward. This isn't about silencing your inner critics forever – it's about learning to live and design alongside them, with more awareness, compassion, and choice. Let's tune in.

(1) Draw your body: where are your brain, heart, and gut?
   Start by sketching a simple outline of your body. Don't worry about making it look nice – just give yourself space to place different voices. You can add a brain (tip: two mirrored Bs), a heart, and a gut (perhaps a bundle of swirling circles). These symbolic zones will help you locate your voices later.

(2) Map distracting voices: what are they saying?
   Think of a time when you wanted to start a prototype, begin a project, or simply get up – but didn't. Go back into that moment and listen to your inner dialogue. What voices held you back? Label each one and write down its typical line.
   For example, the Perfectionist thinks, "Either 150% or not at all." The Anti-Believer thinks, "This is never going to work."
   Now place them on your body sketch. Are they located in your head (analytical), your heart (emotional), your gut (instinctive), or somewhere else?

(3) Map supportive voices: what are they saying?
   Now recall a moment when you did take action, when you prototyped, started something, or followed through. What inner voices were present and helpful? Label and quote them, too.
   For example, the Chill Voice says, "It's going to be alright." The Life Designer says, "Just try it once and see what you can learn – it's only a prototype."
   Place these positive voices on your body sketch as well.

(4) Increase awareness: what's going on inside?
   Step back and look at the full picture. This mapping helps create distance, and neuroscience shows that distancing yourself from your inner voices is one of the most effective ways to handle them more consciously.
(5) Identify focus voices: which ones need attention?
   Circle one to three key voices that have the most influence over your behavior. It could be a negative voice you want to quiet – or a positive one you want to turn up. These are the voices you'll work with on your internal DJ mixer.
(6) Use the DJ mixer: how can you redesign the soundtrack?
   Imagine your inner soundscape like a DJ mixer. What's too loud? What's barely audible? Rate each focus voice from 1 to 10 in terms of volume.
   For example, the Perfectionist is at 10 and the Chill Voice is at 2.
   Now, formulate design questions to rebalance the mix: "How might I turn down the Perfectionist?"; "How might I give more volume to the Chill Voice?"; "How might I respond differently to the Perfectionist?"
   In one workshop, a participant worked with the question, "How might I respond differently to the Perfectionist?" Her team asked: "What would a supportive friend say?" and "How would a kind aunt or favorite character from a movie respond?" They used the Core of Creativity to brainstorm playful and practical strategies. The participant tried several ideas, like listening to Justin Bieber's "Love Yourself," texting a friend when the voice appeared, and saying to herself: "I hear you, Perfectionist. But just for today, I'm going to try 10 percent instead of 150 percent – just to see what happens."

Tips and Tricks

- Embody your voices. A powerful extension of this method is to physically embody inner voices – often done in pairs. One person plays the voice, the other experiences it. For example, we've seen someone bend over their partner, arms pressing toward their head, enacting a perfectionist voice. The result? A strong physical reaction – literally pushing the voice away. It's a visceral reminder of the impact these voices can have.
- Say it out loud. Hearing your inner voice spoken by someone else can be eye-opening. Have a partner say the things you typically tell yourself.

How does it feel when those words are spoken aloud? Then, practice responding with different tones – curious, compassionate, assertive, or even as your Life Designer voice.
- Play with the metaphor. We use the DJ metaphor because it allows you to remix your inner soundtrack – lowering the volume on a negative track or swapping in a more energizing one. But you can also choose another metaphor that resonates more with you, like the Inner Choir, the Inner Team, or even the Board of Advisors. The key is to find a metaphor that helps you relate to your inner voices with more creativity and control.

The Social Support Map

One of the most common reasons we don't get started or struggle to keep going with our prototypes is the feeling of being alone. A lack of support can quietly undermine even our best intentions. The Social Support Map is a method that helps you visualize and activate the network of people who can support you as you move forward with your ideas, prototypes, or life transitions. It invites you to reflect not only on who might help, but also how. Emotional encouragement, hands-on collaboration, resource-sharing, or gentle accountability – different kinds of support serve different needs.

While the DJ of the Inner Sound focused on reshaping the voices inside your head, the Social Support Map turns your attention outward. Because sometimes, what holds us back isn't an inner critic – it's the quiet absence of connection, encouragement, or shared momentum.

This method helps you spot where support already exists in your life and where it might be missing. By mapping out your Cheerleaders, Joiners, Connectors, and GKITBs (those who give you a "gentle kick in the butt"), you can begin to design a support system that feels intentional, personal, and energizing. For example, let's say your goal is to run a marathon, a half-marathon, or even a 10k. The following steps will show you how to identify the right people to support you – each in their own unique way. Whether you're starting something new or trying to keep going, this map helps you remember you don't have to do it alone!

Procedure and Steps

In the steps ahead, you'll create a visual map of your current and potential support system – centered around a project or prototype you've been putting off or struggling to act on. You'll identify people who lift you

Part III Life Design Toolbox

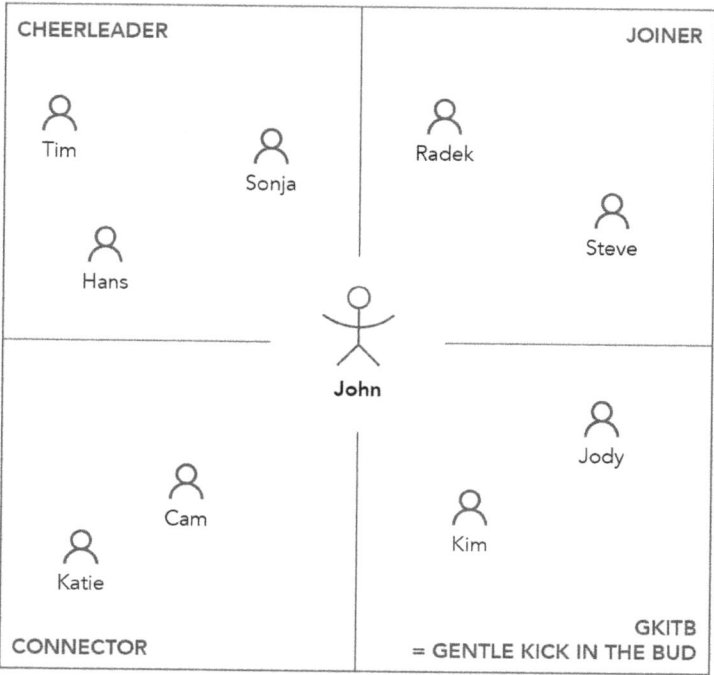

Figure 11.3 The Social Support Map.

up, those who might join you in action, connectors who open doors, and those who lovingly hold you accountable. You'll walk away not only with a clearer sense of who's in your corner, but also with concrete next steps to invite that support in. Let's start mapping and move from stuck to supported.

(1) Draw your map: who's around you?
Start with a blank sheet of paper. Draw yourself in the center – a simple smiley or stick figure works – and write your name next to it. This map is about you and the support around you.

(2) Cheerleaders: who lifts you up?
In the top-left corner, list the people who give you moral support. These are your encouragers – those who celebrate your efforts, offer comforting words when things get tough, or simply believe in you. They may not join your journey directly, but their presence matters.

Write down their names and how they cheer for you – each person might do it in their own unique way.
(3) Joiners: who might jump in with you?
In the top-right corner, name the people who might actually join you in action. These are your running buddies, your painting partners, your fellow workshop explorers. They share the experience, add energy, and might even cocreate something with you. Write their names and how they might participate.
(4) Connectors: who could connect you?
In the bottom-left corner, list people who might not join you directly but could open doors – by introducing you to others, sharing useful resources, or pointing you toward communities or opportunities. For instance, someone who knows a running coach or can connect you with a local creative meetup.
(5) GKITBs: who gives you a gentle kick in the butt?
This category – coined by Stanford DCI fellows – is for those who lovingly nudge you forward. Who holds you accountable in a supportive way? Maybe they check in with you, remind you of your goals, or just say, "Come on, do it!" Write down who gives you that push – and how they do it.
(6) Take action: who do you reach out to next?
Once your map is complete, take a moment to appreciate the support you already have. Then ask yourself: who could I thank? Who could I talk to next? Maybe you reach out to a Joiner or Connector. Maybe you ideate how to find someone new. You can even turn it into a "How might I..." question, like, "How might I find someone to run with?" or "How might I connect with others in the creative community?"

This method helps you recognize not only who is in your circle, but also what kind of support you need – emotional, practical, motivational, or connective. It's a powerful way to turn isolation into momentum.

Tips and Tricks

- One person, multiple roles. Some people might show up in more than one category – and that's great! If someone supports you in multiple ways, draw them in each relevant corner of your map. This makes their

different forms of support more visible, depending on where your focus lies (e.g., cheerleading versus joining).
- Create your own category. Category 4, GKITB, was coined during a seminar at Stanford, and it stuck because it resonated with many. But feel free to personalize your map. If another category would better reflect the kind of support you need, swap it in! The goal is to make the map work for you.
- Play with the visual. Customize the look and feel of your map. You can draw people who offer stronger support as larger figures or use shapes to distinguish between work (squares) and personal (circles) contacts. Add hearts to those closest to you – turn it into a heartstorming rather than a brainstorming. Let the visual express what matters most.

PART IV

Life Design Secrets
What 10000+ People Taught Us

This part focuses on the learnings we have collected from working with thousands of people around the world. These are learnings you cannot Google, but they are essentially valuable and often represent things everyone thinks but rarely speaks about.

We start with curated method mixes, which are focused on a collection of twelve typical challenges organized into four transition types. We map each of these frequent challenges with a proven mix of methods that help people to better deal with these challenges, from not knowing where to start, to regaining agency when life feels overwhelming, to finding new ways to create ideas, and finally staying relevant and living big dreams even if they seem far away. You'll find guidance on how to string together methods across phases to meet your current needs with clarity and creativity.

Chapter 13 then introduces special methods – three powerful practices we've seen consistently empower Life Designers to sustain change beyond a workshop or coaching session. These power enablers offer an additional layer of support for real-life application: cultivating your energy competence, creating tangible outputs, and building a supportive social environment. Together, they help you anchor your Life Design journey in daily routines and relationships, making it more likely that insights turn into lasting shifts.

Finally, in Chapter 14 we explore the silent truths – the questions and quiet struggles many of us carry but rarely voice. These invisible transitions often surface only in private moments, after a seminar ends. In this chapter, we name what has long remained unnamed, because naming is where redesign begins. We invite you to reflect on five silent truths: the desire to combine passions and security in a portfolio, the identification of shifts in retirement, the distractions of social media, the quest for life satisfaction, and finding time to act – so you can begin shaping a life that feels truly your own.

CHAPTER 12

Method Mix by Transition Type

In this chapter, we present curated method mixes designed to address typical transition challenges and real-life situations that arise when we seek to change, grow, or take a more proactive role in shaping our future. The method combinations are crafted to meet you where you are and guide you through a tailored journey of reflection, ideation, and action.

Based on the most frequent intentions and design needs shared by Life Designers, we've identified twelve typical scenarios clustered into four key transition types that share a similar design challenge. We hope you'll recognize your current situation among them and find not only a deeper understanding of what you're experiencing, but also practical tools and concrete next steps to start designing your path forward. The following is an overview of the different scenarios.

- Transition type A: the Unsettled Starter.
  Main challenge: finding direction and energy to start the journey.
  Scenario 1: "I want to change something, but I don't know where to start."
  Scenario 2: "I wonder what's next in my career and life."
  Scenario 3: "I know what I don't want any more, but not what else to do."

- Transition type B: the Overwhelmed Navigator.
  Main challenge: regaining agency when life feels overwhelming.
  Scenario 4: "I have no control over so many things. Can I still design my future?"
  Scenario 5: "I have the fear of missing out."
  Scenario 6: "How can I realize my potential?"

- Transition type C: the Stuck Creative.
  Main challenge: unlocking creativity to find new possibilities.
  Scenario 7: "I always have the same ideas. How could I come up with something new?"
  Scenario 8: "I have many ideas but end up doing nothing."

Scenario 9: "I'm stuck in either-or thinking, like 'shall I stay or shall I go?'"
- Transition type D: the Meaning-Maker.
Main challenge: living big dreams, finding purpose, and staying relevant.
Scenario 10: "I want to finally fulfill my big life dreams, but they seem so far away."
Scenario 11: "I want to stay useful, be interested, and stay interesting."
Scenario 12: "What should I do with my life?"

Transition Type A: The Unsettled Starter

Main Challenge: Finding Direction and Energy to Start the Journey

The Unsettled Starter is someone who senses the need for change but is unsure where or how to begin. This type's core challenge is navigating that foggy in-between space – feeling the pull toward something different, but lacking the clarity, confidence, or momentum to take the first step. The method mix offered here is designed especially for people in this early phase of transition. Whether you're stuck in a routine, uncertain about what's next, or simply longing to feel more energized and aligned, these tools help you begin – gently, but intentionally.

In the following scenarios, you'll meet Lena, Maya, and Marianne – three people who didn't have all the answers, but who began by paying attention to what gave them life. Through reflections like Me at My Best, mapping strengths, and testing ideas with low-pressure prototypes, they moved from uncertainty to momentum. Their stories show that you don't need a master plan to begin – you just need the willingness to notice, explore, and take one small, meaningful step. Because every big journey begins not with certainty, but with curiosity.

Scenario 1 "I Want to Change Something, But I Don't Know Where to Start"

Lena sat in yet another Zoom meeting, her mind drifting. She wasn't miserable, but something felt off. A quiet voice inside whispered, "I want to change something." But what? And where to begin?

Three Good Things
That evening, she tried a simple exercise a friend had suggested: writing down Three Good Things from her day: (1) a colleague thanked her for

truly listening; (2) she solved a tricky problem with a creative idea; (3) she felt energized mentoring a junior teammate. Something clicked. She kept going – Three Good Things, every night. Gradually, patterns emerged. She wasn't just reflecting; she was noticing what brought her joy.

Signature Strength
Curious, Lena took a character strengths assessment. From the long list she identified those that resonated most with her inner self. Her top traits? Perspective, creativity, and love of learning. "These aren't just personality traits," she thought. "They're clues – maybe even a compass."

Strengths Portfolio
She began using her Signature Strengths more intentionally: taking on creative projects, mentoring others, learning new skills. Work felt lighter – less like a grind, more like a playground. She didn't quit overnight. But she started exploring, talking to people, trying small experiments.

The Biggest Shift?
Lena stopped waiting for a grand answer and started following her energy and small clues. Sometimes the first step isn't dramatic. It's quiet. But it changes everything.

Box 12.1 Method Mix 1: From Stuck to Starting

When you don't know where to start, begin with what already gives you energy.

Here are three small but powerful methods to help you reconnect with what matters and gain momentum.

(1) Three Good Things: notice what's working.

> Write down three positive things from your day and why they mattered. This builds emotional awareness and highlights what brings joy.

(2) Signature Strengths: discover your natural fuel.

> Take the VIA Character Strengths survey to uncover core traits like curiosity, creativity, or perseverance – often invisible sources of energy. This is the first part of the Strengths Portfolio method.

(3) Strengths Portfolio: use your superpowers.

> Identify different areas of life that allow you to use your top three to seven strengths more regularly. Start applying them more often and more intentionally – in conversations, decisions, and small daily choices. This is the second part of the Strengths Portfolio method.

> **Box 12.2 Action Prompt**
>
> Designing your future begins with noticing what already gives you life. That's your starting point. Write down Three Good Things today – just once, to start. Then take the free VIA strengths survey. Highlight three strengths that feel most energizing. Can you recall a moment when you brought them to life? How might you use them more?

Scenario 2 "I Wonder What's Next in My Career and Life"

It started with a quiet question that wouldn't leave Maya alone: "What's next for me?" Not in a crisis kind of way, more like a gentle nudge toward something more meaningful, more aligned. She didn't want another plan. She wanted direction.

Strengths Portfolio

She began with mapping out what energized her, what she was naturally good at, and what others often turned to her for.

Connecting the Dots

Then, she laid out her past experiences, interests, and patterns. Slowly, a bigger picture came into focus – one that sparked curiosity.

Future Scenarios

She moved on to imagining different versions of her future: running a retreat in nature, creating learning spaces for women in transition, hosting a podcast while working remotely. Each scenario felt bold, playful, and possible. One idea stood out.

Magic Circle

She brought it into the Magic Circle, where imagination turns into intention. "What if I cocreate a weekend workshop to test this?" she thought.

Stairway to Heaven

She shaped the idea and translated it into action using the Stairway to Heaven – a practical plan to test the waters. Step 1 was to talk to someone who'd done it. Step 2 was to host a tiny version with friends. Step 3 was to reflect and iterate. She started prototyping her way forward, not needing to know it all – just the next step.

Growth Journey Map

With each action, she checked in with her Growth Journey Map to reflect on what energized her, what challenged her, and where new insights were emerging. It wasn't a straight path. But it felt right. And that first question? It evolved: "What else might be possible?"

The Biggest Shift?

Maya realized she didn't need to wait for clarity – she could create it through action. Each small step gave her new information, new energy, and a deeper sense of alignment. It wasn't about finding the one right answer – it was about staying in motion, guided by what felt true.

Box 12.3 Method Mix 2: From Question to Possibility

You don't need a final answer – just the courage to explore your own possibilities.

If you're standing at a crossroads, these five methods help you explore options and move forward with creativity and confidence.

(1) The Strengths Portfolio: gather your energy sources.
    Map out what you're good at, what energizes you, and what others rely on you for.

(2) Connecting the Dots: find meaning in your past.
    Lay out key experiences, interests, and turning points to spot patterns and possibilities.

(3) Future Scenarios: imagine bold new paths.
    Use what you've uncovered to draft several future storylines – serious, playful, or surprising.

(4) The Magic Circle: turn ideas into testable prototypes.
    Choose one scenario and turn it into a prototype idea that's creative but grounded.

(5) The Stairway to Heaven: get moving in small steps.
    Break your prototype into doable steps – what can you try now, soon, and later? Use each small action to explore, learn, and refine your direction.

(6) The Growth Journey Map: reflect, adapt, and grow.
    Capture what energized you, what challenged you, and what surprised you. Use your reflections to deepen insight and guide your next iteration.

> **Box 12.4 Action Prompt**
>
> You don't design your future all at once – you design it one bold question, one small step at a time. Reflect on: what energizes you right now? What stories, strengths, and interests have shaped you? What are three possible future paths you'd love to explore? Pick one future scenario and bring it into the Magic Circle. Break it into steps using the Stairway to Heaven. Try the first one. Then reflect using the Growth Journey Map: what did I learn? What surprised me? What do I want to try next?

Scenario 3 "I Know What I Don't Want Anymore, But Not What Else to Do"

Marianne had been a team leader for over six years. She was good at it – respected, efficient, the one people turned to in a crisis. But something had shifted. The meetings, the metrics, the nonstop urgency – none of it energized her anymore. She found herself thinking, "I know what I don't want. But I have no idea what's next."

Connecting the Dots

One quiet Sunday, she sat down with a blank page and did the Me at My Best reflection (as part of the Connecting the Dots intervention). She wrote about a time when she led a messy, high-stakes project with a crossfunctional team. It had been chaotic – but also energizing. There was collaboration, purpose, and creative flow.

Strengths Portfolio

As she reread the story, something clicked. She started highlighting moments when she had felt most alive. From there, she built her Strengths Portfolio: systems thinking, focus under pressure, making complexity simple, holding space for teams to thrive. "These are my core ingredients," she thought, "and I haven't used some of them in years."

Opportunity Bingo

Feeling curious again, she pulled out her Opportunity Bingo sheet. She mixed and matched strengths, past roles, random ideas, and hidden passions.

- Strategy + facilitation + nature = leadership retreats in the wild.
- Systems thinking + empathy = coaching ops leads through burnout.
- Storytelling + experience design = designing energizing offsites.

None of these were final answers, but they were fresh directions. She didn't need to figure it all out. She just had to follow the energy and prototype forward. For the first time in a long time, the unknown didn't feel like a threat. It felt like an invitation.

The Biggest Shift?
Marianne stopped trying to find the perfect answer and started listening to her own energy. Instead of chasing clarity, she gave herself permission to explore. What once felt like an empty space became a playground for new possibilities.

> **Box 12.5 Method Mix 5: From "Not This" to "Maybe That"**
>
> When clarity is missing, creativity can lead the way.
> When you know what's no longer right but don't yet know what's next, these tools help surface clues and spark creative direction.
>
> (1) Connecting the Dots: uncover energizing moments.
>   Reflect on a time when you were at your best. What were you doing? How did you feel? What made it meaningful?
>
> (2) The Strengths Portfolio: name your active ingredients.
>   Map out the skills, traits, and energies that show up when you thrive. What do others rely on you for? What lights you up?
>
> (3) Opportunity Bingo: mix the expected with the unexpected.
>   Combine your strengths, experiences, curiosities, and wild ideas to generate new career directions. Playfully. No pressure.

> **Box 12.6 Action Prompt**
>
> You don't need a perfect answer. Just a few good questions and the courage to play. Do the Connecting the Dots exercise: when were you last at your best? What were you doing? What strengths or skills showed up in that moment? Highlight the actions, feelings, and values that matter most. Then build your Strengths Portfolio. Try one round of Opportunity Bingo: mix your skills with passions or past roles to invent three possible directions. Don't evaluate – just explore.

Transition Type B: The Overwhelmed Navigator

Main Challenge: Regaining Agency When Life Feels Overwhelming

The Overwhelmed Navigator is someone who feels caught in the storm – pulled in too many directions, drained by decision fatigue, or weighed down by the pace of life. This type's core challenge is reclaiming a sense of control and direction when everything feels too much. Whether it's external pressure, emotional overload, or fear of falling behind, the result is the same: stuckness. The method mix offered here is designed for people in this state of overload – offering small, grounding steps that restore clarity, energy, and momentum without adding pressure. These tools help you shift your attention, build emotional resilience, and reconnect with your own ability to move forward.

In the following scenarios, you'll meet Nico, Ava, and Jonas – three individuals navigating different forms of overwhelm. Through practices like identifying micro-habits, reframing comparison, using nudges, and activating social support, they each begin to design their way out of paralysis. Their stories show that regaining agency doesn't require big change – it starts with tiny shifts in mindset, environment, and conversation. Sometimes, even a gentle nudge or a well-timed pause can begin to turn the wheel.

Scenario 4 "I Have No Control Over So Many Things. Can I Still Design My Future?"

Nico sat on the edge of his bed, scrolling the news. Another crisis. Another wave of uncertainty. Work was stressful, the world felt heavy, and everything seemed beyond his influence. "I have no control over so many things," he thought. Then a quieter question emerged: "Can I still design my future?" The answer didn't roar in – it whispered: Start small. Start with something you can shape.

Routine Redesign

So, Nico turned to his morning routine. He realized he usually started the day with stress – email, headlines, notifications. Instead, he made a simple shift. For the first ten minutes, no phone. Just a cup of tea. A quiet stretch. A window open to fresh air. A slow breath. Nothing fancy – just a moment of agency before the day took over. That shift changed more than his morning. It gave him a foothold.

Three Good Things
He built on it gently. Each night, he added a quick ritual: Three Good Things. A small laugh during a meeting. The smell of his tea. A kind message from a friend. These moments, once invisible, became reminders of what still worked – of where he could find light.

Connecting the Dots
One evening, he wrote about a time when he felt truly at his best: leading a team through a messy project with humor, calm, and creativity. "That's still me," he realized. Not a different version. Just a forgotten one. He didn't need a grand plan. Just a reclaimed morning, a few good things, and a true story to hold onto. The world was still uncertain. But his days? They began to feel like something he could shape again.

The Biggest Shift?
Nico stopped waiting for the world to calm down – and started creating moments of calm within it. By reclaiming just a few minutes each day, he rediscovered a sense of agency that had felt lost. Small rituals became anchors. And from that steadiness, the future began to feel less like something happening to him – and more like something he could participate in.

Box 12.7 Method Mix 4: From Overwhelmed to Empowered

You don't need to fix everything. Just reclaim a small space and begin.

When things feel chaotic or beyond your control, these small practices help you find stability, clarity, and a path forward.

(1) Routine redesign: begin where you are.
   Redesign a small routine, choose a part of your day – morning or evening – and make one intentional change. A ritual, a pause, or a practice that centers you. Have a look at the Quick Tour of the Life Loops framework, where we introduced the morning routine as an example of driving change with a small, risk-free routine that happens every day.

(2) Three Good Things: shift your focus toward the positive.
   End your day by writing down three things that went well. No matter how small, they remind you that joy and progress are still present.

(3) Connecting the Dots: reconnect with your capable self.
   Reflect on a time you felt alive, strong, and engaged. What strengths were present? Let that story guide your next steps.

> **Box 12.8 Action Prompt**
>
> A new future begins in the first ten minutes of your day. Redesign your morning by asking yourself: "how do I currently start my day – and how does it affect me? What's one small change I could make to begin the day with more intention? When did I last feel like the best version of myself?" Try one new element: no phone, a five-minute walk, a quiet cup of tea. Then start noting Three Good Things each night. Finally, write your Connecting the Dots story. Let it remind you who you already are.

Scenario 5 "I Have the Fear of Missing Out" (FOMO)

Ava was in her second year of university, and her calendar was packed – club meetings, study sessions, weekend trips, networking events. And yet, every time she scrolled through her feed, a familiar feeling crept in: the fear of missing out – FOMO. Everyone else seemed to be doing something big. Launching startups. Studying abroad. Landing dream internships. And Ava? She was doing a lot, but still felt behind.

DJ of the Inner Sound
One night, after skipping an event just to rest, she tried something different. She imagined herself as the DJ of Her Inner Sound. She turned down the loud voice saying, "You should be doing more" and turned up the one whispering, "You're doing enough. You're finding your way."

The Social Support Map
The next day, she worked on her Social Support Map during a workshop. It helped her see something surprising: she wasn't alone. She had people in her corner – each offering a different kind of support.

- Cheerleaders like her roommate Sonja, who was always reminding her she was doing great.
- Joiners like her project partner Sam, who shared late-night brainstorming sessions.
- Connectors like her cousin Leah, who had links to cool internships.
- GKITB types like her mentor Jana, who lovingly pushed her to follow through.

Seeing those names in front of her helped quiet the noise. FOMO thrives in isolation – but Ava realized she was already supported, already connected.

Signature Strengths

Later, she discovered her Signature Strengths – curiosity, humor, and perspective. They weren't just things she liked; they were how she moved through the world when she felt most alive. She didn't need to say yes to everything. She just needed to follow what felt true to her – with the right people around her. FOMO didn't vanish. But now, Ava had a compass – and a crew.

The Biggest Shift?

Ava stopped measuring her worth by what others were doing and started tuning in to what mattered to her. She realized that being deeply connected beats being constantly busy. With her inner compass and outer circle in place, she trusted she was on her own path.

Box 12.9 Method Mix 5: from Fomo to Focus

You don't need to chase every opportunity – just the ones that feel right with the right support.

When everything looks appealing and you fear missing out, these tools help you turn inward, focus on what matters, and lean into your support system.

(1) DJ of the Inner Sound: tune your inner volume.
    Visualize your thoughts like a soundboard. Lower the volume on external pressure and amplify the voices that reflect your values and energy.

(2) The Social Support Map: you're not alone.
    Map your network into four support types: Cheerleaders, Joiners, Connectors, and GKITBs. Seeing your people clearly helps you activate support more intentionally.

(3) Signature Strengths: let your strengths guide you.
    Identify three to five character strengths that feel most like you. Use them as filters for choosing opportunities that align with who you are. This is the first part of the Strengths Portfolio method.

Box 12.10 Action Prompt

You're not falling behind – you're designing your own rhythm. Try the DJ of the Inner Sound: what voice do you want to hear more of? What needs to be turned down? Draw your Social Support Map: who are the people you can count on for support in different ways? Fill in names for each type of support. Reach out to one person this week. Then, take the VIA Character Strengths survey and highlight your top three to five strengths: which strengths help you feel like yourself and how can you use them more? Let them guide your next decision.

Scenario 6 "How Can I Realize My Potential?"

Jonas was forty-two. He had a solid career, a respected title, and a creeping question: "Is this it?" He wasn't unhappy – just... unfinished. There was a quiet sense that more was possible. But where to begin? He treated the question like a project. Not to blow everything up – but to redesign things from the inside out.

Three Good Things

First, he trained his attention. Instead of doomscrolling or dwelling on what wasn't working, he started a simple habit: writing down Three Good Things each night. A good conversation. A successful presentation. A peaceful moment during a run. The good hadn't disappeared – it had just been drowned out by stress. Noticing it made a difference.

The Strengths Portfolio

Second, he rediscovered what gave him energy. Through reflection and feedback, he identified his Signature Strengths: strategic thinking, mentoring, storytelling. These weren't just skills, they were clues. He began using them more intentionally, especially in ways that lit him up – coaching younger colleagues and leading creative projects.

Third, he shifted his identity. He stopped defining himself by his job alone. Instead, he created a Strengths Portfolio. His career became one part of a broader landscape. He started a podcast, joined a nonprofit board, and created space for ideas that had long been on hold. Each piece added depth and meaning.

The Magic Circle

Fourth, he brought his dreams into the real world. In a peer group – his own Magic Circle – he prototyped a new workshop series. It didn't have to be perfect. Just *real*. Testing it gave him insight, momentum, and a sense of possibility.

Nudging Nuggets

Fifth, he got out of his own way. Procrastination had many masks – perfectionism, busyness, distraction. So, Jonas set up *nudges*: calendar blocks, accountability buddies, and music that helped him focus.

DJ of the Inner Sound

Last, he became, as he joked, the DJ of His Inner Sound – curating not just his schedule, but his mindset. Jonas didn't quit his job. He reimagined his life. Realizing his potential wasn't about a big leap. It was about a series of thoughtful steps toward a fuller version of himself.

The Biggest Shift?

Jonas realized he didn't have to choose between security and possibility – he could create both. By treating his potential as something to explore, not prove, he gave himself room to grow without blowing everything up. Redesigning his life became less about escape and more about expansion.

Box 12.11 Method Mix 6: From Unused Potential to Intentional Growth

You don't need to start over. You just need to start with what's already in you.
    When you feel there's more in you to express, these five tools help you move from vague longing to clear, grounded action.

(1) Three Good Things: shift your lens toward what works.
    Build awareness of the positive by writing three meaningful moments each day. This rewires your attention toward strengths and possibilities.

(2) The Strengths Portfolio: use what energizes you and think beyond your job.
    Identify the three to five strengths that feel most like you. These are your natural fuel – align your choices with them to stay energized and authentic. Map the roles, projects, and activities where you use your strengths. Build a life portfolio – not just a career path.

(4) The Magic Circle: prototype your dreams.
    Bring an idea into a safe, playful environment. Turn dreams into testable prototypes and learn by doing.

(5) Nudging Nuggets: design for action.
    Create small nudges to stay on track.

(6) DJ of the Inner Sound: curate your mindset.
    Adjust your internal soundtrack by turning down doubt and tuning up courage, clarity, and focus.

> **Box 12.12 Action Prompt**
>
> Your potential isn't a one-time decision – it's a design process. Start by writing down Three Good Things each night for a week: what moments or actions recently made you feel alive or proud? Identify your top three to five signature strengths and sketch out your Strengths Portfolio: work, side projects, passions. Choose one dream or idea and bring it into a Magic Circle: what's one idea that you have been postponing – and how could you test it? Then set up one or two nudges to help you act: a calendar block, a buddy check-in, or a music cue. And finally, what internal "soundtrack" do you need to adjust?

Transition Type C: The Stuck Creative

Main Challenge: Unlocking Creativity to Find New Possibilities

The Stuck Creative is someone caught between too many options and too few fresh ideas. This type's core challenge is escaping the loop of overthinking – replaying old stories, cycling through familiar solutions, or being paralyzed by too many possibilities. The method mixes that follow are designed to help you get unstuck, break out of binary thinking, and rediscover creativity as a practical tool for momentum. Whether you're tired of circling the same idea, unsure how to choose among competing paths, or longing for a new direction, these tools offer playful structure and actionable clarity.

In the following scenarios, you'll meet Jana, Sofia, and Daniel – each facing their own version of mental gridlock. Through methods like story-based reflection, generative creativity, and low-risk prototyping, they shifted from indecision to insight. Their stories show that you don't need a brilliant idea to begin – just the willingness to experiment, the courage to question the obvious, and a creative nudge to move forward.

Scenario 7 "I Always Have the Same Ideas. How Could I Come Up with Something New?"

Jana stared at her journal, frustrated. Another brainstorming session, another round of the same three ideas. "Why do I always come up with the same stuff?" she sighed. She wasn't lacking effort – just stuck in a negative loop.

Connecting the Dots
So, she tried a different entry point. No pressure. No sticky notes. Just a story. She sat down and wrote a reflection called Me at My Best. It was about the

Every transition has a map, let's unfold it together.

summer she helped organize a community music festival. She was everywhere – hyping the crowd, coordinating chaos, fixing last-minute surprises with a smile. She felt alive, engaged, in flow. As she reread the story, she circled the phrases that jumped out: creativity, people energy, solving messy problems with joy, creating spaces where others thrive. These weren't just good memories – they were clues. Hidden ingredients: interests, strengths, values.

Opportunity Bingo

Next, she brought them into Opportunity Bingo – a playful tool where you mix what you love with wild possibilities. She invited a few friends to join, turning it into a low-stakes idea jam. Together, they stretched the boundaries.

- "What if I designed team-building workshops through freestyle rap?"
- "What if I ran learning retreats in unusual places?"
- "What if I helped people write their career origin stories?"

The loop evolved. New doors opened. Turns out, she didn't need more ideas – she needed the right ingredients and a space to play.

The Biggest Shift?

Jana realized she wasn't out of ideas – she was out of fuel. Once she reconnected with what gave her life, the creativity flowed naturally. The biggest shift wasn't more brainstorming – it was better listening: to her past, her values, and her joy.

Box 12.13 Method Mix 7: From Idea Loop to Creative Spark

You don't need to force new ideas – just remix what's already inside you.

If you keep cycling through the same ideas, these tools help you shift from recycling to remixing, tapping into your energy, values, and imagination.

(1) Connecting the Dots: find your energy formula.
   Write about a time you felt fully alive – a Me at My Best story. What were you doing? Who was there? From your story, pull out recurring themes: skills, values, interests, emotions. These become the building blocks for idea generation that feels meaningful.

(2) Opportunity Bingo: mix, match, and multiply.
   Take those ingredients and playfully combine them with unexpected formats, contexts, or challenges. Play alone – or, better, invite others and stretch the ideas together.

> **Box 12.14 Action Prompt**
>
> You don't need a bigger ideation session – you need better ingredients and room to play. Write your Me at My Best story: when were you last fully alive and energized? What were you doing? Underline the moments, actions, and feelings that stand out: what patterns show up in that story – skills, values, interests? Extract five or six ingredients from it – these are your creative fuel. Then, play one round of Opportunity Bingo: mix those with wild formats, random ideas, or social themes. What strange or playful combinations can you create from these ingredients? Do it with a friend for extra fun.

Scenario 8 "I Have Many Ideas but End Up Doing Nothing"

Sofia's notebooks were full – lists of business ideas, workshop formats, side projects. She loved brainstorming. But when it came time to choose or start, she froze. "I just can't decide," she admitted. "I get overwhelmed and end up doing... nothing." One morning, while walking with a mentor, she shared her frustration. The mentor replied with a metaphor: "You don't have to silence the voices in your head. Just learn to DJ them." That stuck.

DJ of the Inner Sound

Sofia began experimenting with the DJ of the Inner Sound. When the voice saying, "You'll fail anyway" crept in, she turned it down. When the one whispering, "Why not try?" came through, she turned it up. It wasn't about being fearless. It was about choosing which voice led the mix.

The Social Support Map

Next, she worked on her Social Support Map. She didn't just list people – she reflected on how they could help.

- Mila: her reliable accountability buddy.
- Tom: a thoughtful cousin who asked sharp questions.
- Lina: her Cheerleader at work, always celebrating small wins.

She reached out to each of them – not for advice, but for support. That alone got her unstuck.

Nudging Nuggets
Finally, Sofia designed a few nudges into her routine, gentle ways to move from intention to action: a recurring calendar block labeled "Build, not scroll"; a browser homepage that opened directly to her project tracker; a weekly check-in text with Mila to celebrate any tiny progress. Sofia didn't become wildly productive overnight. But her ideas slowly shifted from clutter to motion – emails, sketches, conversations. Not perfect. But moving. And that made all the difference.

The Biggest Shift?
Sofia stopped waiting for motivation and started designing for motion. She no longer judged herself for not acting – she just made action easier. With the right voices and support around her, momentum became something she could shape.

Box 12.15 Method Mix 8: From Idea Overload to Action Flow

You don't need more ideas – you need movement. One small step at a time.
When too many ideas leave you stuck, these three methods help you clear mental noise, activate support, and move forward – gently but consistently.

(1) DJ of the Inner Sound: curate your mindset.
  Your inner voices are like a playlist. Turn down the critics and amp up the curious, brave, or calm voices that help you take action.

(2) The Social Support Map: build a support system with intention.
  Map the people around you by support type: Cheerleaders, Joiners, Connectors, GKITBs. Reach out to one person who can help you take the next step.

(3) Nudging Nuggets: design your environment for momentum.
  Use small design tricks – calendar prompts, tech tweaks, check-ins – to make starting easier and staying on track more natural.

Box 12.16 Action Prompt

Progress doesn't start with a big leap – it starts with turning the volume toward your next move. Try the DJ of the Inner Sound: identify and adjust your mental mix. Which inner voice do you want to turn down? Which one needs more volume? Then draw your Social Support Map – and contact one person this week. Who could support you right now – and how? Finally, create one or two Nudging Nuggets: a calendar block, a check-in text, or a small change in your workspace that invites action. What's one tiny nudge I can build into my day to reduce friction?

12 Method Mix by Transition Type

Scenario 9 "I'm Stuck in Either-Or Thinking, Like 'Shall I Stay or Shall I Go?'"

Daniel was halfway through his MBA, juggling case studies, job interviews, and late-night WhatsApp chats about "what's next." But one question kept looping: "Should I stay in my current job, or leave to do something completely different?" The more he thought about it, the more trapped he felt. Staying meant stability, credibility, a proven path. Leaving meant freedom, purpose, uncertainty. He was stuck in either-or mode – so he stayed stuck. Then, during a leadership module, he encountered a different mindset: "Design your life like a portfolio – not a single bet."

The Strengths Portfolio
First, he created a Strengths Portfolio. He mapped not just what he was good at, but what energized him: strategic thinking, storytelling, empathy in high-pressure situations. He realized he was already using many of his signature strengths, but only in narrow ways. What if he brought more of them into more areas of his life – no matter where he was?

Future Scenarios
Next, he stepped beyond the binary. Instead of one 'right answer," he sketched out three Future Scenarios: (1) stay at his company, but redesign his role for more meaning; (2) join an early-stage impact startup as a strategy lead; (3) take a sabbatical to explore teaching and coaching across cultures. It wasn't about choosing now – it was about opening possibilities.

Start–Stop–Continue
To gain clarity, he reflected using Start–Stop–Continue. This simple tool helped him see what mattered – without forcing a binary decision.

- Start: bringing more coaching and mentoring into his current role.
- Stop: saying yes to projects that drained his energy.
- Continue: leveraging his storytelling skills to influence with empathy.

Instead of asking "stay or go?" he started asking: "What do I want to keep – and how?"; "What do I want to grow?"; "What do I want to let go of?" That shift changed everything. He didn't need one big leap. He needed small, clear steps rooted in what energized him most.

The Biggest Shift?
Daniel stopped framing his life as a decision and started designing it as a portfolio. Letting go of the pressure to choose "the one right thing" opened space for many meaningful things. He didn't escape uncertainty – but he learned to move with it.

> **Box 12.17 Method Mix 9: From Either-Or Thinking to Design Thinking**
>
> You don't need to choose between this or that. You can build a life that includes what matters most.
>
> When you feel boxed in by two choices, these tools help you open space, reconnect with what matters, and move from stuck to strategic.
>
> (1) The Strengths Portfolio: map your energy and identity.
> List your key strengths and where you're using them now. Ask: "Where could I bring these alive more fully?"
>
> (2) Future Scenarios: imagine beyond the binary.
> Design three distinct futures – realistic, bold, and playful. Each is a lens, not a commitment.
>
> (3) Start–Stop–Continue: shift the question.
> Use these three prompts to reflect: "What do I want to keep – and how?"; "What do I want to bring in or grow?"; "What do I want to reduce or eliminate?"

> **Box 12.18 Action Prompt**
>
> Real clarity often lives beyond "yes" or "no." It starts with the courage to ask better questions. Sketch your Strengths Portfolio. What are your key strengths – and where are you underusing them? Then write out three Future Scenarios – even rough ones. What are three distinct directions your future could take? Use Start–Stop–Continue to reflect across each. What energizes you and should stay? What do you want to invite in and grow? What drains you and could be reduced?

Transition Type D: The Meaning-Maker

Main Challenge: Living Big Dreams, Finding Purpose, and Staying Relevant

The Meaning-Maker is someone who carries ambitions that haven't faded – but haven't fully taken flight either. This type's core challenge is navigating the space between what has been and what's still possible – while seeking purpose, creative expression, or renewed relevance at any age or life stage. Whether you're stepping into newfound freedom, sensing the end of a chapter, or simply wondering how to keep contributing meaningfully, the method mix offered here supports you in bridging aspiration and action.

12 Method Mix by Transition Type

In the following scenarios, you'll meet Eva, Simon, and Tariq – three other individuals at different life stages who paused not because they were done, but because something deeper was calling. Through reflection, prototyping, and connection, they began to breathe life into long-held dreams, expand their sense of contribution, and embrace transitions not as endings, but as invitations. Their stories remind us: meaning doesn't retire, and it's never too late to evolve what matters most.

Scenario 10 "I Want to Finally Fulfill My Big Life Dreams, But They Seem So Far Away"

At fifty-four, Eva had spent years holding space for others – raising kids, leading teams, caring for aging parents. Life had been full of purpose, but something kept whispering louder each year: "What about my dreams?" She had them. Big ones. A writing retreat by the sea. A coaching practice rooted in wisdom, not hustle. A slower, more creative rhythm of life. But they felt far away. Maybe even out of reach.

The Magic Circle
Then she discovered the Magic Circle – not fantasy, but a structured space to explore her dreams with action in mind. She entered it with intention and grounded herself in the five core Life Design abilities.

- Appreciation, curiosity, and empathy: she began by listening to her own longings without judgment.
- Co-creation with a "Yes, and..." mindset: she stopped dismissing her ideas and began building on them with supportive peers.
- Prototyping low-risk experiences: she didn't wait for perfection. She tested.
- Applying a growth mindset: she focused less on getting it right and more on learning from each step.
- Moving to multioptional thinking: she stopped asking, "Is this realistic?" and instead asked, "What's one way I could try this now?"

Ten Ways of Prototyping
From there, she explored the Ten Ways of Prototyping. Suddenly, her dreams transformed into real-life experiments: interviewing someone who runs a boutique retreat center, hosting a micro-writing circle at her kitchen table, offering one coaching session to a friend of a friend, shadowing a creative coach, designing a mock website – just for play.

The Stairway to Heaven
She mapped her steps on her Stairway to Heaven – a ladder from smallest to boldest actions. And with every rung, her dreams got closer. Not all at once. But week by week, she was building momentum. Eva didn't need to start over. She needed to start. Because her dreams weren't too far away. They were waiting for her to show up.

The Biggest Shift?
Eva stopped seeing her dreams as distant destinations and started seeing them as active invitations. The gap between idea and reality shrank – not because she leapt, but because she stepped. Slowly, consistently, she remembered that dreaming is a form of doing.

Box 12.19 Method Mix 10: From Distant Dreaming to Purposeful Doing

Dreams become real when you start doing – even just a little.

When life dreams feel too big or too far off, these tools help you bring them closer – starting with small, energizing steps.

(1) The Magic Circle: begin designing from your dream.
   Use this creative space to hold your ideas with curiosity and possibility. Anchor it with the five Life Design abilities to bring clarity, empathy, action, and play.

(2) Ten Ways of Prototyping: test before you commit.
   Choose low-risk, real-world ways to try out parts of your dream. Prototyping helps you learn, adapt, and stay energized – without pressure to get it perfect. This is part of the Stairway to Heaven method.

(3) The Stairway to Heaven: turn inspiration into action.
   Plot your ideas on a ladder of steps – from tiny to bold. Small moves create progress and momentum, one step at a time.

Box 12.20 Action Prompt

Your dreams aren't too far. They're on the other side of a single, courageous action. What's one dream you've been quietly holding for a long time? Enter your Magic Circle and sketch your dream – big or small. Use the five Life Design abilities to explore and reframe it. Which of the Life Design abilities could help you bring it to life? Then pick two or three ideas from the Ten Ways of Prototyping. Map them on your Stairway to Heaven, starting with the easiest. What's one small way you could prototype it this month?

Scenario 11 "I Want to Stay Useful, Be Interested, and Stay Interesting"

Simon had just wrapped up his final strategy meeting. After thirty years in leadership, his retirement celebration was full of warm praise, laughter – and a quiet fear he rarely shared. He wasn't afraid of slowing down. He was afraid of disappearing. "I still want to be useful," he told a friend. "I want to stay interested... and interesting." But what did that even mean now that he wasn't running the show?

Cultivating Empathy
He began again – not with a plan, but with empathy. He started asking people around him to "Tell me more..." He listened: to young professionals navigating burnout; to former colleagues reinventing themselves; to his granddaughter launching an online business from her bedroom. Each conversation sparked something in him.

The Magic Circle
Then, one morning, he sat down with the Magic Circle. He asked himself: "What do I really mean by being useful, interested, and interesting?" He unpacked it.

- "Useful" wasn't about being in charge – it was about helping others feel confident.
- "Interested" meant staying curious and learning new things.
- "Interesting" was about sharing meaningful stories that sparked connection.

The Ten-Minute Prototype
From that clarity, he built a ten-minute prototype: He offered to host a "story swap" session at a local coworking space – just a space for people to share challenges while he listened and asked thoughtful questions. It was simple. But powerful. Simon left that session buzzing – not because he was leading, but because he was connecting. Retirement didn't mark the end of his usefulness. It marked the beginning of a different kind of presence – less loud, but more real.

The Biggest Shift?
Simon realized relevance isn't earned once – it's reimagined again and again. He didn't need a title to matter; he needed connection, curiosity, and a way to offer presence. Staying interesting, he discovered, was really about staying deeply engaged.

> **Box 12.21 Method Mix 10: From "Still Useful" to "Deeply Engaged"**
>
> Relevance isn't something you keep. It's something you design again – differently.
>
> When you're entering a new chapter but want to remain meaningful, connected, and curious, these tools help you discover what that looks like for you.
>
> (1) Cultivate empathy: start with, "Tell me more…"
>   Use this simple question in conversations. It invites deeper dialogue, builds connection, and helps you better understand others – and yourself. This is part of the five Life Design abilities.
>
> (2) The Magic Circle: clarify what truly matters.
>   Sit down and explore what words like "useful," "interested," or "interesting" mean to you. Define them in your terms. Let them guide what comes next.
>
> (3) The Ten-Minute Prototype: act on insight immediately.
>   Turn your insight into a very tiny experiment. Imagine what you could be doing within ten minutes, for example, offering something, testing an idea, or sparking a conversation. If you don't know what to do, try something new for ten minutes, for example, walking backwards, exploring your street, or finding a new fruit in the supermarket. This is an add-on to the Ten Ways of Prototyping, which are part of the Magic Circle method.

> **Box 12.22 Action Prompt**
>
> Staying relevant isn't about staying busy. It's about staying connected to yourself and others. Have three "Tell me more…" conversations with people of different ages or stages. What do their stories spark in you? Then sit down with the Magic Circle and define what "useful" and "interested" mean to you now. Design a Ten-Minute Prototype – a small act that brings one of those values to life. Try it. Reflect. Then ask: "What might I do next?"

Scenario 12 *"What Should I Do With My Life?"*

In different corners of the same city, three people woke up with the same quiet question: "What should I do with my life?"

Mia, Twenty-One: The Student

Mia was surrounded by options – majors, internships, exchange programs. But none of them felt quite right. At the campus library, she picked up a book: *Design Your Future*. One line hit home: "Life isn't a straight line. It's something you design." That changed things. She joined a workshop, met others who were just as unsure – and just as curious. Slowly, the pressure lifted. She didn't need a master plan. She needed a prototype.

Tariq, Forty-Three: The Midlife Manager
On paper, Tariq had made it. Leadership title, steady income, a polished LinkedIn profile. But inside? Restlessness. So, he started talking to people outside his professional bubble – creative freelancers, younger colleagues, even a retired neighbor. He asked deeper questions and listened – really listened. The answers didn't come from a spreadsheet. They came from stories. And they sparked something new.

Eva, Sixty-Seven: The Retiree
Eva had closed the door on full-time work, but not on learning. She signed up for a storytelling course. Mentored a student. Took walks with neighbors who challenged her thinking. Every conversation was a spark. Every new project a reminder: she wasn't done. She was still *becoming*.

Three People, One Question
Three people. Three life phases. The same question. And, in their own way, the same approach.

- Do something that shifts your thinking, either small, like the Three Good Things, larger, like the Strengths Portfolio, or approach big life dreams with the Magic Circle.
- Connect with people who expand your view.
- Stay in growth mode – always learning, always becoming.

Because purpose doesn't follow a schedule. And there's no deadline for designing a future that fits.

The Biggest Shift?
They each saw that "What should I do with my life?" isn't a question to solve, but a conversation to live. The future stopped being a burden and became a canvas. They didn't find all the answers – but they found the courage to begin.

> **Box 12.23 Method Mix 12: From Existential Question To Creative Exploration**
>
> You don't find your life's purpose. You design your future, one insight, one action, one connection at a time.
>
> When you're faced with the big, timeless question – "What should I do with my life?" – these three moves help you break the paralysis and start designing forward.
>
> (1) Read this book: take action.
>   Books like this one introduce fresh ideas, frameworks, and language to reframe your path. A small insight can spark a big change.
>
> (2) Connect with others: learn through real stories.
>   Talk to people across generations, industries, and backgrounds. Ask open-ended questions. Listen not for advice, but for possibility. Human conversations create clarity.
>
> (3) Stay in growth mode: learning is lifelong.
>   Try something new. Take a class. Join a circle. Mentor or be mentored. The goal isn't to find the answer – it's to stay in motion, curious and evolving.

> **Box 12.24 Action Prompt**
>
> The question isn't, "What's the plan?" It's, "What's your next prototype?" Is there a book, quote, or idea that has recently shifted how you see things? If not, pick a book or podcast that stretches your thinking. Who in your life could you talk to who sees the world differently? Reach out to someone from a different background or generation – ask them about their turning points. What's one new skill, project, or topic you'd be excited to explore? Sign up for one learning opportunity – big or small. Then ask, "What's one thing I'm curious enough to try next?"

CHAPTER 13

Special Methods
Sustainable Life Design

In practicing what we preach, this chapter is dedicated to the key learnings we've gathered from running countless Life Design programs, workshops, and coaching sessions with thousands of people – from age eight to eighty-eight across the globe. Over the years, we've seen what truly resonates with participants and, more importantly, what helps them carry the energy, clarity, and momentum of a workshop into the reality of daily life.

Beyond the foundational practices – for example, performing Life Design abilities, starting small, and prototyping in iterations – we've identified three powerful pillars or Special Methods that function as power-enablers and consistently help Life Designers sustain change beyond the moment, for example, the classroom, the coaching session, or the retreat. These elements are mentioned throughout this book, but their transformative potential deserves special focus here. The three pillars of sustainable Life Design are as follows.

The Three Pillars of Sustainable Life Design

- Energy competence: learning to design your energy, not just manage your time. Energy is the fuel for all action, and the foundation for productivity, self-compassion, and well-being.
- Tangible output: externalizing your thoughts and emotions in a visual and tangible way. Creating tangible output will make your ideas more accessible and shareable – for both you and others.
- A supportive social environment: building psychological safety and surrounding yourself with people who support your growth. This means engaging in meaningful Life Design conversations and minimizing the influence of those who don't share a proactive mindset.

Psychologist Robert Sternberg, known for his work on intelligence, proposed a "triarchic model of successful intelligence," which included not only analytical and creative intelligence, but also practical intelligence – the ability to shape one's environment to support desired outcomes. These pillars can be seen as strategies to do just that: to intentionally design your environment so it supports the life you want to create. As psychologist Mihály Csikszentmihalyi, father of the "flow concept," put it: "You can make a person more creative not by giving them new ideas, but by changing their environment." By managing your energy, making your ideas visible, and cultivating a supportive cultural, psychological, and rhythmic environment, you're shaping the conditions for meaningful action and long-term transformation – at work and in life.

Energy Competence

One of the most overlooked, but absolutely essential, elements for greater productivity, well-being, and life satisfaction is energy. We rely on energy to stay motivated, tackle challenges, and follow through on what matters most. And yet, most people focus on managing their time – not the energy that fuels it. This shift in perspective is captured beautifully in the now-classic *Harvard Business Review* article, "Manage Your Energy, Not Your Time." It reminds us that time is fixed, but energy is dynamic and with the right awareness and strategies, we can actively design it. With these three special methods, you'll explore how to better understand, manage, and redesign your energy. In fact, energy often proves to be even more critical than time when it comes to productivity and well-being. While we may not go as far as the *HBR* article, we do believe this: "Design your energy first and time will follow."

Therefore, energy competence is a powerful tool in the empathy phase, offering deep insights into how your energy unfolds throughout the day, what lifts you up, and what drags you down. This awareness lays the foundation for designing a future that brings more of you into your life. From this empathic understanding, you can continue through the Life Loop. In this section, we'll explore three practical ways to better understand and work with your energy.

(1) The Energy Curve. Learn about your chronotype and how it shapes your natural energy highs and lows throughout the day.

13 Special Methods

(2) The Energy Map. Identify the activities, people, and routines that either boost or drain your energy – so you can redesign your day more intentionally.
(3) The Energy–Tension Matrix. Discover how to develop micro-strategies that help you reduce tension, increase energy, or ideally both at the same time.

We've tested these exercises in workshops around the world – from executives to students, and from early career professionals to people in retirement transitions. Across the board, participants consistently highlight these energy-based methods as among the most practical, eye-opening, and immediately useful tools for improving their daily lives. In the pages ahead, you'll find simple, science-informed steps to help you work with your energy, not against it. Let's begin.

The Energy Curve

We often hear people label themselves as either early birds or night owls, but this either-or view doesn't capture the full picture. Chronobiology research shows that there are at least five chronotypes: two morning types, two evening types, and one indifferent type. Each type experiences energy differently throughout the day.

Understanding your chronotype helps you map out your personal Energy Curve: when you're at your best (prime and high time), when you need to recharge (low time), and when you're most creative and reflective (alpha time). So, how do you figure this out? The Energy Curve tool will help you visualize your natural rhythm and design your day around it.

Procedure and Steps

The following steps will help you map your Energy Curve so you can align your most important activities with the rhythms of your natural energy. The Energy Curve helps you become aware of when you're most energized and when you're not – so you can make more intentional choices throughout your day.

(1) Identify your chronotype: what type are you?
Begin by identifying your chronotype, which is based on when you naturally prefer to wake up. Instead of simply dividing people into morning and evening types, we refer to Olov Östberg's five chronotypes.

(2) Identify your prime time: when are you at your best?

Your prime time is the two- or three-hour period each day when your energy is at its peak – physically, mentally, and emotionally. Physical energy supports action and movement, mental energy allows for focus and complexity handling, and emotional energy gives you patience, willpower, and the capacity to stay present with yourself and others.

Morning types reach their prime earlier in the day, while evening types peak later. Everyone, regardless of chronotype, has two to three hours of prime time – it just unfolds at different times. The variation for morning types tends to be tighter, while for evening types it can spread more evenly across the day.

(3) Identify your high time: when do you still feel strong?

In addition to your prime time, you also have a second window of elevated energy: your high time. It's not quite as intense as prime time, but still well above average. This second wave usually lasts for two to three hours. For morning and indifferent types (chronotypes I–III), high time often falls in the afternoon or early evening. For evening types (IV and V), it may arrive earlier in the day.

(4) Identify your low time: when does your energy dip?

Low time is your daily slump – typically lasting one or two hours – when your energy drops noticeably across all three dimensions. This is a natural rhythm and usually falls between prime time and high time. For many people, especially morning types, this coincides with the post-lunch "soup coma." Use this time for low-effort tasks or rest. Recognizing this dip can help you avoid unnecessary frustration or pressure.

(5) Identify your alpha time: when are you most creative?

Alpha time is the dreamy, intuitive space just before and after sleep – when your brain operates in a relaxed, creative state. It's often the moment when surprising ideas or solutions emerge. This happens in the morning, as you wake, and in the evening, as you wind down. Protecting this time can boost your creativity significantly.

To preserve your alpha time, try not to let your smartphone be the first or last thing you interact with. Einstein understood the power of alpha time: he would nap while holding a large set of keys in his hand. When he fell into deeper sleep, the keys would fall, waking him up in the alpha state with fresh insights.

(6) Draw your Energy Curve: how does your energy unfold?

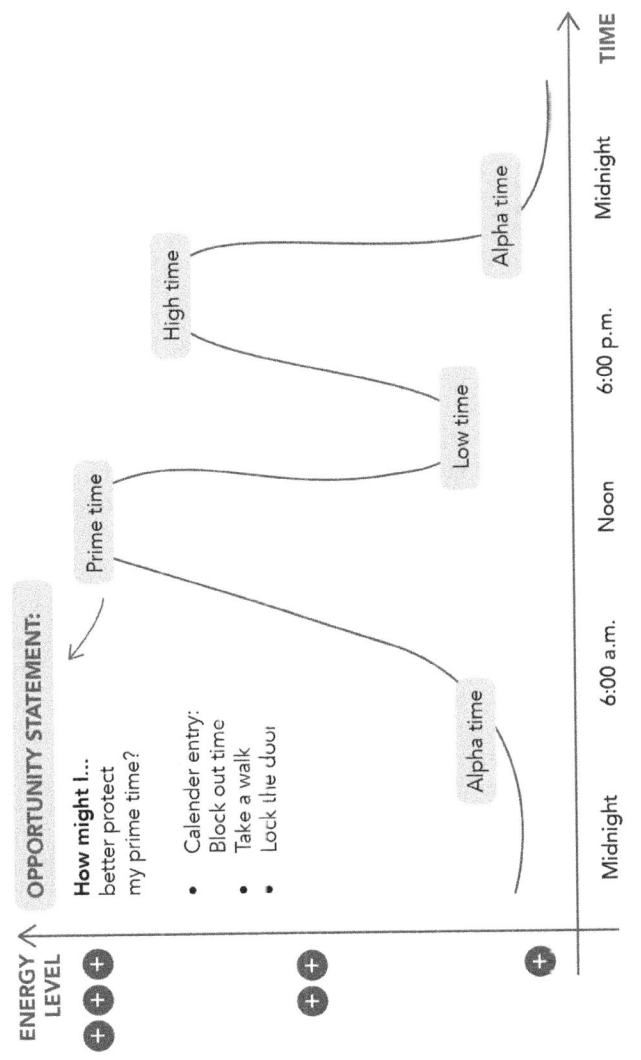

Figure 13.1 The Energy Curve.

CHRONOTYPES

	CHRONOTYPE	PREFERRED WAKE-UP TIME	PRIME TIME	PREFERRED BEDTIME
I	Strong Morning Type	05:00 - 06:30	05:00 - 08:00	20:00 - 21:00
II	Moderate Morning Type	06:30 - 07:45	08:00 - 10:00	21:00 - 22:15
III	Indifferent Type	07:45 - 09:45	10:00 - 16:00	22:15 - 00:30
IV	Moderate Evening Type	09:45 - 11:00	16:00 - 21:00	00:30 - 01:45
V	Strong Evening Type	11:00 - 12:00	21:00 - 01:00	01:45 - 03:00

Figure 13.2 Chronotype overview.

Now it's time to sketch your Energy Curve. Mark your prime time, high time, low time, and alpha time on a typical day. Use your chronotype as a guide, but also trust your intuition. The curve doesn't have to be mathematically precise; just draw it in a way that feels right to you.

You can also create two curves if your rhythm differs between weekdays and weekends. If you're waking up at 7:00 am for work but naturally prefer sleeping until noon, your energy will adjust but won't match the power of your natural rhythm.

You might also draw and compare Energy Curves with a partner or colleague. This can spark helpful conversations and deeper understanding of each other's work and rest styles.

(7) Use your Energy Curve as a starting point for change.

The Energy Curve is a powerful empathy tool for understanding yourself better. Once you've mapped your rhythm, ask questions like: "How might I protect my prime time from distractions?"; "How might I make better use of my low time?"; "How might I use my alpha time more intentionally?"

One Stanford professor in our course realized her mornings – her prime time – were consumed by emails and meetings. After this exercise, she blocked off 9:00 am to 12:00 pm each day for deep, focused work, and posted a note on her door: "No meetings or calls before noon." That one change significantly improved her productivity and satisfaction.

Tips and Tricks

- Use energy as a tool of self-compassion. Your Energy Curve reflects your ideal daily rhythm – but life isn't always ideal. A poor night's sleep, a heavy meal, ongoing stress, or an intense work session can all affect your physical, emotional, or mental energy. Understanding the three types of energy can help you be more compassionate with yourself. Instead of blaming yourself for being tired or unfocused, ask: Which type of energy is low right now – and what can I do to restore it?
- Work smarter, not longer. One of the most powerful insights from the Energy Curve is that you don't need to be "on" all day to be productive. Research shows that most people have only four to six hours of high energy per day – ideal for deep thinking, decision-making, and emotional presence. In other phases, you can shift to lighter, routine tasks. Aligning your workload with your energy levels allows you to sustain performance and well-being over time.
- Match task intensity with energy levels. Not all tasks are created equal. Based on neuroscience research, we distinguish three levels of cognitive demand: routine tasks – low-effort, automated (e.g. sorting emails, updating slides); demanding tasks – moderately effortful, semi-automated (e.g., writing a report, preparing for a meeting); proactive or novel tasks – high-effort, nonautomated (e.g., strategic planning, idea generation, creative work). Map these task types to your Energy Curve: schedule proactive and novel tasks during prime time, demanding tasks during high time, and routine activities during low time. Matching the right task to the right energy window is one of the smartest design decisions you can make in daily life.
- Be kind to your curve. Don't expect to draw the perfect Energy Curve right away. It takes time to observe your rhythms and become more attuned to the different energy phases throughout your day. But the more you pay attention, the better you'll become at using your prime time for meaningful action – and that can be a game-changer for your productivity, well-being, and Life Design journey.

As Life Designers, we know that prime time is when we're most likely to take action. That's why it's worth aligning your most important tasks – especially prototypes and creative work – with this high-energy window.

It's also important to recognize the social biases that exist around energy patterns. Morning chronotypes tend to fit better into traditional nine-to-five schedules, and cultural sayings like "The early bird catches the worm" unfairly frame early rising as more disciplined or productive. Evening types often experience what scientists call social jet lag – their natural rhythms are out of sync with societal norms, leaving them tired, misunderstood, or even unfairly judged.

This is where Life Design comes in. Following your Energy Curve – rather than a rigid schedule – can help you perform better, feel more satisfied, and take care of your health. We've heard powerful and liberating reframes from participants, like: "How might I use my prime time in the evening, even if my colleagues prefer after-work drinks?" or "How might I enjoy my low time without feeling guilty?" Proactivity means putting yourself in the driver's seat. It's not just about pushing harder – it's about choosing more wisely. Sometimes that means using prime time for big action. Other times, it means fully embracing rest. Either way, it's still Life Design.

The Energy Map

The Energy Map helps you become more aware of the people, activities, and situations that either energize or drain you. You'll explore not just who or what gives or takes energy, but how strongly they impact you, and why. With these insights, you'll be able to take a more deliberate, thoughtful approach to redesigning your energy – bringing more of what fuels you into your life and finding creative ways to reduce or reframe what depletes you.

Procedure and Steps
The following steps will guide you in creating your Energy Map, so you can use your energy more intentionally, shift from passivity to agency, and design more energizing days.

(1) Set the stage: who is this for?
Take an A3 or tabloid sheet (or two A4 or letter pages taped together) and find a quiet space to work. Write your name in the center and draw a simple symbol or smiley to represent yourself. This map is all about you – your energy and your needs.

(2) List energy elements: who or what gives or drains your energy?
Around your name, write down people, activities, or things that either give you energy or take it away. Spread them out so you have space to work with each one. Don't overthink – anything that comes to mind is valid. Aim for five to twenty-five elements.

13 Special Methods

ENERGY MAP

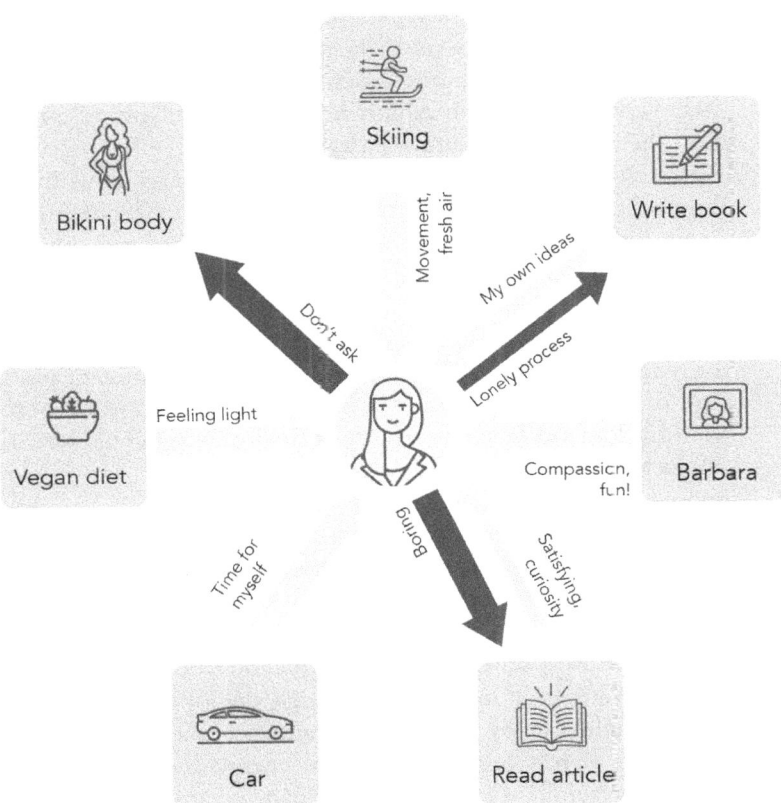

Figure 13.3 The Energy Map.

(3) Make it visual: which icons help you remember?
   For each element, add a small icon or doodle. Visuals make your energy map more engaging and easier to recall later. You can find inspiration on sites like TheNounProject.com or through a quick image search.
(4) Color-code the energy: what's the flow of energy?
   Now connect each element to yourself with a line to represent the energy flow: green = energy-giver; red = energy-drainer; red and green = mixed (only if truly balanced).

Use one line per element and resist the urge to label everything as "mixed." Be honest about the dominant energy dynamic.

(5) Describe the energy: what's behind it?
On one side of each line, write a few keywords to describe why that element gives or drains your energy. For example, for "skiing" as a green arrow: "fresh air, movement, freedom." These insights will help you later when you explore how to redesign your energy.

(6) Adjust the strength: how much energy is involved?
Use line thickness to show the strength of the energy flow: thicker lines = stronger effect (positive or negative). Start by identifying your biggest energy-givers and -drainers, then scale the rest accordingly using two- or three-point line weights.

(7) Spot patterns: what stands out?
Take a step back and look at your full energy map. Is there more green or red? Are your energy-givers mostly people, activities, or places? Are the drainers clustered in one part of life (e.g., work, home, health)? Patterns help you see where small changes could have big impacts.

(8) Choose focus points: where do you want to act?
Circle one energy-giver you'd like more of and one energy-drainer you'd like less of. Choose the ones that stand out as most urgent or most meaningful. You don't have to fix everything – just start somewhere.

(9) Create opportunity statements: how might you redesign your energy?
Now turn your insights into Life Design questions. For example: "How might I enjoy more of what energizes me – like beautiful views?" or "How might I make this energy-draining task more social or playful?" These statements invite creativity, compassion, and forward motion.

Tips and Tricks

- Make it yours. Intentionally keep the categories broad – people, activities, and things – so you can adapt the Energy Map to your needs. If helpful, you can also break it down further into physical, mental, and emotional energy, or zoom in on just one category, like people or work-related tasks.
- Go slow and stay honest. This exercise can bring up strong emotions, especially when you're honest about what's draining or nourishing you.

Give yourself time and space. Many participants find it helpful to take a short break or go for a walk afterward to process what came up.
- Combine with your Energy Curve. Link your Energy Map to your Energy Curve by aligning tasks and energy sources with your natural rhythms. For example, schedule emotionally or cognitively demanding tasks during prime or high time. Use energy-giving activities during low time to recharge. One Nike manager, for instance, prioritizes his energy rhythm so strongly that he sticks to his home schedule even across time zones and books only hotels with twenty-four-seven gyms to support his key energy source: fitness.

The Energy–Tension Matrix

Understanding your energy isn't just a helpful insight – it can be a powerful lever for improving daily life. It allows you to protect your prime time, ease into your low time, and tap into alpha time for creative thinking. In an ideal world, we would live fully in sync with our Energy Curve. But life happens. Meetings land in your low time, deadlines loom, and instead of resting, you push through.

And yes – your body can keep up for a while. But when you override your natural rhythms too often, you shift into what's called "hyperaggressive energy" – a state of high energy combined with high tension. This mode might help in the short term, but over time, it drains you and can lead to stress, burnout, and even health issues.

This is where the Energy–Tension Matrix comes in. It helps you map where you currently stand and discover actionable ways to shift toward a more sustainable state. The ideal zone is known as calm energy – a five-star state for performance, according to energy researcher Robert Thayer. It's the sweet spot where you're energized but not stressed, focused yet relaxed. From here, you're not just active – you're proactive, confident, and able to act with intention. The matrix outlines four key states.

- Calm energy: high energy, low tension – focused, proactive, grounded.
- Hyperaggressive: high energy, high tension – rushed, edgy, unsustainable.
- Relaxed fatigue: low energy, low tension – passive, low motivation.
- Tense fatigue: low energy, high tension – exhausted and overwhelmed.

By placing yourself on the Energy–Tension Matrix, you gain clarity on where you are and how you might move closer to calm energy. That's what this next method is all about.

ENERGY-TENSION-MATRIX

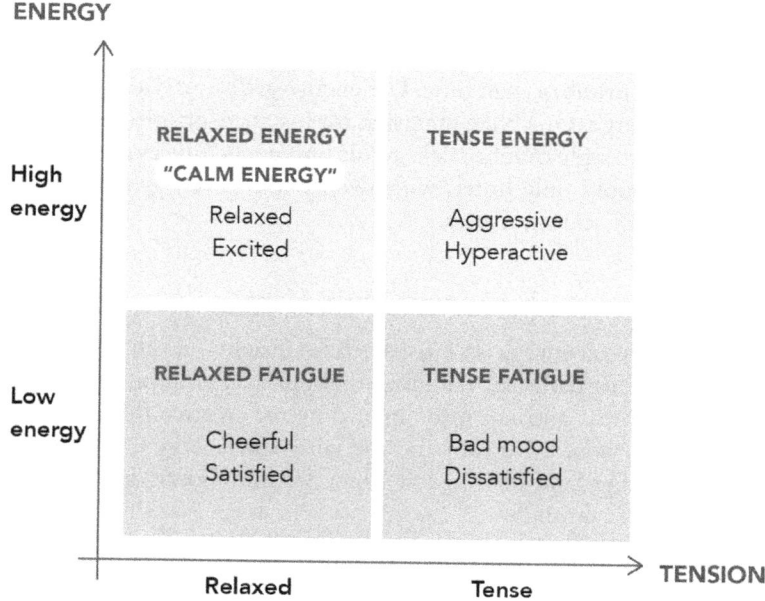

Figure 13.4 The Energy–Tension Matrix.

Procedure and Steps

The following steps will help you assess your current energy and tension levels, locate yourself on the Energy–Tension Matrix, and explore small, actionable ways to move toward the ideal state of calm energy.

(1) Assess your energy: how energized do you feel?
Start by tuning into your physical, mental, and emotional state. Do you feel alert, active, and open – or more sluggish and drained? Rate your current energy on a scale from 0 to 10, or simply ask yourself: "Am I feeling more like 'Oh no...' or 'Oh yeah!' right now?"

(2) Check your tension: how relaxed or stressed are you?
Now consider your level of tension. Are your thoughts flowing freely, or does your mind feel tight and impatient? Notice physical signs too – like a clenched jaw or tight shoulders. Again, rate it from 0 to 10, or ask: "Am I calm and loose, or tense and wound up?"

(3) Place yourself on the Energy–Tension Matrix: where am I right now?
Use your energy and tension scores to find your current zone on the Energy–Tension Matrix. Are you already in the calm energy quadrant, or do you find yourself in a state of relaxed fatigue, hyperaggression, or tense fatigue?

(4) Explore your shift: what do you want to change?
If you're not yet in calm energy, define a question to guide your next move. Try prompts like: "How might I release some tension?"; "How might I refuel my energy right now?"; "What small thing could help me reset?"

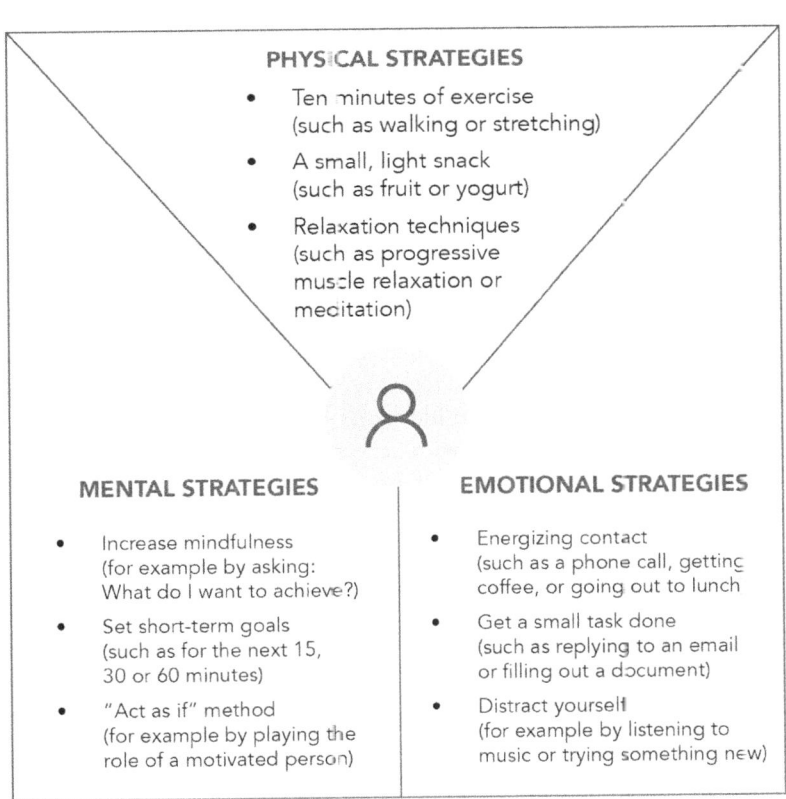

Figure 13.5 Microstrategies for calm energy.

(5) Design microstrategies: What helps you recharge?

Research shows that just five to ten minutes of intentional physical, mental, or emotional activity can make a meaningful difference. You might: go for a brisk walk (physical); do a brain dump or breathing exercise (mental); listen to an uplifting song or message a friend (emotional).

Look at the Energy–Tension Matrix for more inspiration and test what works best for you. Small shifts can lead to big changes.

Tips and Tricks

- Keep it short and simple. Design microstrategies for boosting physical, mental, or emotional energy that only take five to ten minutes – or even just one. The shorter the activity, the more likely you'll actually try it, especially during busy days. Once you're comfortable with these small time windows, thirty or sixty minutes will feel like a luxury.
- Calm energy = prime time. When you connect the Energy–Tension Matrix with your Energy Curve, you'll notice that calm energy often occurs during your prime time. That's why many people guard this time from distractions – even if it's just once a week. In a Life Design workshop in South Africa, MBA students coined the motto: "Protect your prime time like a tiger." Maybe that works for you too.
- Don't stress about it. Seeing your ideal Energy Curve or aiming for calm energy can sometimes feel overwhelming. That's okay. Don't pressure yourself to live the ideal every day. Use these reflections as awareness tools first. Begin with self-compassion, then redesign small elements – like giving yourself permission to rest during low time instead of pushing through.

Tangible Output

One of the most powerful insights we've gained over the years is this: getting ideas out of your head and into the world – through something tangible, physical, and visual – can make all the difference. It shifts your perspective, sparks creativity, and helps you take action. Here are three visual strategies that have proven especially effective – for both personal use and in workshop settings.

Life Design that sticks uses:

ENERGY
VISBILITY
CONNECTION

(1) Visual thinking: draw it out with pen and paper.
   Creating simple visuals with pen and paper reduces overwhelm, sparks conversation, and creates something you can take with you beyond the moment. It doesn't require artistic talent – just the willingness to sketch ideas, emotions, or structures. We've found that even quick drawings make abstract thoughts more concrete and easier to engage with.
(2) Life Design Spaces: create your design walls and collages.
   Another great practice is to build Life Design Spaces. Whether in a workshop setting or your home office, a visual collage of your thoughts, goals, and inspirations helps you see the bigger picture. These visual anchors offer daily reflection, reinforce intention, and give physical space to what truly matters to you.
(3) Visual artifacts: use the power of a mini-zine.
   One of our favorite tools is the mini-zine: a small, eight-page booklet made from a single A4 sheet or tablet-sized paper. Fast and fun to make, it's a perfect way to wrap up a session, reflect on what you've learned, and take your insights with you. Participants of all ages love it and it often becomes a meaningful keepsake or reminder to take action.

These visual tools invite playfulness, deepen learning, and help Life Designers stay connected to their own ideas – long after the workshop ends. You can learn more about each tool in the following chapters.

Visual Thinking

As you've seen throughout this book, visual thinking and knowledge visualization are essential parts of the Life Design approach. Grounded in research, they help Life Designers clarify their thoughts, engage more deeply, and move from reflection to action. Importantly, you don't need to be good at drawing or consider yourself "creative" to benefit from visualization. Visuals are not about artistic talent; they're about making ideas tangible and easier to work with.

What Is Visual Thinking?

At its core, visual thinking is the use of simple visuals – like sketches, diagrams, maps, or frameworks – to structure, express, and develop ideas. These visuals make complex or abstract information tangible, accessible, and easier to work with. You don't need to be good at drawing. If you can sketch a box and an arrow, you already have everything you need to benefit from visual thinking. Visuals help on three levels.

- Cognitive: they reduce mental overload and help you think more clearly.
- Emotional: they make your ideas more engaging and personally meaningful.
- Behavioral: they support taking action by making your thoughts visible and shareable.

You can use visuals both for yourself and with others. When used privately, visuals help externalize and clarify thoughts – Einstein, Darwin, and Freud all used this practice. Our minds can only process about five to nine pieces of information at once (see "cognitive load theory"), so getting ideas "out of your head" onto paper acts like a brain dump and creates space for new insights. In conversations, visuals are powerful tools: they structure your thinking, act as conversation-starters, and invite feedback, suggestions, or encouragement from others.

Analog or Digital?
You can use a tablet, laptop, or any digital tool, but we recommend pen and paper whenever possible. Why? Because physical paper lets you spread out multiple sheets side by side, which creates a powerful effect known as "one eye-span." Coined by Yale professor Edward Tufte, this principle says that if you can see everything within your field of vision at once – without clicking between windows or slides – you free up cognitive capacity. That's why PowerPoint often falls short and why flipcharts or paper walls are so effective. That said, if you prefer digital tools, go for it. Doing it digitally is far better than not doing it at all.

Visuals as Conversation-Starters
Creating visuals not only deepens your own thinking but makes it easier to share your ideas with others. Many Life Designers use their Energy Curve to explain the concept of energy competence to a friend or colleague – and teaching others is a powerful way to reinforce your own learning. If you're a coach or facilitator, visuals also create a tangible record of progress. Unlike digital handouts or slide decks that might get lost in a folder, a hand-drawn visual can sit on a desk or wall – visible, present, and actionable.

Keep Your Visuals Alive
The value of a visual lies in its ongoing use. Visuals help you pick up where you left off, even weeks or months later. They make it easier to keep

momentum after a workshop, act as informal prompts for conversations, and encourage you to express and iterate on your ideas. They're snapshots of your thinking – fixed for now, but open to development.

Start Simple
Any visual can begin with a line – splitting top and bottom, left and right – or a two-by-two matrix. You'll find plenty of templates in this book, but don't hesitate to create your own. Life Designers in our courses often start with quick, simple sketches and end up with meaningful tools they return to again and again. You can explore some examples of two-by-two matrices as visuals created by Life Designers in Figure 13.6 and see how you might create your own. The Career Matrix shows you how you can develop new career ideas by changing either industry/context or role/identity or both. The Action Matrix displays strategies of what to do when you feel stuck organized into different social strategies and according to the effort needed.

Life Design Spaces

Life Design Spaces are a powerful and playful way to externalize what matters most – literally putting your values, dreams, and insights on the wall. Whether in a physical seminar room or at home during a virtual session, creating a Life Design Space brings movement into reflection. It's not just a mental exercise – it's physical and embodied.

Making What Matters Visible
The setup is simple and flexible. You might start with a theme like "This is how I want the next year to feel" or use the space to gather and visualize insights from a one-day or multiday workshop. Begin by pinning up your visual templates, then layer them with post-its, quotes, images, or drawings. Some participants add headlines or group their content into sections. What makes these spaces effective is rooted in the science of knowledge visualization – especially the principles, "overview first, details on demand" and "permanent visibility." When you can see all your ideas at a glance – what Edward Tufte calls the "one eye-span" effect – you reduce cognitive load and make it easier to see patterns, discover insights, and decide what matters most.

Bringing Energy and Interaction into Reflection
Life Design Spaces are not just cognitive – they're energizing. Standing up, walking around, and creating something with your hands invites deeper engagement. Add music to set a playful tone, or let participants tune into

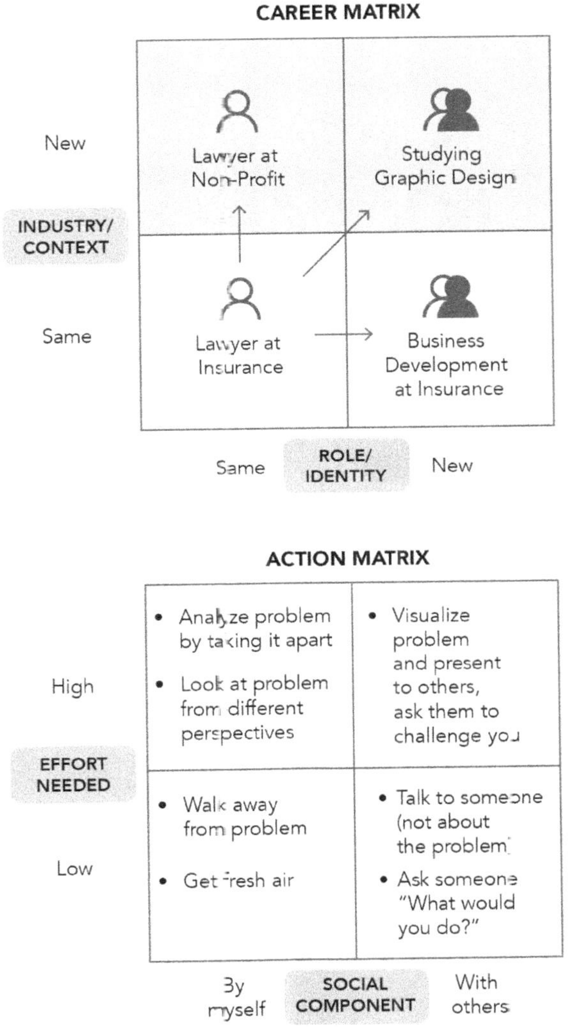

13 Special Methods

CAREER MATRIX

[Career matrix diagram: Industry/Context (New vs Same) on vertical axis, Role/Identity (Same vs New) on horizontal axis. Quadrants: Same/New — Lawyer at Non-Profit; New/New — Studying Graphic Design; Same/Same — Lawyer at Insurance; Same/New — Business Development at Insurance. Arrows point from Lawyer at Insurance to the other three quadrants.]

ACTION MATRIX

Effort Needed	By myself	With others
High	• Analyze problem by taking it apart • Look at problem from different perspectives	• Visualize problem and present to others, ask them to challenge you
Low	• Walk away from problem • Get fresh air	• Talk to someone (not about the problem) • Ask someone "What would you do?"

Figure 13.6 Visualization examples: career matrix and action matrix.

their own soundtracks for personal focus. In group settings, a gallery walk invites participants to explore each other's spaces – sparking inspiration, conversation, and connection.

Figure 13.7 shows Life Design Spaces created at the African Doctoral Academy by doctoral candidates, postdocs, and science managers. We

198

LIFE DESIGN SPACES

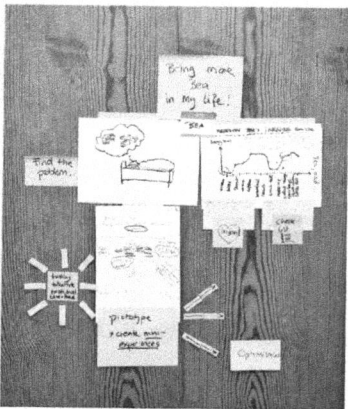

Figure 13.7 Life Design Spaces.

often use this method to open up divergent thinking and then narrow focus using the Magic Circle method – choosing one key idea to bring forward into prototyping.

Design Your Environment
You can use Life Design Spaces not only in workshops, but also in your own home or office. Having your thoughts and insights visible – rather than hidden in a notebook or a folder – acts as a gentle nudge to stay connected to your intentions. It supports continuity: when you return to your Life Design work days or weeks later, you'll remember where you left off. Many Life Designers go further: they start redesigning their environments to be more conducive to creativity and reflection. Some keep pens and post-its notes close by. Others set up personal whiteboards. These are not just tools – they are part of a Life Design mindset that shapes surroundings to support growth and insight. This approach echoes Robert Sternberg's model of successful intelligence, which includes the ability to shape your environment in ways that help you achieve what matters most.

Visual Artifacts

The third and one of the most energizing and effective visual strategies we've seen is creating visual artifacts. Creating and using visual artifacts is a small act with lasting impact. Whether for yourself or with others, it helps turn reflection into something visible, memorable, and shareable. In Life Design, that's the kind of action that sticks.

The Power of a Mini-Zine
Especially mini-zines have proven to be a very effective visual artifact. The beauty lies in its simplicity and visibility. Made from a single sheet of A4 paper, folded into eight small pages, the mini-zine is a tangible takeaway packed with meaning. We've used this technique with audiences ranging from schoolchildren to senior executives and every time, it sparks joy, focus, and creativity. Whether in-person or virtual, participants can fold a blank mini-zine in just a few minutes. What they fill it with is up to them: key workshop takeaways, personal reminders, affirmations, or teaching messages they want to pass on. The front and back covers are often used to highlight what matters most – something to carry forward or share with others. Unlike slides or digital notes tucked away in folders, the mini-zine

stays close – on a desk, in a notebook, or even in a jacket pocket – subtly reminding you of what's important. It becomes a physical signal for the mindset, values, or actions you want to bring into daily life.

INSTRUCTIONS FOR PRODUCING A MINI-ZINE

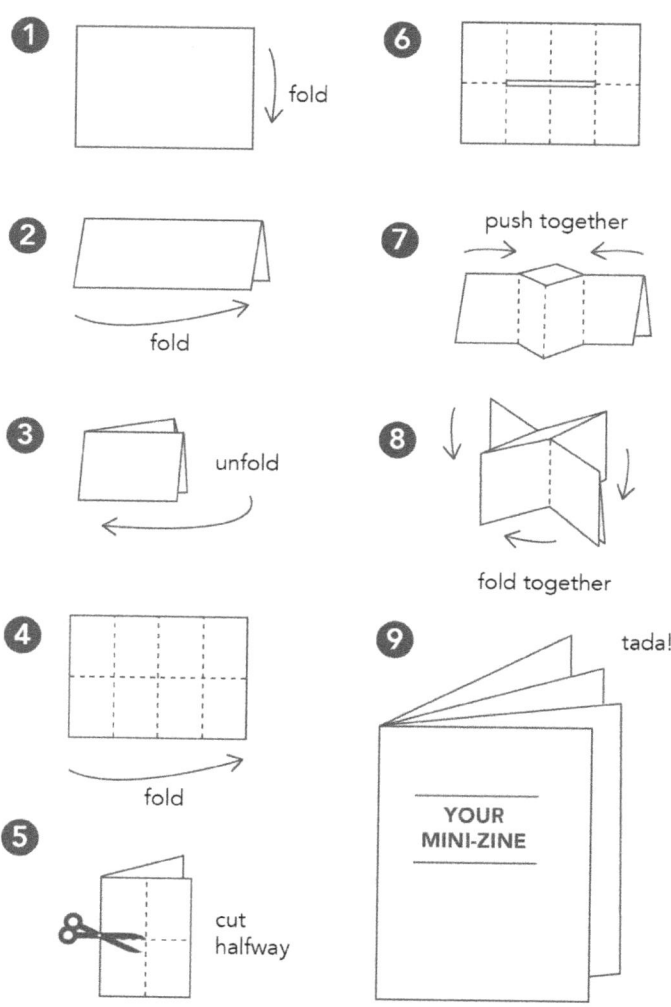

Figure 13.8 Instructions for producing a mini-zine.

Make It Personal (Not Perfect)
Some people get highly creative – drawing, coloring, and even crafting mini-masterpieces. Others prefer to jot down simple notes with a black pen. Both are equally valuable. What matters is that each mini-zine reflects your own style. We always encourage people to make it theirs: it's not about being artistic – it's about being authentic.

Endless Possibilities for Use
Over the years, we've seen the mini-zine used in all kinds of ways:

- as a workshop takeaway summarizing learnings and insights
- as a reminder of Life Design phrases like "Tell me more..." or "What can I learn here?"
- as a reflection tool for daily practices like Three Good Things
- as a space for capturing prototyping ideas or a Social Support Map

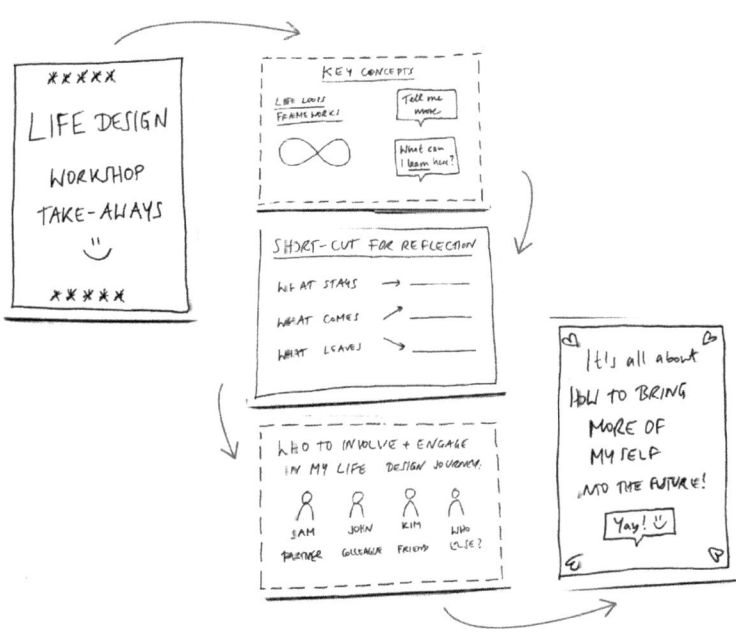

Figure 13.9 Life Design mini-zine.

- as a transition companion with prompts like "What stays, what stops, what starts?"
- as a heartfelt gift – like "Ten Reasons Why I Love You" – that people keep for years

It may seem playful, but it's also powerful. A mini-zine becomes a cognitive and emotional anchor. Some participants place it next to their laptop or on their wall to be reminded daily of what they want to cultivate – whether it's empathy, a growth mindset, or the courage to take action.

Not Just Fun: A Smart Learning Tool
While some may initially see the mini-zine as a playful or even trivial activity, it's actually backed by solid behavioral and cognitive science. The mini-zine works as a subconscious signal – a visual and tactile reminder of what matters to you. Many participants place their mini-zine on their desk, computer, or fridge, letting it nudge them daily toward empathy ("Tell me more...") or reflection ("What can I or we learn here?"). It also serves as a teaching device, helping you pass on insights and ideas to others – making the act of learning social, visible, and shareable. When something is tangible, we're more likely to revisit it, act on it, and build habits around it. So yes, the mini-zine is simple and fun, but it's also a meaningful tool for consolidating insights, stimulating reflection, and igniting action. Whether used for yourself or with others, it's a tiny booklet with a surprisingly big impact.

Supportive Social Environment

One of the biggest insights we've gained over the years is that no matter how skilled or motivated you are as a Life Designer, your environment matters. Just like we've explored how physical spaces and visual artifacts support your journey, it's equally important to consider your social, psychological, and temporal environment – the people, culture, emotional climate, and rhythms around you. These factors can either fuel your momentum or quietly drain it. In this section, we explore three key elements for crafting an environment that helps you move from intention to sustained action.

(1) Shape the cultural–social environment.
(2) Create psychological–emotional safety.
(3) Establish meaningful rhythms and rituals for ongoing progress.

13 Special Methods

Together, these pillars help you not only maintain energy and insight after a seminar or coaching experience, but create the scaffolding to carry your Life Design practice into everyday life.

Shape the Cultural–Social Environment

Many participants join our courses, executive programs, and workshops not only to design their future, but to be part of a community. During the sessions, we intentionally build a safe space and foster a shared mindset rooted in the Life Design framework and abilities. But after the program ends, it's essential to maintain that sense of connection and support.

Reflect on Your Inner Circle

Start by reflecting on your immediate circle – friends, family, colleagues, or teams you belong to. How do they respond when you share a new idea or talk about a dream you want to pursue? Do they listen and encourage you, or are they dismissive, critical, or skeptical? Just like with the Energy Map, you can ask: "Who are my energy-givers? Who are my energy-takers?" Sometimes, even those closest to us may struggle with our change, especially if it challenges the version of us they've come to know. This isn't a reason to stop, but it is a reminder to seek out people who energize and support you.

Un/Supportive (Sub)Cultures

Beyond your inner circle, there's also the broader cultural influence: the country you live in, the organization you work for, or the norms of your upbringing. In countries with strong risk-averse cultures – like Germany or Singapore – failure can be more stigmatized than in places like the US, where experimentation is more normalized. You might not change the culture around you, but you can choose your subculture. We know Life Designers who spend more time with jazz musicians or skateboarders – communities where mistakes are essential and even celebrated. In skateboarding, it's said you need to fail a trick 10,000 times before you land it well.

Create Psychological–Emotional Safety

A psychologically safe environment is crucial for Life Design. Without it, we won't feel free to share openly, test new ideas, or learn from failure. According to Harvard professor Amy Edmondson, psychological safety is the shared belief that a team is safe for interpersonal risk-taking. For Life Designers, this means creating an environment where every idea – no matter how unconventional – can be shared without fear of judgment. A major internal study at Google found psychological safety to be the defining trait of effective teams. Your Life Design conversations should reflect this – free of criticism, full of mutual respect. This ethos aligns with principles of Marshall Rosenberg's "nonviolent communication." As a Life Designer, you're also a space-holder. You help shape a physical, social, and emotional environment that feels safe. That's why we've built a strong alumni community in our programs – people say they can skip small talk and dive straight into what matters most. To foster this kind of safety in your own environment, consider:

- setting shared ground rules
- printing and posting the Life Design abilities as reminders
- sharing stories that illustrate what psychological safety looks like in action

Even small gestures – like active listening or asking, "Tell me more..." – can help create an atmosphere where others feel seen, heard, and safe to grow.

Establish Meaningful Rhythms and Rituals for Ongoing Progress

While energy management and visibility help spark and sustain Life Design momentum, daily and weekly rhythms and rituals form the invisible scaffolding that makes meaningful change stick. Life Design isn't just about intense bursts of insight – it's about turning those insights into ongoing practices that anchor your progress, even when motivation dips or life gets busy.

Research in behavior change, habit formation, and even ancient wisdom traditions shows that humans thrive on repetition, structure, and meaningful rituals. The trick is not to rely solely on motivation, but to create rituals that carry you forward – even on the days you feel tired, stuck, or overwhelmed.

Examples of Rhythms and Rituals

- Weekly reflection prompts: every Friday, ask yourself, "What gave me energy this week?" or "What do I want to continue, stop, or start?"
- Morning journaling: make time for a three-minute check-in – "What am I grateful for? What would make today meaningful? What's one small prototype I can try?"

- Mini-rituals for prime time: create a ritual to open and close your prime time work slot, like lighting a candle, playing a specific song, or writing a post-it with your one goal.
- Sunday Life Design sessions: take thirty to sixty minutes to revisit your Magic Circle, Energy Map, or Stairway to Heaven and plan your next steps.
- Accountability rituals: share your next prototype with a friend every Monday – or post it in a community space like a WhatsApp group or whiteboard.

What turns routines into rituals is intention and meaning. Even the simplest act – like drinking coffee while sketching your thoughts – can become a ritual if it marks a moment of tuning into yourself. Rituals help Life Design move from something you do to something you live.

Box 13.1 The Importance of Life Design Teams

Even with the best intentions, many people find themselves stuck after reading about Life Design or completing exercises on their own. What makes the real difference? Having a Life Design Team.

A Life Design Team is a small, supportive group – ideally two to four people – who meet regularly (at least every two weeks) to reflect, prototype, and grow together. Without this rhythm, it's easy to lose momentum or fall back into old habits. Your team can include friends, acquaintances, or even strangers – what matters most is shared commitment and psychological safety. If you're just two, each of you can invite someone else to form a team of three or four. Start with an informal first meeting in a relaxed setting to get to know one another. Over time, your team becomes a space where you listen deeply, affirm each other's efforts, share ideas, and respond with curiosity – not judgment.

One of the authors met with his Life Design Team for three hours every two weeks over three months. Together, they explored the full Life Loops process – from empathy to continuity – using the tools and methods in this book. A great place to start is redesigning your morning routine: it's low-risk, highly visible, and a perfect way to run through the entire loop quickly. After your first experiments, regroup to share what you've tried and what you've learned. These follow-up sessions are often where the real insights surface – when you say things out loud, you realize what has actually changed.

Think of your Life Design Team as your sounding board. They're not there to give you the answers, but to help uncover your strengths, encourage your experiments, and nudge you gently forward. By showing up for one another with empathy and appreciation, you'll also begin to treat yourself with more compassion, clarity, and confidence.

Box 13.1 (cont.)

In one of our studies, we found that participants in Life Design Teams moved more rapidly and effectively from reflection to action. The process of being seen and supported catalyzes momentum. Most importantly, it helps you bring more of yourself – authentically and intentionally – into the future you want to create.

CHAPTER 14

Silent Truths
What We Don't Say Out Loud

There are thoughts we all carry but rarely share – the quiet crises, private doubts, and invisible transitions that shape our lives far more than we often admit. In our dozens of seminars, workshops, and projects, we've seen how these truths rarely surface in the group, but instead emerge in quiet one-on-one conversations – after the sessions, when most people have left the room. In this chapter, we give voice to what many didn't dare ask out loud, not to solve everything at once, but to name what has long remained unnamed. Because naming it is where redesign begins.

In the pages that follow, we explore five silent truths that many people hesitate to voice, yet quietly wrestle with.

- The desire to combine passions and security through a portfolio career, as people wonder how to honor multiple interests without sacrificing stability.
- The hidden identity shifts of retirement, where the joy of freedom can unexpectedly mingle with loss of purpose and routine.
- The quiet toll of social media, as comparisons and curated lives subtly erode self-confidence and clarity about our own path.
- The yearning for greater life satisfaction, where people hope for simple ways to feel more fulfilled yet often overlook the strengths they already possess.
- The challenge of finding time to take action, which we address through micro-prototyping – showing how even sixty seconds can spark meaningful change.

By shining a light on these quiet dilemmas, this chapter invites you to reflect, experiment, and begin designing a life that feels more authentic, resilient, and your own.

Passion and Security? The Rise of the Portfolio Career (and Portfolio Life)

Many people in our seminars and projects ask us quietly different questions that all lead to one answer. They ask, "I have this dream job, but I cannot make a living from it, how can I still integrate it into my life?" Some ask, "I have so many interests and feel overwhelmed, is there still a way to make some of them happen in parallel?" And another group of people says, "I have to bring food to the table to feed me (and my family), but I really want to try something else. How can I make it happen?" All of these questions have one answer: "Creating your own career and life portfolio could be a good option!"

First coined by Charles Handy in *The Age of Unreason*, the term "portfolio career" describes a career built like a portfolio of investments – diversified, adaptive, and purposefully mixed. It may look like one "anchor" job supported by creative side gigs. Or it may take a seasonal rhythm, shifting focus throughout the year. Some prefer multiple part-time roles that offer variety without the volatility of full self-employment. A portfolio career can take many different forms and shades, but all of them share the idea of living your life and career as a flexible, evolving portfolio of time and energy investments, in which work engagement, hobbies, or side projects can fluidly come, stay, or go in a variety of scopes or rhythms to ultimately find your own perfect mixture of activities at different times and stages of life.

A portfolio career is not a fallback for the indecisive, but a bold expression of multiplicity. It reflects a growing cultural awareness: we are multifaceted beings, wired for variety, capable of thriving across diverse domains. Whether you're juggling consultancy with part-time teaching, freelancing while parenting, or combining artistry with analytics, the portfolio career allows you to honor your evolving interests and values over time.

Therefore, applying a portfolio career to life design resonates strongly with modern career theories. For instance, the "boundaryless career" and "protean career" frameworks describe how today's working lives are increasingly self-directed, shaped by personal values, and fluid across organizational borders. A portfolio career embodies these principles – it thrives on adaptability, lifelong learning, and the pursuit of meaning beyond any single employer or job title. Empirical studies reinforce this view: portfolio careers can enhance psychological resilience, support a stronger sense of purpose through diverse roles, and foster skill development that boosts long-term employability. They have even been linked to well-being, cognitive health, and satisfaction later in life. In short, a portfolio career isn't just a practical option – it's a scientifically supported path to a resilient, meaningful, and sustainable working life.

This chapter encourages you to question the outdated scripts of linear careers. If you've ever felt torn between options, stifled by the nine-to-five, or called to do more than one thing, a portfolio career might not just be an option – it could be your path to greater alignment, energy, and meaning. You don't need to fit into one job title. You need to fit into your life. So, what could your career portfolio look like? Here comes an overview of why choosing a portfolio career can be relevant to you, the different types of portfolios, and how you can get started to design your portfolio.

Why Choose a Portfolio Career?

A portfolio career lets you design a working life as multifaceted as you are – blending different roles, interests, and income streams into one cohesive path. For those who thrive on variety – for example, personality types like "Scanners," who are multipassionate and curious about many different things – it offers a natural fit. But its appeal goes far beyond personality types.

In an unpredictable world, a portfolio career provides freedom, creative expression, and resilience. By diversifying what you do, you're not just following your passions – you're building flexibility and security into your livelihood. One role may energize you, another may pay the bills, and together they create a balanced, meaningful life. A portfolio approach to work and life can give you the following.

- Diversity and freedom. You'll not be limited to one label or job title. Instead, you have the freedom to define your own professional identity. For instance, you can be a teacher and a visual artist, a business consultant and a yoga instructor, or a marketing professional and a musician.
- Stability and security. You'll gain stability from multiple income streams. Just as financial advisors recommend diversifying your investments, diversifying your income can protect you from economic shocks, offer autonomy in times of uncertainty, and let one income stream support you if another slows down.
- Personal expression. You'll feel empowered if you are striving for variety and will find joy in ongoing growth and self-expression. The portfolio career supports creative and intellectual freedom, joy in switching contexts, lifelong learning, and skill growth – which is especially important for personality types such as Scanners.
- Work–life alignment. You'll gain the flexibility to shape your work around your life – not the other way around. As it provides more

control over schedules, the capacity to scale work up or down and the balance between professional growth and family life, it can be especially appealing to parents or caregivers.

Types of Career and Life Portfolios

Different portfolio structures emerge depending on individual preferences, market contexts, and life stages. There is no one-size-fits-all – what matters is that your portfolio reflects your values, needs, and ambitions. Table 14.1 shows some common types.

Table 14.1 *Types of career and life portfolios*

Type of portfolio	Description	Example roles
Hybrid portfolio	Main occupation + side gigs: a stable primary job with additional income or passion projects.	Full-time manager + freelance writer + tutor
Patchwork portfolio	Freelance/multiple gigs: no main employer; a mix of contract work, projects, gigs.	Consultant + trainer + podcaster + artist
Cyclical portfolio	Seasonal gigs: activities shift depending on season or demand cycles.	Ski instructor in winter + gardener in summer
Balanced portfolio	Income + non-income gigs: a mix of income-generating work and meaningful unpaid roles.	Part-time consultant + community volunteer
Entrepreneurial portfolio	Entrepreneurial gigs: several entrepreneurial initiatives or businesses run simultaneously.	Online store owner + coaching practice + app developer
Transition portfolio	Combined life stages gigs: a portfolio intentionally designed for a life transition (e.g., retirement, parental leave, study sabbatical).	Mentor + artist + part-time lecturer
Encore portfolio	Legacy-focused gigs: designed around giving back, usually during retirement; could also include paid and nonpaid activities.	Community advisor +pottery lab + local guide

Each of these models can evolve over time, blending elements as your circumstances and aspirations shift. The key is intentionality: designing a mix that brings both security and fulfillment. Portfolios are as unique as the people who create them – shaped by personal priorities, passions, and life circumstances. The examples below show how individuals at different ages design portfolio combinations that align with their values, needs, and aspirations.

- Patchwork portfolio: Jonas, age twenty-five.
  Jonas embraces the flexibility of multiple gigs to build skills, networks, and a reputation while testing entrepreneurial ideas. This structure supports learning and agility early in his career. His portfolio activities include freelance UX design for startups (main income), tutoring for coding bootcamps (income + community engagement), and DJing at local clubs on weekends (creative expression).
- Hybrid portfolio: Sara, age thirty-eight.
  Sara combines stable employment with purpose-driven and creative side activities, balancing financial security with personal growth and contribution. She designed the following portfolio: full-time HR management at a midsized company (main income + stability); certified life coaching, offering weekend workshops (purpose + side income); membership of a community theater group (creative expression).
- Cyclical portfolio: Thomas, age fifty-two.
  Thomas structures his work around seasonal rhythms, integrating income streams and roles that reflect his passions, community ties, and expertise. His portfolio includes: vineyard management (seasonal cycles – spring-to-autumn focus); ski instructing during winter (seasonal income + passion); organizing a local food festival (community contribution + side income).
- Transition portfolio: Asha, age sixty.
  Asha is in a transitional phase, shifting from full-time work to more selective, meaningful engagements while cultivating personal interests and legacy activities. His portfolio combination involves part-time lecturing at a university (meaning + modest income), being a board member at a local NGO (community leadership), and dedicated time for painting (creative expression).
- Encore portfolio: René, age seventy-two.
  René's portfolio focuses on giving back, staying intellectually engaged, and earning modest income from passion projects in retirement. His portfolio activities include his reputation as a retired architect (no

longer in full-time practice), mentorship to young architects (non-paid, meaning-driven), and his part-time work as a guide for city architecture tours (income + passion).

What these examples illustrate is that life and career portfolios are highly versatile. They often combine paid work with unpaid activities, mix short-term gigs with long-term commitments, and bring together purpose-driven, creative, and income-generating roles. This blend allows individuals to design a working life that reflects their full identity, while offering flexibility and resilience in a changing world.

Portfolios also evolve across life stages. Younger individuals frequently use them to experiment, explore different interests, and build skills. In midcareer, portfolios tend to balance stability with side ventures that offer personal growth or creative expression. Later in life, portfolios often shift toward contribution, flexibility, and joy – enabling people to give back, stay engaged, and find meaning beyond financial gain.

Getting Started: Three Entry Paths to a Portfolio Career

Starting doesn't require a leap off the cliff. Many people ease into a portfolio career by experimenting on the side – testing ideas, adjusting schedules, and learning as they go. Whether you start small or take a bigger leap, the process is iterative: try, learn, refine. There are three practical ways to begin, each offering a different pace and level of risk. Choose the one that fits your life.

- Moonlighting. Starting with moonlighting means launching a side project outside your regular work hours – on evenings, weekends, or during breaks. It's a low-risk way to explore new interests, test your skills, and build confidence without giving up the security of your main job. This approach is ideal if you're curious but cautious, allowing you to learn and grow gradually while keeping your financial stability intact.
- Rejigging. Rejigging your current work setup gives you more time and mental space to develop your portfolio career. This could mean shifting to a part-time role, compressing your workweek into fewer days, or working remotely to cut out commuting. By reshaping your existing schedule, you create room for new opportunities without needing to make a drastic change.
- Jumping in. This means taking a bigger leap – leaving your primary job to focus fully on your portfolio career. It's bold, but with the right preparation, it can be a smart move. Importantly, you must have designed and tested your new path before committing fully. This route suits those who

have already explored their direction and are ready to go all in while savings, part-time gigs, or a transitional buffer provide financial security.

As a simple and effective starting point for building your portfolio career, we additionally recommend using the Strengths Portfolio exercise found in Chapter 7. This tool will help you identify your signature strengths and clarify what energizes you – insights that form a strong foundation for designing a fulfilling and authentic portfolio path.

Key Takeaways

Portfolio careers offer exciting opportunities for creative freedom, resilience, and growth – but they also require mindful design, planning, and self-management to navigate the challenges that come with juggling multiple roles. There's no one to tell you to stop at 5 pm, and fewer safety nets. But for those willing to learn, iterate, and design intentionally, the rewards are significant. The following is a summary of the benefits and challenges.

Here is what's great about portfolio careers.

- Creative expression: you get to share your full self.
- Stability: one stream slows down? Others pick up.
- Autonomy: set your own hours, pace, and priorities.
- Income potential: many earn more after one or two years.
- Learning by doing: you grow with each experiment.

Watch out for the following.

- Energy management: juggling takes planning.
- Work creep: there's no built-in end-of-day.
- Admin load: you're your own finance, HR, and PR team.
- Identity blur: "So, what do you do?" isn't easy to answer.

In a world where more and more people quietly wonder how to integrate their dream job, multiple interests, or new aspirations into a sustainable life, the portfolio career offers a powerful answer. Far from being a fallback, it is a scientifically grounded and future-fit strategy that blends resilience, meaning, and skill diversity.

Whether hybrid, patchwork, seasonal, entrepreneurial, or designed for a life stage, a portfolio can reflect your unique needs and values while helping you thrive amid complexity and change. As you consider your own next steps, remember, you don't have to choose just one path – you can design a working life that fits you.

> **Box 14.1 Reflection Prompt**
>
> Is this career model for you? Ask yourself:
>
> - "Do I thrive on variety and change?"
> - "Am I excited about exploring multiple interests?"
> - "Can I self-manage and adapt to ambiguity?"
>
> There are no wrong answers. Only starting points.

> **Box 14.2 Action Prompt**
>
> To start exploring and planning a possible career portfolio, your first steps may include the following.
>
> (1) Talk to portfolio careerists: learn how others structure their weeks, manage energy, and find clients.
> (2) Visualize your ideal portfolio: use Life Design tools to explore combinations that reflect your needs and values. You can go straight to the Strengths Portfolio method and visualize your current or ideal portfolio.
> (3) Launch a "shift project": try one project on a small scale – test, reflect, iterate on one client, one volunteer role, or one mini-course or workshop.

The Finish Line? Retirement as Life Reboot

Another question we often hear is how to navigate the uncertainty that comes with preparing for, entering, or living in retirement. People wonder: "How can I continue to feel relevant, useful, curious, and engaging?" Society often promotes unhelpful myths – like the idea that retirement is just an endless vacation – yet many discover that this fantasy leads to boredom sooner than expected. The dream of finally doing nothing usually lasts only a few weeks or months.

We had a doctor in one of our programs who proudly displayed his retirement date in large letters at his practice, eagerly counting down to June 30, only to return to part-time work just six weeks later. This isn't everyone's story, but we hear examples like this often in our courses. Retirement might be the long-awaited reward after decades of hard work – a time of freedom, relaxation, and self-indulgence. No more meetings, no more deadlines, no more grind. But what if we treated retirement less like a finish line and more like a life reboot?

Why you don't need ONE PERFECT JOB?

You can create a PORTFOLIO OF ACTIVITIES

that gives you:
MEANING + INCOME + JOY

Far from being a simple transition into leisure, retirement marks one of the most significant identity shifts in adult life. Beneath the surface of financial plans and celebratory farewells lies a profound psychological and social transformation – one that can bring surprising joys and unexpected challenges. In our work with people in transition, we've seen again and again that retirement isn't just about how you'll spend your money – it's about how you'll spend your days, and who you'll be without your work identity. Let's explore both the positive and negative surprises that often accompany this life stage.

The Hidden Side of Retirement: What Really Happens When Work Ends

While many people look forward to the freedom of retirement, the reality can feel less like floating into paradise and more like falling off a cliff. The loss of title, routine, and social connection can leave even the most prepared retirees asking: "Who am I without my work?" But thankfully, retirement can also bring remarkable and unexpected gifts. With intention and openness, many retirees discover that this life chapter offers opportunities for growth, connection, and joy.

Retirement is a major life transition – one that comes with both unexpected challenges and hidden gifts. What often surprises people isn't just the shift in daily life, but how emotionally complex that shift can be. Let's take a closer look at some of the common surprises retirees face – first the challenges, and then the joys that often emerge when the dust settles.

Common Negative Surprises

(1) Loss of structure and routine. Work provides invisible scaffolding for our lives – shaping when we wake, eat, move, and socialize. Without this structure, days can blur together. Time feels abundant, but also hollow. Studies show that retirees lacking daily routines report higher levels of depression and anxiety.

(2) Shrinking social circles. Many friendships are forged at work – through colleagues, clients, and daily interactions. When these connections fade, loneliness can creep in. Studies reveal that one in three adults over fifty experiences chronic loneliness, with retirement often acting as a trigger.

14 Silent Truths: What We Don't Say Out Loud

(3) Unexpected financial anxiety. Even those who are financially secure sometimes worry more than anticipated. The absence of income replenishment means each expenditure can feel weightier, particularly during market dips or health scares. Behavioral economists describe this as "loss aversion on steroids" – a heightened fear of spending.

(4) Drop in self-worth and visibility. In societies that tie value to productivity, leaving the workforce can feel like becoming invisible. Without their professional identity, some retirees struggle to feel relevant. Research indicates that those who fail to find a new sense of purpose are more prone to depressive symptoms in the first year.

Common Positive Surprises

(1) Rediscovery of curiosity and creativity. Freed from work demands, retirees often dive into new passions or long-forgotten hobbies – from painting and music to learning languages or even launching businesses. Creativity can flourish when time is finally on your side.

(2) Richer personal relationships. With work out of the way, many find their relationships deepen. There's more space for meaningful conversations, presence, and shared experiences with partners, children, and friends.

(3) Improved health and energy. The stress of work gone, many retirees sleep better, eat healthier, and move more – and feel younger in the process.

(4) A new sense of purpose. Volunteering, mentoring, and contributing to meaningful causes provide purpose that can rival, or even surpass, the fulfillment once found in professional life.

From Retirement to Life Reboot: How Life Design Can Help

The truth is retirement isn't just a financial transition – it's an existential one. And the upsides don't come automatically. Without preparation – emotional, social, and psychological – retirement can feel disorienting. That's why more people are turning to Life Design as a way to navigate this phase. Life Design encourages you to prototype your future – experimenting with new roles, routines, and relationships that reflect your values and aspirations.

Many people in this phase ask us, "What should I focus on to prepare for or navigate retirement successfully?" The answer comes down to building, sustaining, or strengthening three key elements that strongly shape daily happiness and well-being.

- Structure. For some, structure might mean a detailed daily schedule; for others, it's enough to have weekly touchpoints like a regular hike, or even looser anchors like annual trips or holidays. Life Design offers practical tools to help you consciously shape your rhythm. For instance, the exercise of redesigning your morning routine can guide you in creating a routine that suits your mornings, afternoons, or evenings. By exploring your energy patterns – through identifying your chronotype and mapping your Energy Curve – you can align activities with the times you feel most energized. Perhaps you'll choose to enjoy the news and music during your morning peak and save social interactions or exercise for the afternoon – or tailor it in whatever way fits you best.
- Activities. When it comes to activities, research from positive psychology shows that well-being is highest when we combine fun, pleasurable pursuits with meaningful, purpose-driven ones. Put simply, it helps to wake up with something to look forward to. To uncover what brings you joy and meaning, you might try the Three Good Things exercise, which helps highlight smaller and bigger activities that resonate with you. The Connecting the Dots method encourages reflection on past experiences when you felt very authentic – from your past years even to childhood – to rediscover sources of pleasure and purpose. Identifying your Signature Strengths can also point you toward pursuits that naturally fulfill and energize you.
- Social connections. Social connections form the foundation that ties it all together – woven into both our routines and activities. What matters most isn't the number of connections, but the quality. As the longest-running study from Harvard on adult development shows, the depth and strength of our relationships are what truly make the difference. Strengthening your relationships starts with understanding your current network. The Social Support Map helps you recognize and appreciate the people already in your life and may also inspire you to expand your circle. Alternatively, focusing on the social dimension of your Energy Map can help you identify your energy-givers – those who uplift you – and prompt small steps to reconnect, reach out, or plan shared experiences.

> **Box 14.3 Reflection Prompt**
>
> Is this new chapter calling for a reboot? Ask yourself the following questions.
>
> - What parts of my identity feel most at risk – or most free – as I think about life beyond work?
> - When do I feel most energized and fulfilled now – and how can I build more of that into my days ahead?
> - Which connections do I want to strengthen, rekindle, or newly build to feel supported and engaged in this next phase?
>
> There are no wrong answers. Only starting points.

> **Box 14.4 Action Prompt**
>
> To start exploring and planning a possible career portfolio, your first steps may include the following.
>
> (1) Redesign a routine: Use the Energy Curve tool to test different ways to structure your day and observe how it affects your mood, energy, and sense of purpose.
> (2) Prototype purpose. Choose one small project or role (e.g., volunteering, mentoring, learning a skill) that aligns with your strengths and gives your week a sense of direction – even for just one hour.
> (3) Social scan. Map your current relationships using the Social Support Map and identify one energy-giving person you want to reconnect with or one community you'd like to explore.

By rebooting these three key elements through Life Design methods, you'll be well equipped to master a positive transition into the life stage of "retirement." Remember that you can always actively shape the structure of your days, the activities that enrich them, and the connections that sustain you. Rather than being a passenger in retirement, you'll take the driver's seat – a vital mindset for navigating this transition with patience, health, and joy. With thoughtful preparation, retirement can be less about what we leave behind and more about what we choose to create next.

We hope this section has offered you a richer, more multidimensional understanding of retirement and the transition it entails. May it inspire and empower you to take an active role in shaping your retirement – building it with intention through meaningful structure, engaging activities, and strong social connections.

Scrolling through Illusions? Social Media's Hidden Impact

Another big topic that comes up frequently in our Life Design programs is how to deal with the distractions, comparisons, and seemingly attractive "feeds" offered by social media platforms such as Instagram, TikTok, or LinkedIn. While this is a challenge for people at any stage of life, it seems especially potent for those in early adulthood or during key transition periods. Participants often share how hard it can be to stay focused on their own path when bombarded with endless images of other people's successes, adventures, or milestones.

When surveying our students or speaking with late teenagers in gap year programs, we repeatedly hear anxieties about facing a flood of lifestyles and choices on social media – and the fear of missing out on a better or more exciting life. As one participant put it, "If I study something for three years, then I'm locked up and can't do anything else," reflecting the sense of limitation that arises after seeing dozens of alternative paths online within minutes – from people who travel the world to those building camper vans or launching businesses. Another shared, "I see so many people celebrating their professional milestones on LinkedIn that I sit at home and wonder what I am actually doing here, not celebrating anything."

Based on these insights and recurring questions about how to better navigate social media, this section offers an overview of how platforms like Instagram and TikTok can affect us – often in ways that quietly derail our Life Design efforts. Social media represents just one contemporary example of how external voices and images shape our views and choices. This is not new – films, television, and cultural narratives have long played similar roles – but today's platforms amplify these effects with unprecedented reach and speed. The following sections outline an overview of some social media's hidden impacts, alongside reflections on how Life Design can help us see through these illusions and stay grounded in designing lives that are authentic, meaningful, and our own.

Effects of Social Media on Life Design

Before we can make conscious, values-driven choices about how to engage with social media, it's important to first understand how these platforms may be shaping us – often without our awareness. What seems like harmless scrolling can quietly influence our emotions, thoughts, behaviors, and even our sense of self. In Life Design, we aim to increase self-awareness so we can live and act with greater intention. That begins by noticing the hidden costs of social media usage. The following section outlines some of the most common negative effects of social media and how they can silently interfere with our ability to design a life that feels true and fulfilling.

- Psychological distress. Social media platforms like Instagram often act as powerful amplifiers of social comparison and self-doubt – challenges that can quietly undermine our efforts to design fulfilling lives. When we constantly see curated, idealized snapshots of others' achievements, adventures, or appearances, it becomes easy to question our own path, to feel inadequate, or to lose sight of what truly matters to us. Fear of missing out (FOMO) reinforces this tension: we may find ourselves anxious about what we aren't doing rather than engaged with what we are. Recognizing these dynamics is a vital first step in Life Design – it helps us reclaim attention and emotional energy, and shift focus back to our own meaningful experiments and choices.
- Cognitive distortions. In Life Design, we aim to see clearly so we can act intentionally. Yet social media often clouds this clarity by fostering cognitive distortions that reshape how we see others' journeys and our own. The "highlight reel fallacy" tempts us to believe that the polished images and short videos we consume reflect entire lives, when in reality they show only selective moments. Similarly, compressed time narratives – the illusion that major transformations happen quickly and easily – can leave us impatient with our own progress. Life Design reminds us that meaningful change is rarely instant. It unfolds through real effort, experimentation, and resilience – not in the span of a thirty-second reel.
- Behavioral consequences. From a Life Design perspective, our behaviors are the small steps that build (or block) the life we want to create. Social media, by design, can pull us into patterns that make intentional design harder. The addictive pull of infinite scrolling and doomscrolling consumes time and focus that could be invested in our own prototypes, connections, and growth. At the same time, the constant pressure to present a perfect, filtered self encourages us to perform rather than live authentically. Life Design invites us to notice these patterns and gently redirect our energy from passive consumption toward active creation and genuine experience.

- Developmental and identity challenges. Life Design is, at its heart, a journey of identity – of discovering who we are, what matters to us, and how we want to contribute. Social media can complicate this journey, especially for young people navigating life's early transitions. The search for external validation through likes and comments can overshadow the slower, deeper work of building an intrinsic, grounded sense of self. Fear of public failure may limit the playful exploration and risk-taking that are so essential for learning and growth. Life Design encourages us to create space for reflection, experimentation, and self-authored identity – beyond the metrics and performances of digital platforms.

While it's important to be aware of the challenges, social media is not all distortion and distraction. When used with intention, it can also be a powerful tool for connection, creativity, and inspiration. Many participants in our Life Design programs have shared how platforms like Instagram, YouTube, or LinkedIn sparked new ideas, helped them find like-minded communities, or made them feel less alone in their struggles. Social media can expose us to diverse life paths, global conversations, and unexpected opportunities we might not otherwise encounter. It can help us express ourselves, build networks, learn new skills, or stay close to loved ones across distance. For those designing their lives, it can even serve as a mirror – reflecting aspirations, highlighting patterns, or pointing to what resonates most deeply.

The key is not to reject social media, but to engage with it consciously. Life Design invites us to become active curators of our digital environments, using these tools to support growth rather than comparison, and creativity instead of conformity. In the next section, you'll find practical ways to strengthen that intentional relationship – so your screen time becomes aligned with the life you truly want to create.

Design Your Future Beyond Illusions: Exercises for the Social Media Age

As a companion to these insights, we offer a set of practical reflections and Life Design exercises to help you see through the illusions of social media and stay grounded in your own path – even in the face of highly curated, fast-paced, and comparison-driven world of social media.

First of all, it's worth pausing to name the deeper issue beneath much of social media's negative influence: comparison. Maybe you have already heard some of the following life wisdoms: "Don't compare your inside to someone else's outside"; "Comparison is the end of happiness and the beginning of discontent"; or "The shortest path to unhappiness is comparing yourself to others." These truths feel timeless – and yet, they've become especially urgent in the digital age.

A helpful reflection to leave the spiral of comparison enforced by social media is to understand that – generally speaking – there can be three types of comparison.

(1) Comparison with the norm describes measuring us against what is socially expected or considered "typical" (e.g., timelines for education, career, relationships).
(2) Comparison with others describes looking at peers, influencers, or friends and judging our worth, pace, or direction against theirs.
(3) Comparison with ourselves describes reflecting on our own growth over time, honoring personal progress and lessons learned.

The first two forms of comparison are often destructive – especially when we are not at peace with ourselves. They can amplify self-doubt, paralyze decision-making, and shift focus away from what actually matters to us. The third, however, can be powerful: when we compare ourselves only to our past selves, we can begin to track growth, resilience, and self-discovery on our own terms. Therefore, reminding ourselves of the focus on learning with the growth mindset, one of our five core Life Design abilities, can also become a crucial pillar when it comes to healthy handling of social media. When we shift from external validation and comparison to internal alignment and growth measurement, Life Design can become truly sustainable. It invites us to live less in reaction and more in creation. To give our attention not to the loudest feeds, but to the quiet signals of our own energy, values, and curiosity.

Additionally, there are some Life Design methods that invite you to engage more mindful with digital life, shifting your energy away from passive consumption and toward purposeful creation. They might help you counteract the pressures of digital life, recenter your attention, and reconnect with your authentic direction. We consider the following three methods as the most impactful exercises.

- Energy Map. When we feel drained by comparison or overwhelmed by input, we often lose touch with what truly energizes us. This exercise helps you notice which activities, people, and environments give or take energy – so you can design more of what fuels you. Reconnect to your

sense of self by better understanding and mapping out who and what gives you energy and how – you can refer to the Energy Map method in Chapter 13.
- The Social Support Map. In a sea of followers and online connections, it's grounding to reconnect with the real people who know, support, and care about you. Mapping your key relationships can help you strengthen meaningful ties and shift your focus away from superficial approval. Who are the people that matter to you and why do they matter? Map them out and do one random act of kindness for them – you can refer to the Social Support Map method in Chapter 11.
- DJ of the Inner Sound. Social media doesn't just amplify outer voices – it also affects the voice inside your own head. This method helps you notice which inner tracks are playing (e.g., comparison, self-criticism, doubt) and invites you to remix them. What would your inner voice sound like if it spoke with the care, compassion, and encouragement of a best friend? A powerful way for many participants in our seminars is to create distance to these outer and also your inner voice through the DJ metaphor – you can refer to the DJ of the Inner Sound method in Chapter 11.

These exercises are not about disconnecting from the digital world entirely – but about engaging with it from a place of self-awareness and sovereignty. They help you become the designer of your attention, not just a consumer of images or algorithms. As you experiment with these tools, remember there is no one "right" path – only a path that is right for you. Life Design is not about optimizing for perfection or competing with others. It's about honoring your unique rhythm, your personal strengths, and your evolving understanding of what makes life meaningful.

This section explored how social media platforms like Instagram, TikTok, and LinkedIn quietly shape our identities, decisions, and transitions – often pulling us into cycles of comparison, distorted expectations, and performative living that can derail our Life Design efforts. By uncovering these hidden dynamics and offering practical exercises, we invite you to shift from passive scrolling to intentional designing – reclaiming focus, authenticity, and agency in an age of digital illusions.

A Fast Track to Life Satisfaction? Five Key Strengths

One question that often comes up quietly is whether there's a faster way to improve life satisfaction, given how busy and time-pressed people feel.

> **Box 14.5 Reflection Prompt**
>
> Take a few quiet minutes and reflect on the following questions.
>
> - In what ways do you find yourself comparing your life to others?
> - Which type of comparison shows up most for you (against the norm, others, or yourself)?
> - What might help you shifting the focus on your own growth and learning?

> **Box 14.6 Action Prompt**
>
> Try one of the following small shifts to reclaim focus and authenticity.
>
> (1) Mute the noise. Unfollow or mute two accounts that trigger comparison – and replace them with creators or communities that inspire you in a grounded way.
> (2) Track your energy. For one day, notice how you feel before and after scrolling – and record your energy shifts using the Energy Map method.
> (3) Reclaim a moment. Choose one hour this week to go screen-free and do something that reflects your values, not someone else's highlight reel.

While searching for shortcuts isn't always the most helpful mindset, positive psychology does point to five character strengths – out of the broader set of twenty-four – that have a particularly strong link to greater life satisfaction.

These are: gratitude, the capacity to recognize and appreciate life's blessings and the kindness of others; hope (or optimism), the confidence in and positive outlook toward the future; zest, an energetic and enthusiastic engagement with life; curiosity, the drive to explore, learn, and discover; and love, the deep valuing of close, caring relationships. These strengths together help nurture resilience, build deeper connections, and create a richer sense of purpose and joy. When seen through the lens of time, you can look back with gratitude, live the present with zest and curiosity, and face the future with hope – while love serves as the thread that connects past, present, and future.

As a Life Designer, you can:

- cultivate gratitude by practicing Three Good Things, tuning into the positives in your daily life, or reaching out to someone from

your Social Support Map with a message of thanks or a personal meetup;
- spark zest by experimenting with Ten-Minute Prototypes – try walking backward, exploring a new street, touring your apartment like a traveler, or drawing inspiration from the Ten Ways of Prototyping or your Energy Map to engage with activities that give you energy;
- fuel curiosity by stepping into the unknown: listen to unfamiliar music, see a challenge through an adventurous lens, or ask, "Tell me more..." in deep conversations with yourself or others;
- strengthen hope by using the Micro-Practices method in Chapter 13 to ease tension and boost energy, by fostering a growth mindset by asking "What can I learn here?" and by viewing your prototypes through the Prototyping Prism method to uncover learning in each feature; and
- live love by actively nurturing relationships – in work, at home, and in side projects, hobbies, or volunteering. Share kind words, protect your prime time using the Energy Curve, and make space for meaningful moments with family and friends.

In Life Design, these strengths aren't about finding shortcuts – they are about designing small, intentional actions that create a more fulfilling, joyful, and resilient life. This section of the book connects these strengths to practical Life Design tools, helping you move from insight to action in shaping your future.

Too Busy? A Hundred Ways to Prototype in Sixty Seconds

People often share with us how busy their lives are – and how hard it feels to find the time or energy to prototype anything at all. This raises an intriguing question: "What's the smallest prototype you could try? What if you had just sixty seconds?" The idea for this micro-prototyping series was sparked by Laura, a participant in one of our executive education programs, who experimented with one minute of conscious breathing while still in bed – and proudly shared it as her prototype to a more relaxed start to the day during our seminar.

Science backs up the power of such small moments. Just sixty seconds of focused breathing with closed eyes can help calm your body and refocus your mind. Slow, conscious breaths activate the parasympathetic nervous system – your body's natural "rest-and-digest" mode – lowering heart rate and stress, while eye closure reduces sensory input and supports emotional regulation. Inspired by Laura's example, we explored how you can turn even a single minute into an active, meaningful prototype – because prototyping is about doing, not just thinking. Here's a collection of one hundred ways to use one minute for micro-prototyping grouped into different category. So, which one will you try right now?

Visualize Your Life or Work

(1) Sketch your ideal day in three symbols.
(2) Draw a map of your energy highs and lows.
(3) Doodle three alternative career paths.
(4) Draw your life as a tree (roots, trunk, branches).
(5) Sketch a "future you" stick figure doing something bold.
(6) Draw a pie chart of where your time really goes.
(7) Create a timeline of your next five years.
(8) Map what gives you energy on a sticky note.
(9) Doodle your current versus desired work–life balance.
(10) Sketch your support network.

Say It Out Loud

(11) Say your life mission in one sentence.
(12) Name three things that make you feel alive.
(13) State one thing you'd change today if you could.
(14) Role-play introducing your future self at a party.
(15) Voice what your "inner critic" says – then what your "inner coach" replies.
(16) Say a new habit you want to try this week.
(17) Describe what "success" looks like in three words.
(18) Tell yourself your proudest moment of the last month.
(19) Say out loud: "What am I curious about right now?"
(20) Give your current chapter of life a title.

Write It Down

(21) Write a one-line resignation letter (just for fun).
(22) Jot three things you'd do if you had no fear.
(23) Write a micro-bucket list of three items.

(24) List three small experiments you could try this week.
(25) Write your "why" for your current job.
(26) List three people you'd like to learn from.
(27) Draft a personal motto.
(28) List three strengths you want to use more.
(29) Note one thing you want to say no to.
(30) Write a one-line job ad for your dream role.

Try a New Behavior

(31) Sit differently for one minute (e.g., power pose).
(32) Take a new path in your room/office.
(33) Try saying *no* to a small request.
(34) Close your eyes and take three deep breaths.
(35) Send a thank-you message.
(36) Try a micro-meditation.
(37) Stand up and stretch.
(38) Ask someone nearby a curious question.
(39) Swap your phone with a notebook for one minute.
(40) Smile at yourself in the mirror.

Micro-Interactions

(41) Ask someone what they love about their work.
(42) Ask: "What would you do with an extra day off?"
(43) Say to a friend: "Can I share a wild idea?"
(44) Share one of your life design ideas.
(45) Ask for a one-word description of you.
(46) Ask: "What's one thing I could do differently?"
(47) Compliment someone authentically.
(48) Offer help on something small.
(49) Text a mentor or role model.
(50) Invite someone to coffee/tea for a Life Design chat.

Design Your Environment

(51) Move one object to make your space more inspiring.
(52) Put a sticky note with a positive cue on your laptop.
(53) Delete one app that drains you.

14 Silent Truths: What We Don't Say Out Loud

(54) Set a new wallpaper that reflects your goal.
(55) Put a book within arm's reach that sparks curiosity.
(56) Place a meaningful item on your desk.
(57) Arrange your space to face light.
(58) Write a word of the week on your notebook.
(59) Change your screensaver to a life goal image.
(60) Reorganize your desktop icons.

Imagine Alternatives

(61) Pretend you live in another country – what would you do today?
(62) Imagine you're retired – what would you try?
(63) Imagine you're a beginner at your job – what would excite you?
(64) Imagine you have unlimited energy – what's next?
(65) Imagine you only had six months left in this job – what would you focus on?
(66) Imagine switching industries – what could you transfer?
(67) Pretend you have $1 million – what would you prototype first?
(68) Pretend you could fail safely – what would you attempt?
(69) Imagine you're starting over at eighteen – what's your first move?
(70) Imagine your best friend designed your life – what would change?

Act It Out

(71) Gesture how you feel about your current job.
(72) Walk like your future confident self.
(73) Make a face that represents your current mood at work.
(74) Act out saying "yes" to a new opportunity.
(75) Mimic how you'd celebrate a dream goal achieved.
(76) Act out leaving work with excitement.
(77) Pretend you're giving a speech at your future retirement party.
(78) Act out solving a challenge with ease.
(79) Pretend you're the CEO of your life.
(80) Mimic "pressing pause" on something that drains you.

Design Quick Experiments

(81) Block one minute for focused breathing – does it shift your mood?
(82) Turn off notifications for one minute – what do you notice?

(83) Pick one thing on your to-do list and cross it off mentally.
(84) Write "I can..." at the top of your page and list three ideas.
(85) List three people you could ask for advice.
(86) Set a one-minute timer and brainstorm alternatives to your job.
(87) Time yourself doing one micro-task – does it surprise you?
(88) Say no to multitasking for sixty seconds.
(89) Close your laptop and just reflect.
(90) Wear a small item that symbolizes your life design goal.

Creative Sparks

(91) Draw your life as a mountain path.
(92) Sketch a "values compass."
(93) Doodle your week as a weather map.
(94) Draw a bridge from now to your dream future.
(95) Create a coat of arms with your top three values.
(96) Sketch a ladder – each rung a small next step.
(97) Draw a river – what's the flow; what's the obstacle?
(98) Make a quick vision board (sticky notes or photos nearby).
(99) Visualize your week ahead as a game board.
(100) Draw yourself with wings – what do they help you do?

These micro-prototypes aren't about perfection – they're about sparking new thinking, feeling, and acting, quickly and playfully. They're not about getting it right or creating big change in one go – they're about inviting fresh perspectives and small sparks of momentum in your day. So, take a breath, pick one, and experience how even sixty seconds of intentional experimenting can start to shift your path.

At the end of this chapter, we would like to let you know: if you recognize yourself in any of these silent truths, know that you are not alone – these quiet struggles are far more common than we often admit, and they are part of the shared human experience. The good news is that Life Design isn't about changing everything overnight or striving for perfection. It's about learning to see more clearly, taking small, intentional steps, and building self-efficacy along the way. By accepting where you are, becoming more conscious about what is happening, and experimenting gently with what could be, you can proactively shape a path that nurtures greater life satisfaction.

Box 14.7 How to Travel Wisely

We live much of our lives on autopilot – working, commuting, moving through routines that, over time, blend into a kind of blur. Years can pass this way, with few moments that stand out. And yet, we often vividly remember the pizza we ate on a childhood holiday, the smell of sunscreen on a beach, or the cold drink we had while watching a sunset last summer. Though travel takes up only a tiny fraction of our lives in terms of time, it often takes up a disproportionately large share of our memories. That's because travel activates episodic memory – the kind of memory linked to emotionally rich, novel, and specific experiences – unlike the procedural or habitual memory that governs most of our daily life. In other words, travel helps punctuate the story of our life with memorable chapters. And that makes it especially meaningful and worthwhile.

One of the silent truths in our modern lives is this: many people want to travel, but few stop to ask why. We spend hours searching for the perfect destination, checking the weather forecast, comparing flight prices, and imagining that a change in scenery will also lead to a change in feeling. Travel has become a kind of secular ritual of escape, celebration, or self-discovery. And yet, if we pause for a moment, we might realize that we often focus more on where we want to go than on why we're going in the first place.

In our Life Design workshops, we often explore a simple but powerful question: "What does traveling mean to you?" For some, it's freedom. For others, it's learning, connection, or even escape. You don't need to get on a plane to begin a journey. You can travel with a finger on a map, through a story or a dream, via Google Street View, or by walking a new path in your neighborhood. The point is not only movement – it's meaningful movement. Travel becomes wise when it's connected to your values, your needs, your rhythms, and your aspirations.

The experience of travel isn't just what happens during the trip. It begins with anticipation – the dreaming, planning, and conversations before the journey. And it continues with the storytelling, remembering, and meaning-making afterwards. In that sense, a single journey can stretch across weeks or even years, depending on how we design it. When we zoom out, we see that travel is less about geography and more about identity: "Who are you when you travel? What parts of you come alive when you're somewhere new? And how might you bring that spirit into your everyday life?"

This is an invitation to rethink and redesign what travel means for you. Are you seeking inspiration? Healing? Playfulness? Perspective? Instead of asking, "Where should I go next?" try asking, "What part of me needs movement right now?" When we travel wisely, we don't just collect passport stamps – we expand our sense of self, build rich memories, and nourish our inner world.

> **Box 14.8 Reflection Prompt**
>
> Before planning your next trip, take a moment to look inward. Wise travel begins with self-awareness – understanding not just where you want to go, but what you hope to feel, learn, or release along the way. Use the questions below to guide your inner compass and bring intentionality to your journey.
>
> - When in your life have you felt most alive while traveling – and why?
> - What kinds of travel restore your energy – and what kinds drain it?
> - What are you really hoping to find or feel on your next trip?

> **Box 14.9 Life Design Interventions to Travel Wisely**
>
> (1) Travel map of the self.
>   Draw three maps: one of places you've been that have shaped you; one of places you dream of going (real or imagined); one of places in your daily environment where you can experience similar feelings (e.g., awe, calm, curiosity). Reflect on the emotional qualities you associate with each place and how to integrate more of those into your current life.
>
> (2) Reverse bucket list: travel edition.
>   Instead of listing where you want to go, list the types of experiences you want to have. For example, "I want to get lost in a local market"; "I want to feel small under a big sky"; "I want to laugh over dinner with someone from another culture." Then brainstorm multiple ways (including local or virtual ones) to have these experiences.

Key Insight: Travel Is a Path to Meaningful Self-Discovery

Travel holds a unique power to create vivid, lasting memories because it breaks the routine of daily life and aligns with our emotional, episodic memory. Traveling wisely means going beyond destinations to connect movement with personal values, purpose, and identity – turning each journey into a meaningful chapter of self-discovery and growth.

PART V

Horizons of Life Design

Life Design doesn't begin and end as an individual method or with group workshop – it unfolds across time, roles, and systems. As a mindset that evolves with us, it's not confined to individual reflection or personal change; it's a way of approaching the world that can scale across age groups, workplaces, institutions, and even societies. From classrooms to boardrooms, from early dreams to late reinventions, and from the search for personal meaning to the urgency of global challenges, Life Design offers more than reflection – it offers pathways for action.

This part expands the horizon of what Life Design can become and invites you to explore how Life Design is already making an impact at multiple levels – and how you might contribute to what comes next. You'll find real-world stories and applications that showcase how Life Design grows in scope: from empowering children to uncover their strengths, to supporting transitions and well-being in organizations, to shaping societal conversations around longevity, AI, and sustainability. It's also where we open the door to what else we do. We'll give you a behind-the-scenes glimpse into the ongoing work of the Life Design Lab at the University of St. Gallen – our programs, partnerships, and co-creations with individuals, teams, and global institutions.

Whether you're exploring Life Design for yourself, considering how to facilitate it for others, or imagining how to integrate it into your organization or community, the chapters that follow will offer insight, tools, and inspiration. If you've ever wondered how to bring Life Design into the world – or deepen your impact with it – this is your invitation to see what's possible.

CHAPTER 15

Life Design as a Catalyst for Scaling Change

Where can Life Design go? The answer: anywhere people are navigating change. In this chapter, we explore how Life Design supports transformation across multiple levels – individual, organizational, and societal – and acts as a catalyst for scaling change. From curious kids to seasoned professionals, from forward-thinking companies to global institutions, Life Design meets people where they are and helps them move forward with purpose.

We'll look at how individuals of all ages – from children and college students to midcareer professionals, elite athletes, and best-agers – use Life Design to turn restlessness into reinvention, and curiosity into action. At the organizational level, we explore how teams and leaders use Life Design to foster growth, inclusion, and agility across the employee lifecycle. And at the societal level, we highlight Life Design as a powerful response to pressing global shifts, such as demographic change, longevity, and the future of work.

You'll encounter real-world examples from universities, nonprofits, coaching programs, and international institutions. Whether you're leading a team, raising a child, rethinking your role, or planning your encore chapter, this chapter invites you to see yourself not just as a learner of Life Design, but as a carrier of its possibilities.

Life Design for Individuals: From Children to Best-Agers

When we first introduced Life Design, many assumed it was a tool just for students – something to help them figure out "what to do with their life" before everything else would fall into place. Over time, we've learned something essential: Life Design isn't just for students. It's a lifelong approach that supports people at every age and stage – from children dreaming big to experienced professionals navigating transitions, and retirees seeking renewal and purpose.

Table 15.1 *Life Design for Individuals*

Type of audience	Courses, initiatives, and programs
Children and teenagers	– Children's University – Courses and projects in schools – Collaboration with nonprofits for disadvantaged teenagers – EU Horizon Project for Life Design Youth Toolkit
Young adults and students	– Bachelor/undergraduate – Master/graduate – PhD/postdocs – Gap year programs
Experienced professionals	– MBA programs – Senior Scientist programs – Executive education – Life Design coaching – Life Design leadership – Certificate of Advanced Studies (CAS) in Life Design
Best-agers and senior professionals	– Design Your Retirement – Design the 100-Year-Life – Midlife transition program NEXT – The Nexel Collaborative – The Stanford DCI Program

In this chapter, we explore how Life Design is applied across different life phases: with children and teenagers, young adults and students, mid-career professionals, athletes, and those in later life. Through diverse programs we've seen the power of Life Design not only in building clarity and direction, but also in cultivating energy, well-being, and a sense of meaningful contribution. An overview of our courses, initiatives, and programs can be found in Table 15.1.

Children and Teenagers

Our youngest participants – children between the ages of eight and thirteen – engage with Life Design in a so-called Children's University at the University of St. Gallen. Here, more than 500 students from different regional schools come together to explore their dreams and discover their science-backed character strengths. We encourage them to identify what matters to them, envision possible futures, and begin shaping their own journey. Life Design is introduced not just as a method, but as a future skill. We map out their dreams and connect them with their core five character strengths. They identify their strengths using the VIA Youth twenty-four character strengths test available via the VIA Institute: www.viacharacter.org. In addition, we use a simple version of the DJ of the Inner Sound method to help the children cultivate the health of their inner dialogue to reach their dreams.

Beyond the university, we work with schools that integrate Life Design either as a regular subject or through project-based learning masterclasses. In partnership with organizations supporting disadvantaged youth, we've found that the nondogmatic, person-centered approach of Life Design is particularly empowering. One popular activity is identifying personal "superpowers" – the top five character strengths that, as students say, "no one can take away – not siblings, teachers, or parents." These strengths form the foundation for designing action-oriented, strength-based activities.

In collaboration with social workers and educators across Europe, as part of an Erasmus Plus project, we've also developed a Life Design Toolkit – ELDeM YOU: European Life Design Method for Youth – for teenagers struggling to enter the workforce. Funded through an EU Horizon project, this Toolkit is now available in English, German, Spanish, Dutch, and Ukrainian.

Young Adults and Students

Young adults and students frequently tell us, "I wish I had known Life Design five years earlier." From undergraduates to doctoral candidates, many discover Life Design just as they are beginning to question their direction and options.

We offer Life Design courses at bachelor's and master's levels under titles such as "Design Your Future" – framed as personal development, creativity training, or transition competence. Doctoral and postdoctoral researchers engage with Life Design at institutions including Stanford University (the Creativity in Research Scholars Program), Columbia University (the Design Studio), and Stellenbosch University (the African Doctoral Academy). Across these programs, we support students in overcoming procrastination, navigating uncertainty, and creating meaningful career portfolios that go beyond binary decisions like: "Stay in academia or leave?" The Strengths Portfolio empathy method is especially helpful and popular since it helps academics to think of their careers as more differentiated within academia to discover roles beyond research, and also beyond academia – to pivot into consulting, industry, or nongovernmental organizations (NGOs).

We are also proud collaborators of a new German gap year initiative called the Orientation Program, initiated by Kreatives Unternehmertum (KU), where Life Design is the guiding framework for self-discovery, prototyping career options, and staying healthy while working toward big goals. It is usually taught in 24h special workshops from 2pm to 2pm integrating social evenings and good sleep. Especially for young people passionate about contributing to the UN Sustainable Development Goals, Life Design offers strategies to stay grounded, energetic, and resilient – so they can change the world without burning out.

Midcareer Professionals

For experienced professionals – typically in their thirties to fifties – Life Design often begins with a sense of restlessness. Many know what they don't want anymore, but they're unsure what should come next. This phase is frequently shaped by "either-or" dilemmas: "Should I stay or leave? Should I pursue stability or something more meaningful?"

We support professionals through MBA programs at institutions like the University of St. Gallen and Stellenbosch Business School. Life Design helps participants manage complexity, explore transitions, and develop a next chapter that integrates purpose, energy, and experimentation. We also collaborate with senior scientists and engineers at organizations such as the Fraunhofer Institute, ETH Zurich, and NASA. At NASA, for example, we work with engineers to bring more of themselves to the workplace and support their problem-solving and ideation of new inventions.

Through our executive education programs in Life Design Coaching and Life Design Leadership, professionals between their late twenties and late fifties apply Life Design to themselves, their clients, and their teams. The Coaching program focuses on one-on-one and group facilitation, while the Leadership program addresses core topics like AI, biases, transitions, purpose, and sustainability. Each program runs over six months, with participants earning a Certificate of Advanced Studies (CAS, 12 ECTS) in Life Design upon completion.

Across all these formats, we cultivate spaces of psychological safety – where participants discover that they are not alone in their questions and that new paths emerge through conversation, creativity, and community.

Best-Agers and Senior Professionals

For professionals over fifty, often referred to as best-agers, Life Design opens the door to renewal. Many ask: "Is this it? What's next? How can I stay relevant and contribute meaningfully?"

We've offered workshops like "Design Your Retirement" for years, but soon realized that the term "retirement" didn't resonate. Today, we call these programs "Design Your Future." Participants range from those approaching retirement to those in their thirties planning ahead for longer lives. At the University of St. Gallen, we launched NEXT – a pioneering midlife transition program, and the first of its kind in Europe, using Life Design to reflect on the past and create meaningful futures. NEXT is part of a global movement of universities (including Harvard and Stanford) forming the Nexel Collaborative, offering transition support for the fifty-plus generation.

Some of our Life Design methods, such as the Magic Circle and the Stairway to Heaven, have become popular at the Distinguished Careers Institute (DCI) at Stanford University – where fellows redesign life with new clarity, energy, and experimentation.

Special Professions: Athletes

Some professions come with strong identities – and early transitions. Athletes are one of those groups. Their careers often begin young, revolve around intense focus and performance, and end earlier than most others. This creates unique challenges – identity shifts, loss of structure, and questions like "What now?" – long before typical retirement age. Retirement from sports is more than a career shift – it's an identity transformation. Even world-class athletes like Serena Williams and Roger Federer have described this process as "evolving" rather than retiring. It's often accompanied by emotional uncertainty and existential questions.

Our recent research confirms the magnitude of these challenges. A qualitative study with former Swiss athletes revealed widespread struggles with emotional, social, and structural adaptation – regardless of sport popularity. One athlete described their disorientation after retiring as being in a "Nowhere Land," explaining: "I was kind of just floating around, with no sense of direction. Everything I knew about who I was, what I did, and how I structured my day – gone." Another reflected, "When I was an athlete, I had a schedule, but without basketball, I didn't have a schedule and had to figure life out."

Our study further highlighted that athletes from more popular sports often face additional challenges, particularly financial and vocational, due to stronger public identities and later career-ends. These findings reinforce the need for proactive Life Design support – not just to ease the landing, but to help athletes create what comes next with purpose.

Together with athletes, associations, and institutions like the International Olympic Committee (IOC), we are currently exploring further typical challenges and opportunities during and after athletes' careers. In addition, we aim to contribute to a framework on successful athlete transition with the Life Design approach.

Life Design offers athletes a powerful framework to navigate this pivotal phase and start redesigning before and after the finish line – as a whole-life athlete support – not only to redefine what comes next, but to reconnect with who they are beyond the game. Our work with athletes shows both their strengths – discipline, motivation, goal-setting – and their vulnerabilities: the loss of structure, team identity, and purpose. By reflecting on core strengths, experimenting with new roles, and designing fresh routines, athletes can begin to translate the discipline and drive of their first chapter into meaningful futures. We also help recalibrate their powerful inner voices – once trained for performance – toward self-compassion, adaptability, and new forms of contribution.

Life Design for Organizations: From Onboarding to Retirement

When people first encounter Life Design, they often imagine a personal tool – something for individual reflection or career planning. But its potential reaches much further. Over time, we've discovered how Life Design can transform not just individual lives, but teams, workplaces, and entire organizational cultures.

In this section, we explore how Life Design is applied across organizational contexts – from onboarding programs to leadership development, from diversity, equity, and inclusion (DEI) initiatives to retirement transitions. We've worked with organizations across sectors, adapting Life Design to meet diverse needs: sometimes named explicitly, sometimes seamlessly integrated into broader programs (e.g., a senior manager program at the International Olympic Committee was labeled "From Surviving to Thriving," using the methods and abilities of Life Design). It ranges from forty-five- to sixty-minute input sessions, to twelve-month-programs for new employees, high-potentials, and other talent initiatives along the employee life cycle. Whether it's helping new employees feel anchored, supporting midcareer professionals through change, or

Every age.
Any stage.
All sectors.

A movement in the making.

Table 15.2 *Life Design for organizations*

	Courses, initiatives, and programs	Organizational focus
Transitions	Career Transitions Onboarding Youth Orientation Outplacement (Pre-)Retirement	Leading the Future Meeting Culture Working with AI Inter-Generational Collaboration
Everyday work and culture	Empowering growth Design Your Home Office Design Your Potential Design Your Leadership	Cultivating Culture Diversity, Equity, and Inclusion Retention and Mental Health Human Potential

reimagining the future of work, Life Design offers a flexible, human-centered approach to organizational development.

We structure the impact across four key areas: (1) designing transitions, (2) empowering growth, (3) cultivating culture, and (4) leading the future. What follows are examples for each of the four areas on how Life Design has made an impact.

Designing Transitions

- Main focus: supporting people through key career moments.

From the moment someone joins to the day they leave, transitions shape our careers. Life Design provides a scaffolding for organizations to support employees in navigating these liminal moments with clarity and agency. Just as the pioneer in transition management William Bridges puts it, "Transitions are the most vulnerable places in a career. But also, the most powerful." The following are typical transitions that we have accompanied through programs in organizations.

- Onboarding transitions. We have used Life Design to help a big Swiss bank in designing a creative and meaningful onboarding program with the ability for new employees to connect with each other with empathy, curiosity, and appreciation, despite virtual meeting setups.
- Orientation transitions. When it comes to Gen Z and other young employees, we have used Life Design as youth orientation and a way to take away the pressure that one job has to fulfill all requirements, and

have transformed (sometimes unrealistic) expectations into meaningful actions using the portfolio approach.
- Outplacement transitions. In hard times of outplacement, we have used Life Design as a way to not only find the next job as quickly as possible, but to make sense of the past and the current situation to proactively shape the future in smaller and bigger ways. We use the Connecting the Dots method to make sense of the past and celebrate accomplishments. We use the Three Good Things method to appreciate and change perspective toward the good things happening in everyday life. We use the Magic Circle method to uncover smaller and bigger dreams, and build the Stairway to Heaven to take immediate action.
- (Pre-)Retirement transitions. One insurance company approached us to create a pre-retirement "Life Design Atelier" for managers and employees aged fifty-plus to keep them motivated to work beyond retirement age, which included self-discovery, doing a portfolio approach within and beyond the organization. Inspired by our NEXT program, we were asked to design a customized retirement transition program for a large organization with the hunch to hopefully keep some of them in part-time work due to a shortage of labor.

Empowering Personal Growth

- Main focus: unlocking human potential at work.

Organizations are rethinking personal growth: not as a ladder to climb, but as a garden to cultivate. Life Design programs foster lifelong learning, empowering personal agency and people to own their paths, and create meaningful careers through experiments and unlocking dormant potential. Just as Buckminster Fuller put it: "The best way to predict your future is to design it." The following are a few examples of how we collaborate with organizations to empower growth among their employees.

- Design Your Home Office. We have used Life Design for programs around topics such as the future of work as well as encouraging flourishing and productivity working from home, with energy competence, nudging to take action, and redesigning routines, among others, with organizations such as Porsche Consulting. We use methods such as the Energy Curve for better performance and well-being. We use the method of redesigning morning or evening outines to find more peace of mind and calmness despite the busyness of work and life.

- Design Your Potential. We have worked with NASA on how Life Design can support engineers to bring more of themselves to the workplace and find ways to leverage their human potential. We worked on their strengths and how they could bring what they are naturally good at into existing projects and new ideas. We use the Core of Creativity method as a way to approach creative problem-solving alone and collectively. We use the Signature Strengths method and connect them with the current tasks to perform better and also come up with new tasks and projects in connection with their signature strengths.

For the Senior Managers at the International Olympic Committee (IOC), we developed a program with the title "From Surviving to Thriving," which was about developing a growth mindset, the empowerment of teams, and ultimately increasing influence in the organization.

- Design Your Leadership. For high-potentials at the Swiss Stock Exchange, we developed a twelve-month leadership and high-potential program with the title "Design Y/our Future," which was about developing themselves as leaders and shaping entire organizations. They worked on their leadership goals and career aspirations. We did a two-day kick-off and every six weeks a half-day virtual workshop and they had their individual coaches. We worked both on their direct leadership goals and also their bigger career aspirations using methods such as Connecting the Dots, the Strengths Portfolio, and the Magic Circle.

Cultivating Culture

- Main focus: designing for inclusion, well-being, and belonging.

Inclusive, empathetic, and mentally healthy workplaces don't emerge by accident – they need to be intentionally designed. The following experiences show how Life Design can become a cultural catalyst from the inside out. As the globally recognized expert on DEI Verna Myers puts it: "Diversity is being invited to the party. Inclusion is being asked to dance."

- Diversity, equity, and inclusion (DEI). Life Design was used at Bosch to strengthen the human side of the organization. We used Life Design as an innovative approach for an empathy-driven culture for employees to really connect with one another. A Life Design seminar during the Bosch International DEI week empowered employees and managers with various empathy exercises. One example was the Three Good Things method, which we connected to the idea of what matters to you, what excites you, or even to the idea of what makes you weird. The goal was listening with attention and practicing "Tell me more..." and really connecting with what excites another person (and maybe not you). Another example in a similar context at Bosch was the emphasis on celebrating uniqueness and differences among employees and managers, which led to another seminar on Life Design with positive psychology and strengths in combination with empathy at Bosch International DEI week.

- Retention and mental health. At Deloitte, we were able to show how Life Design can work as a retention strategy to keep and grow talent with career development and adaptability as well as a focus on mental health. It was also the focus on mental health and resilience that we could use for global reinsurance company Swiss Re to set up a program called "Design Your Work Life Experience" that we rolled out for more than 1,500 employees globally. It was essentially about overcoming the gap of employees knowing what they could do for their health and resilience, but not doing it. We recalibrated inner beliefs through methods like the DJ of the Inner Sound. We used the Nudging Nuggets method to build small signals through post-it notes and other signs into their lives to take care of their mental health. We took the Social Support Maps method and built support systems within and beyond the organization.
- Human potential. Part of modern work cultures is to help employees discover their full potential and thrive in their careers. We have used Life Design at organizations such as IBM, Google, and the International Red Cross to uncover employees' hidden potential, reframe the stories about their careers and lives, as well as to realize their human potential at work and also beyond. Ways to uncover hidden potential consisted of the Signature Strengths and Strengths Portfolio methods to be more conscious about natural strengths and where they could add value for themselves and others. Another method was the Growth Journey Map to more consciously and reflect with structure about past projects and find new ways to bring more strengths into future projects.

Leading the Future

- Main focus: innovating how we work together.

The way we work is shifting faster than most organizations can adapt. Life Design offers a flexible compass to navigate the unknown – enabling leaders, teams, and entire cultures to thrive in complexity. Work is no longer a place we go; it is something we create. As Bill Gates puts it: "Work is no longer a destination, but an activity."

- Meeting culture. While Life Design was developed to support personal development and managing oneself working at home, at the office, and in other places, we can now see after many projects that a byproduct is connecting with others in a meaningful way and setting up new positive standards for meetings, workshops, and collaboration in general. This is what employees repeatedly report back to us. We can see that Life Designers who have become used to using visual thinking in their journey adapt it to their daily practices in conversations and meetings, making remote work more engaging and energetic by using visualization with themselves and others. In addition, people have taken ways of collaborating in Life Design to their meetings in general. Instead of doing classical brainstorming, where everyone shares their ideas aloud and immediately, they use "brainwriting" as a method to ideate first for themselves and then share it with others, which leads to more ideas and more variety within the ideas.
- Working with AI. We can see in our executive education program that AI is often perceived as a threat that is going to take away jobs. When we introduce AI in the realm of Life Design, we start by framing AI as a collaboration partner. We start with daily tasks, integrate AI into existing Life Design methods, and develop AI as a Life Design sparring partner. A participant recently reported back, "Before our seminar, I was not working with AI at all. Now, I'm the role model for my young colleagues, and that at the age of fifty-eight."
- Intergenerational collaboration. When we collaborate with organizations on questions such as "What's next in my career and life?" we can see that employees and managers at different ages and stages ask themselves the same questions. When tackling these questions, we can see that Life Design enables participants to have crossgenerational conversations and sparring sessions, where each can benefit from different age perspectives.

Life Design for Society: From the UN to the WEF and Beyond

Life Design not only empowers individuals – it also shapes collective conversations around longevity, transitions, well-being, and meaningful

Table 15.3 *Life design impact on society*

	Problem	Solution/action	Example/initiative
Lack of institutionalized support	People manage transitions alone; default behaviors prevail; mental health issues rise	Institutionalize transition support to improve career/life match-ability	Life Design programs: NEXT at St. Gallen, DCI at Stanford, Nexel Collaborative, La Caixa/Dnovo 50+, Global Transition Report with WDA
Legitimizing prototyping for adults	Prototyping is seen as only for youth; adults lack safe spaces to experiment	Create a culture and platforms for lifelong prototyping of roles, skills, and identities	Prototyping discussions at WEF Davos, creating a prototyping platform
Strategies for emotional stability despite uncertainty	Transitions create uncertainty, which impacts emotional stability	Use Life Design practices: appreciation, specific language (prototyping, portfolio), and visual thinking	Life Design courses, storytelling of NFL player using "portfolio" language
Developing psychological capital as transition support	Low engagement at work; lack of psychological resources for transition	Boost psychological capital (PsyCap): self-efficacy, hope, optimism, resilience	Life Loops framework, small redesigns, growth mindset experiments, emotional tools for resilience
Bias to action and overcoming procrastination	Procrastination blocks personal and societal transformation	Normalize procrastination and provide strategies to build a bias to action	Life Loops framework includes procrastination acceptance; supports tackling finite and infinite procrastination (e.g., SDGs, life dreams)

engagement. This section explores how Life Design is increasingly being recognized not only as a personal development tool, but as a public innovation framework.

Across our work with global institutions like the UN Goals House, the World Economic Forum (WEF), and the World Demographic & Ageing Forum, we've seen how Life Design contributes to urgent societal conversations: from longevity and workforce transformation to sustainable development and inclusive transitions. These aren't abstract issues – they are real-life challenges affecting millions navigating change without support, identity shifts without tools, and futures without clear paths.

At its heart, Life Design offers more than reflective practices: it legitimizes exploration, fosters emotional resilience, and builds psychological capacity. In doing so, it addresses the human side of complex global transitions: the internal shifts that must accompany structural change.

Whether you are a policymaker, educator, NGO leader, or simply someone who wants to bridge personal growth with societal transformation, this chapter shows what's possible when we bring Life Design into the collective sphere. From mindset to method, from individual agency to social impact – it's time to design the future, together.

The Gap: A Lack of Institutionalized Support

Despite longer lives and increasingly nonlinear career paths, most people still navigate transitions without institutional support. Some find coaches or mentors, but many remain stuck, contributing to disengagement, mental health challenges, and unrealized potential. Humans tend to default to the familiar unless prompted by crisis or given structured support.

To change this, we collaborate with organizations and institutions to create transition-support systems grounded in Life Design. At the University of St. Gallen, we launched NEXT for best-agers. At Nova Business School in Lisbon, we support unemployed individuals over fifty through partnerships with foundations like La Caixa and Dnovo. Globally, we co-develop transition programs with the Nexel Collaborative and Stanford's Distinguished Careers Institute (DCI).

Together with the World Demographic Forum, we're also developing a "Global Transition Report" to highlight best practices – such as New York City's municipal transition support or the UN's Immersion Days – to inspire more organizations, governments, and foundations to institutionalize transition programs at scale.

15 Life Design as a Catalyst for Scaling Change

Legitimizing Prototyping as a Pathway for Adult Growth

Prototyping is often associated with startups or student projects, but it's just as vital for adults navigating complex career and life transitions. Life Design promotes the legitimization of prototyping for adults, emphasizing that experimenting with new roles, routines, or identities is not only acceptable but necessary in today's dynamic world.

We create safe, structured environments where adults can try out new directions without fear of failure. While teenagers may shadow a parent for a day or try short internships, adults are often expected to commit fully without first testing the waters. Through Life Design we normalize and legitimize low-risk experimentation at any stage of life – whether that means prototyping a job, testing a side hustle, or exploring a new industry.

At the World Economic Forum in Davos, we discussed this shift with leaders like Moira Forbes. The consensus: organizations need to play a more proactive role in enabling transitions – not just through policies, but through legitimizing learning and exploration at work. Life Design provides both mindset and method to support this evolution.

Strategies for Emotional Stability Despite Uncertainty

Transitions inherently bring uncertainty – but Life Design strengthens emotional resilience by equipping people with tools for psychological and emotional grounding. Research we presented at the Academy of Management Annual Conference highlights three key practices that help people remain centered and capable even during major change.

(1) Empathetic dialogue. Participants who engage in Life Design conversations marked by curiosity, empathy, and appreciation develop more self-compassion and inner clarity. The way we talk to others begins to influence how we talk to ourselves.

(2) Legitimizing language. Words matter. When participants start using terms like prototyping or portfolio, they gain a vocabulary that validates exploration. A former NFL player shared that, instead of vaguely describing his next steps as "this and that," he now says, "I'm designing my portfolio" – a shift that boosts confidence and credibility.

(3) Visual thinking. Using physical templates and visual tools helps participants structure their thoughts, externalize ideas, and invite dialogue with others. Just as Einstein and Darwin used visuals to think, our participants use them to clarify and share their next steps, making transitions feel more navigable and collaborative.

Developing Psychological Capital as Transition Support

Life Design significantly enhances psychological capital (PsyCap) – a critical internal resource made up of four key elements.

(1) Self-efficacy: the belief in one's ability to take on and succeed in challenging tasks.
   Life Design builds self-efficacy through small, achievable prototypes – such as redesigning a daily routine. These quick wins create momentum and a growing sense of agency.
(2) Hope: the ability to set goals and identify flexible paths to reach them.
   Life Design cultivates hope by engaging participants in creative, iterative ideation. They learn to reframe setbacks and use feedback from real-life experiments to reorient rather than retreat.
(3) Optimism: the expectation that positive outcomes are possible now and in the future.
   Through differentiated possibility thinking and the growth mindset, Life Design helps individuals approach uncertainty with curiosity rather than fear – seeing potential rather than limitation.
(4) Resilience: the capacity to recover from adversity, conflict, or even success.
   Resilience is embedded in the Life Loops framework, which embraces iteration and includes procrastination as a natural part of the change process. Participants learn to listen to their inner voices, recalibrate when needed, and keep moving forward.

Higher levels of PsyCap are associated with improved job satisfaction, organizational commitment, and performance. In a time when only 15 percent of employees globally feel engaged at work, according to the Employee Engagement Report by Gallup, this psychological scaffolding is more important than ever.

Bias to Action and Overcoming Procrastination

Procrastination is one of the most widespread obstacles to change – personally, organizationally, and societally. What makes Life Design unique is that it doesn't shame procrastination. Instead, it integrates it into the creative process. We distinguish between finite procrastination: delaying tasks with deadlines (e.g., reports, taxes); and infinite procrastination: postponing meaningful goals without deadlines (e.g., career shifts, personal dreams, climate action).

Life Design acknowledges that 98 percent of people procrastinate. The first step is accepting it; the second is learning how to work with it. Tools like nudging, inner voice work (DJ of the Inner Sound), and peer support help individuals move from inertia to action.

Life Design isn't just a personal toolkit – it's a catalyst for scaling change, helping individuals, organizations, and societies navigate complexity with purpose, resilience, and creativity. As we look ahead, the question becomes: how can Life Design help us not only shape our own futures, but also codesign a world where AI amplifies human potential, longevity is the new normal, and sustainable development becomes a shared, lived practice?

CHAPTER 16

Life Design and the Future (of the Planet)

The future isn't something that just happens to us – it's something we shape, moment by moment, decision by decision. In a world defined by rapid technological shifts, longer life spans, and mounting ecological and social complexity, passive navigation is no longer enough. We need new tools, new mindsets, and new ways of thinking – not just about work or careers, but about life itself. That's where Life Design comes in.

This chapter is about expanding the lens. Beyond personal transformation, Life Design now meets the grand challenges of our time: from collaborating with AI to prototyping longevity, from redefining success to reclaiming attention, Life Design helps us respond creatively and courageously. And it reminds us that designing the future is not only about strategic plans or policy frameworks. It begins with the way we reflect, relate, experiment, and evolve.

To begin this inquiry, we offer ten provocations – ten sharp, hopeful nudges into what a Life Designed future could look like. These aren't predictions. They're invitations. Each one offers a spark to reimagine how we might live, learn, contribute, and thrive in the face of complexity. Some are philosophical. Some are practical. All are meant to stretch your thinking and inspire bold experiments.

So before diving into the specifics of AI, longevity, and sustainability, we invite you to pause here and let your imagination wander. What kind of world do you want to help design? What role might you play? What small experiment could you begin today? The question becomes: "What will you design next?" Let the provocations that follow be your compass. The future is not fixed. It's designed. Let's begin.

Box 16.1 Designing the Future: A Call to Action – Ten Provocations for a Life-Designed Future

(1) Meaningful futures for all.
Let's democratize Life Design through AI – creating life-changing conversations not just for the privileged few, but for kids, teens, adults, and athletes everywhere. No big budgets needed. Just human-centered technology, grounded in science and purpose.

(2) A reward program for happiness.
Why should reward systems only exist for spending? Let's reward the work of becoming – taking care of our mental, emotional, and spiritual well-being. Let's earn our "miles" toward sustainable happiness and meaningful lives.

(3) Prototyping for adults.
Adults deserve permission to experiment, too. In a world of longer lives and career transitions, we must build platforms for safe, smart, inspiring prototyping – so people can test paths, side hustles, and passions before betting everything on assumptions.

(4) Dream toolkits for everyday visionaries.
Dreaming is good. Designing is even better. Let's build accessible, joyful toolkits that help everyone prototype their biggest dreams – and bring them closer, one courageous step at a time.

(5) Sketching out loud.
Visual thinking is not decoration; it's transformation. By sketching our ideas out loud, using visual templates, and sharing them, we ignite action, spark collaboration, and invite others into the design of our futures.

(6) Life design as an intergenerational playground.
Mentoring should not be a one-way street. We envision intergenerational Life Design spaces – where young and old inspire each other, learn from each other, and find new meaning across generations.

(7) Behavior-boosting design.
Furniture is not just decoration – it can be a silent coach. Let's design tables, chairs, beds, and lamps that nudge us toward energy, empathy, conversation, movement, and self-care. Artefacts that inspire action, not just admiration.

(8) Transitions as features, not failures.
Transitions must be celebrated, not feared. Let's create societies and organizations where nonlinear lives are the norm – where career "zigzags," sabbaticals, and portfolio careers are badges of creativity and resilience.

> **Box 16.1 (cont.)**
>
> (9) Design beyond distraction.
>   We must reclaim our attention from the economy of endless scrolling and shallow dopamine hits. Let's build positive AI – technology that nurtures agency, meaning, and positive growth, not just clicks and consumption.
>
> (10) Designing work–life rhythms.
>   Forget work–life balance. Let's design rhythms – fluid, dynamic, personal patterns of energy, creation, connection, and renewal – rhythms that help us thrive over the long arc of a hundred-year life.

Life Design and AI

As artificial intelligence (AI) rapidly reshapes how we live, learn, and work, it also opens new frontiers for Life Design. This chapter explores how AI can become a thoughtful collaborator in our personal and collective journeys – not as a replacement for human intelligence, but as a catalyst for creativity, clarity, and action. By integrating AI into the Life Design process with ethical awareness, emotional intelligence, and critical reflection, we can enhance – not outsource – what it means to design a meaningful life.

We are at a pivotal moment for Life Design. As Life Designers, the question is not whether we will use AI, but how. How can AI become a meaningful ally in designing our futures – without replacing what makes us human? The good news: AI can support every phase of the Life Loops framework. The challenge: to use it wisely – amplifying human intelligence rather than diminishing it.

For too long, the AI debate has focused on threats: job loss, automation, and replacement. We take a different stance: AI and human intelligence (HI) can collaborate to expand creativity, clarity, and capability. But this requires discernment. The integration of AI into Life Design must be paired with a deeper understanding of what humans uniquely offer.

The Future Landscape of AI and Life Design

Looking ahead, we may see roles like Life Design AI coach or AI-augmented transition guide. Life Designers might work with personalized AI systems that support reflection, growth, and purpose. Community-based AI

16 Life Design and the Future (of the Planet)

ecosystems could foster shared learning and collective flourishing. But for this to happen, we need new tools, literacies, and mindsets – not just smarter technologies, but wiser humans.

So, What Are We Going to Do with AI and Life Design?

AI is not the enemy – it's a potential codesigner. Used well, it can serve as sparring partner, creative collaborator, or reflective mirror. The opportunity before us is twofold: to use AI intelligently for our own enhancement, and to explore what AI cannot replicate: human presence, intuition, empathy, embodiment. Life Design invites us to both integrate new technologies and reconnect with what it means to be fully human.

Human Intelligence and Artificial Intelligence as Collaborators

The true potential of AI in Life Design lies in synergy. Human intelligence brings emotion, context, wisdom, and ethical discernment. AI brings speed, pattern recognition, and cognitive augmentation. Together, they can unlock new pathways for learning, creating, and deciding.

Using AI Wisely without Losing Ourselves

Still, AI has its boundaries. It cannot replace embodied experience, moral judgment, or the deep resonance of human connection. Some Life Design

FROM CONTRA- TO CO-INTELLIGENCE

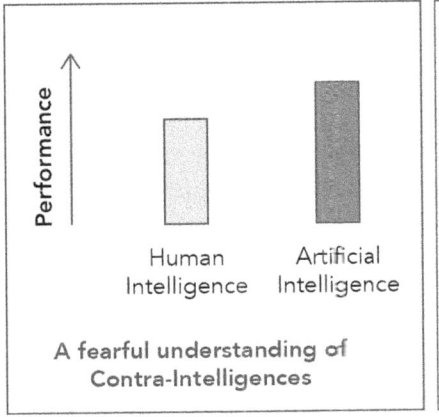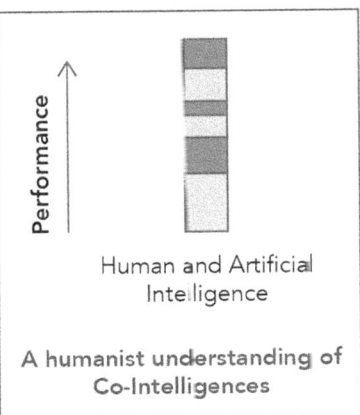

Figure 16.1 Human intelligence and artificial intelligence as collaborators.

moments – like sitting in silence, reading facial cues, or holding someone's hand in uncertainty – remain fundamentally human. These are not limitations to fear, but frontiers to protect. The key is to know where AI supports and where we must turn inward.

Using AI Wisely: Generating, Enhancing, Sparring
AI is often used to generate ideas, texts, or images – useful for automating repetitive tasks. But staying at this level risks declining human creativity. More powerful uses include enhancing our own thinking or using AI as a sparring partner that challenges, expands, and supports ideation. Take the example of someone who wants to combine skiing, travel, and income. You could ask AI: "Give me ten business ideas that combine skiing, travel, and earning money." That's generating. Or you could come up with ideas first and ask AI to expand or improve them: "How could I improve my idea of guiding ski tours for remote workers?" That's enhancing. Better yet, you could ask AI to question your assumptions and stretch your imagination: "What assumptions am I making that might limit how I think about earning money with skiing and travel?" That's sparring (see also fig. 16.2).

AI Along the Life Loops Framework
Each phase of the Life Loops framework can benefit from AI – as a generator in brainstorming, an enhancer in reflection, or a sparring partner during decision-making. Used well, AI becomes a tool for iterative learning and action – not a shortcut, but a catalyst.

New Critical and Creative Skills for Life Designers

AI is shaped by the data and values embedded in its systems. As Life Designers, we must remain vigilant: who built this tool? Whose voices are included or excluded? Does it reflect diverse, inclusive, and life-affirming values? AI offers suggestions, but discernment remains our responsibility. The most important skill is staying in the driver's seat. Every AI output is a starting point, not a verdict. Active questioning, dialogic use, and reflection ensure we use AI with intention rather than by default.

Prompting as a New Language and Micro-Prototyping
Prompting is the new language of human–AI collaboration. It's iterative – like Life Design itself. You give context, set the tone, refine outputs.

16 Life Design and the Future (of the Planet)

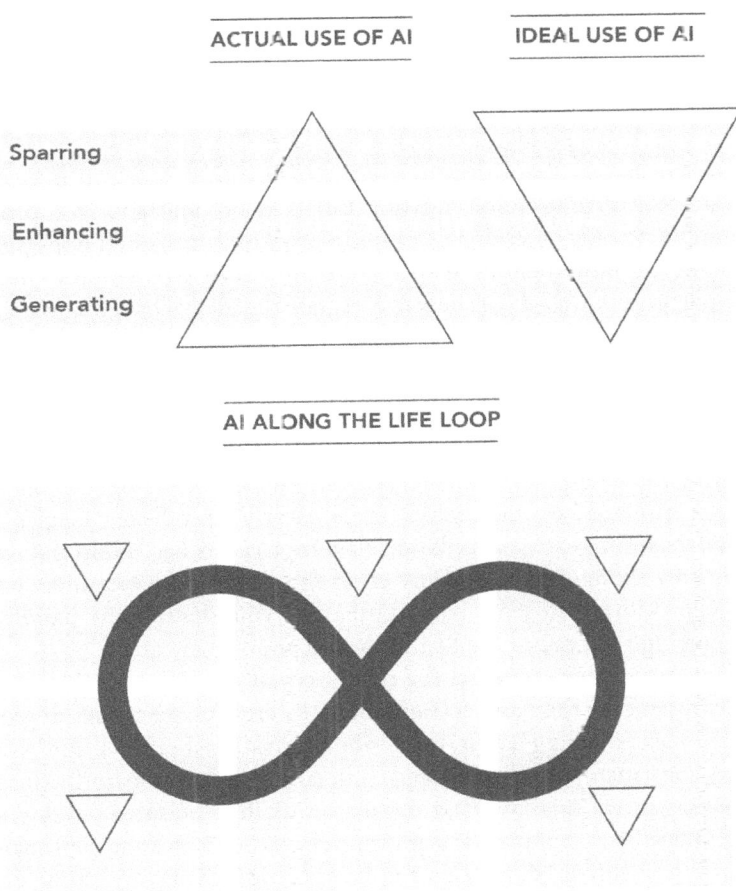

Figure 16.2 Ways of using AI in Life Design and along the Life Loop framework (© Nadine Bienefeld).

Prompting becomes a micro-prototyping practice: not about perfection, but learning. AI is not a magic oracle – it's more like a curious intern that improves with clarity and coaching.

The Social and Community Dimension

Life Design is rarely a solo act. AI can also support collective growth – co-creating ideas in teams, facilitating peer coaching, or enhancing workshop experiences. Imagine AI-assisted group prototyping or a community Life Design bot that supports mutual progress. How might AI amplify not just personal but shared growth?

Meet Your AI Co-Designer: A Typology of Life Design Roles

AI can play diverse roles in your Life Design journey. We propose a tentative typology – each role can appear in multiple Life Loops phases, but some are more helpful at specific points. Each type will also include a sample prompt that shows how to integrate the idea of bringing the topics of skiing, traveling, and making money together.

- AI as a reflective mirror. AI supports self-reflection and insight generation by acting as a journaling assistant, summarizing moods and recurring thoughts, offering self-awareness prompts, recognizing patterns, tracking emotions, and clarifying values. Its primary goal is to help humans see themselves more clearly and foster deeper self-understanding. An example for a prompt could be: "Help me reflect on how skiing, travel, and my efforts to make money connect to my deeper values and sense of purpose. Can you identify any patterns or recurring themes in how I think or feel about these areas?"
- AI as a coach or guide. In the role of coach or guide, AI aids in goal-setting, motivation, and accountability by creating personalized growth roadmaps, tracking habits, delivering motivational nudges, and providing constructive feedback loops. The aim is to support individuals in making intentional progress and mastering their personal development journeys. An example for a prompt could be: "Create a personalized growth roadmap that helps me balance improving my skiing skills, exploring new travel destinations, and building new income streams – with clear milestones, habits to track, and motivational check-ins."
- AI as a teacher or tutor. When acting as a teacher or tutor, AI enhances learning and skill development by crafting adaptive learning plans, simplifying complex concepts, simulating practice situations like conversations or public speaking, and offering feedback on writing, critical thinking, or creative projects. Its goal is to expand the user's knowledge, skills, and overall understanding. An example for a prompt could be: "Design a learning plan that teaches me essential concepts for skiing

technique, smart travel planning (e.g., budget-friendly strategies), and foundational knowledge in earning money through side projects or investments."

- AI as a companion or emotional support. As a companion, AI offers empathetic listening and emotional regulation tools by providing a safe space for venting, supporting mood management, applying techniques like cognitive behavioral therapy (CBT) to reframe unhelpful thoughts, and offering compassion and affirmation. This role aims to enhance emotional well-being and build resilience. An example for a prompt could be: "I sometimes feel overwhelmed trying to pursue my passion for skiing, my desire to travel more, and my goal of making more money. Can you help me process these emotions, offer supportive reframing, and guide me toward inner calm?"

- AI as a collaborator or creative partner. Taking on the role of a creative partner, AI engages in co-creation and ideation by brainstorming ideas for projects, writing, or art, generating creative content like stories or music, exploring visual concepts, and remixing and expanding user ideas. Its purpose is to spark inspiration and amplify creative expression. An example for a prompt could be: "Let's brainstorm creative ideas that combine skiing, travel, and making money – like blog concepts, business ideas, or unique side hustles that could turn my passions into something more."

- AI as a social simulator or practice partner. In the role of a social simulator, AI fosters relational development and communication skills by enabling role-play for tough conversations, practicing empathy and active listening, teaching different communication styles, and assisting in drafting emotionally intelligent messages. The ultimate goal is to boost relational intelligence and confidence. An example for a prompt could be: "Simulate conversations where I confidently share my plans with others – about how I want to integrate skiing, travel, and making money into my life – and practice handling both support and skepticism."

- AI as a Life Design architect or strategist. As a Life Design architect, AI helps users design systems for life optimization by suggesting ways to optimize daily routines and energy flow, proposing life design experiments, recommending tools and workflows, and aiding in prioritization of what matters most. The goal is to align everyday living with deeper purpose and well-being. An example for a prompt could be: "Help me design a life strategy that aligns my passion for skiing, my love of travel, and my financial ambitions – so I can experiment with routines, income sources, and lifestyle choices that support all three."

Ready to change the future you'll live in?

YOUR PROTOTYPES CHANGE MORE THAN JUST *YOUR* FUTURE!

What about your own journey? How might AI help you reflect more deeply, ideate more freely, or act more bravely? What small experiments can you try? AI is not just a tool – it's a test of how we grow. Used with intention, it can elevate our Life Design journey. But the goal is not simply to get more done – it's to live more fully. As we step into this new era, the real invitation is not just to use smarter tools, but to become wiser humans.

So, what might your personal AI Life Design Manifesto look like? What roles will you invite AI to play – and where will you draw the line, trusting your own inner compass? The future of Life Design is not AI versus humanity. It is AI with humanity. Let's design that future – with clarity, curiosity, and compassion.

Life Design and Longevity

As life expectancy reaches into the eighties, nineties, or even over a hundred, the rhythms of life are shifting. One career, one retirement, one identity – these traditional markers no longer suffice. In collaboration with the World Demographic Forum, we explore how Life Design can address both the challenges and opportunities of longer lives. At the UN General Assembly in New York, Life Design was named one of five key strategies for responding to demographic change and extending lifespans.

Life Design provides a toolkit for navigating this new landscape with curiosity, intention, and adaptability. Below are seven key areas impacted by longevity and how Life Design can help you meet the moment.

Multiple Careers and Transitions

Implication
As people live longer, the idea of a single, linear career becomes increasingly outdated. Further ways of career building are emerging, such as the portfolio career. Individuals are likely to move through several professional identities, often in different fields. Reinvention, reskilling, and continuous learning will become the norm, not the exception.

How Life Design Supports You
Life Design builds transition competence through the Life Loops framework, equipping you to navigate change with confidence. You learn to prototype new directions, gather real-world feedback, and iterate as you go. Rather than fearing transitions, you begin to embrace them – normalizing

BEYOND LINEAR CAREERS

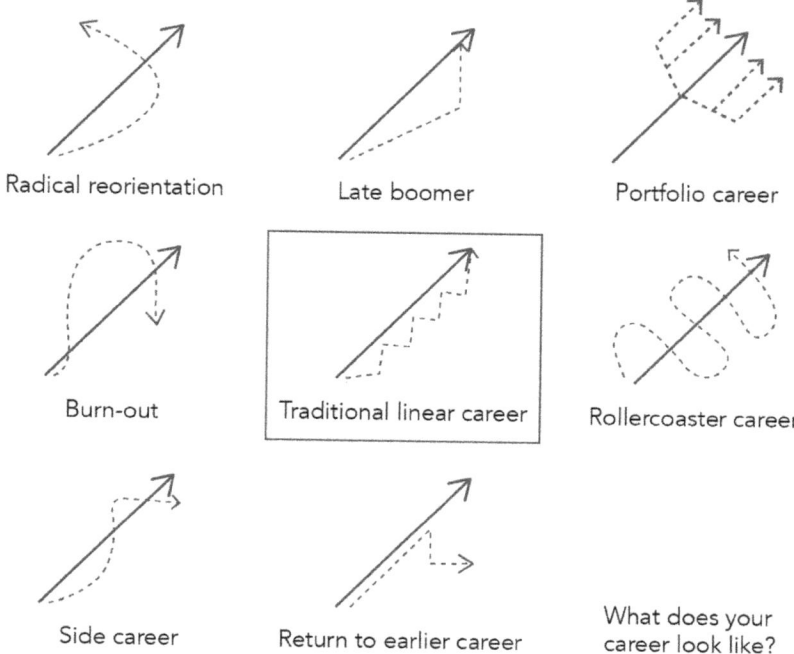

Figure 16.3 Beyond linear careers: new types of nonlinear careers.

change and building the skills needed to navigate evolving professional landscapes across your lifespan.

Extended Retirement Phase

Implication
With lifespans extending into the nineties and beyond, the retirement phase may now span thirty years or more. This period requires more than financial planning – it demands purposeful engagement and reinvention.

How Life Design Supports You
Life Design offers tools like the Future Scenarios and Strengths Portfolio methods to help you envision meaningful post-retirement

paths. Whether through encore careers, creative projects, or volunteering, Life Design helps you stay connected to what matters most — ensuring continued growth, purpose, and vitality in later life.

Financial Pressures

Implication
The risk of outliving one's savings becomes more acute in a longer life. Relying solely on traditional retirement funds may no longer be sufficient. Flexibility, income diversification, and entrepreneurial thinking are increasingly important.

How Life Design Supports You
Life Design encourages portfolio thinking — the idea of building a mix of meaningful and income-generating activities. Through low-risk prototyping of side projects, consulting roles, or part-time ventures, you can explore new opportunities, strengthen financial resilience, and reduce dependence on any single income stream.

Health Management

Implication
Living longer brings the need for proactive, sustainable health management — physically, mentally, and emotionally. Chronic illness, cognitive decline, and stress-related issues are growing concerns that require lifestyle design, not just medical intervention.

How Life Design Supports You
Using tools like the Energy Curve, Energy Map, and Energy–Tension Matrix, Life Design helps you design your days more intentionally — tracking your energy, noticing your patterns, and experimenting with small changes that support well-being. You build habits that promote resilience and vitality across decades, not just days.

Identity Shifts

Implication
Longer lives mean more roles — and more identity transitions. Traditional life stages (education, work, retirement) no longer neatly define who we are. Identity becomes more fluid and complex.

How Life Design Supports You

Life Design helps you develop a resilient, multidimensional sense of self. Tools like the Strengths Portfolio, Connecting the Dots, and DJ of the Inner Sound help you reconnect with your values, talents, and evolving aspirations – beyond job titles or life labels. You learn to carry a strong sense of self through each phase of life.

Relationships and Community

Implication

With longevity comes evolving relationships – through life transitions, relocations, or loss. Without intentional cultivation, people may experience increasing loneliness and isolation, especially in later stages of life.

How Life Design Supports You

Life Design supports meaningful connection through mapping Social Support and engaging with Life Design Teams. You're encouraged to invest in communities of practice, peer learning, and collaboration – helping you stay socially connected, emotionally supported, and embedded in circles of mutual growth across the lifespan.

Generational Mix

Implication

In both workplaces and society, four or five generations now live and work side by side. Each generation brings different values, communication styles, and digital literacies – creating both opportunities and tensions.

How Life Design Supports You

Life Design builds empathy and collaborative skills to help you navigate intergenerational dynamics. Through cross-generational prototyping and shared reflection, you learn to work across differences, co-create inclusive cultures, and unlock the potential of age-diverse teams and communities.

In summary, the traditional life script no longer holds in a world where lives stretch across a century. Instead, you are invited into a new journey – one where careers, identities, relationships, and meanings evolve continuously. Life Design offers you a thoughtful "toolkit" to navigate this unfolding path with intention and creativity. It empowers you to embrace transition, build resilience, nurture community, and stay true to your evolving self over time. A longer life is not simply about adding years – it's about enriching those years with purpose, vitality, and meaning. Life Design helps you craft a future that honors both who you are and who you are becoming.

Life Design and Sustainable Development

One of the most urgent challenges of our time is how to support the planet's development in a sustainable and life-affirming way. The UN Sustainable Development Goals (SDGs) provide a globally recognized framework, bringing together seventeen key areas where action is needed. Yet, only about 12 percent of these goals are currently being pursued in a meaningful way. This gap between intention and action is not just a global issue – it's a human one.

What role can Life Design play in bridging this gap? How can it empower individuals, teams, and organizations to act more effectively on the SDGs? And how does Life Design connect to the increasingly popular Inner Development Goals (IDGs), which focus on the internal capacities we need to navigate complex challenges?

SDGs along the Life Loops Framework

In this section, we explore how Life Design methods and mindsets – especially the five phases of the Life Loops framework – can activate sustainable development from the inside out. We invite you to begin with what matters to you and then design ways to contribute meaningfully, without burning out.

(1) Empathy. If you feel drawn to Goal #3: Good Health and Well-being, you might start by applying empathy. Ask, "Tell me more…" of yourself, of others, of the world. What does health and well-being mean in your context? What do others experience? This process deepens your understanding and builds authentic motivation. By identifying your signature strengths and aligning them with your chosen SDG, you increase both the impact and sustainability of your efforts.

(2) Ideation. Using tools like the Core of Creativity, you can brainstorm how to support your chosen SDG alone or in teams. Let your strengths and interests combine with new methods, technologies

(such as AI), or existing initiatives. You might map ideas using Opportunity Bingo or integrate the goal into a Future Scenario. By expanding your options creatively, you make it easier to take the first step.

(3) Prototyping. Sustainable development efforts often carry assumptions about what making an impact looks like. Life Design encourages low-stakes, real-world experimentation to test those assumptions. Whether through direct action (e.g., cooking for refugees), indirect service (e.g., managing teams who cook food for refugees), systemic change (e.g., improving infrastructures to improve support of refugees), or framework change (e.g., shifting narrative and policies about what is means to be a refugee and treatment of refugees), prototyping allows you to explore the level and type of impact that feels right to you. Try something for a day or a weekend before committing long term. Volunteer platforms and Life Design conversations can help you get started.

(4) Learning. After taking action, reflection is key. Tools like the Growth Journey Map help you make sense of what went well, what was difficult, and what comes next. Did you enjoy the immediate impact of your prototype, or did it feel incomplete? You may choose to iterate your role – from hands-on contributor to organizer, strategist, or systems thinker. Learning is not failure – it's forward motion.

(5) Perseverance. The fact that only a fraction of the SDGs are being fully addressed suggests a collective procrastination. Life Design tackles this gap with methods like Nudging Nuggets, DJ of the Inner Sound, and the Social Support Map. These tools help you ask: "What small nudge would move me forward? Which inner voice needs amplification? Who could support or join me?" In this way, Life Design builds momentum not through pressure, but through compassion and structure.

Importantly, when working with young adults, we often see the desire to go "all in" for a cause, but also the risk of burnout. We've seen this in our courses and gap year programs, where high ideals sometimes meet exhaustion. That's why it's so critical to start with yourself.

Key to Sustainable Success: Start with Yourself

Any contribution to the SDGs becomes more sustainable when rooted in your own strengths, values, and motivations. Your Signature Strengths are not only what you're good at – they're what energizes you. By aligning

16 Life Design and the Future (of the Planet)

them with your approach to sustainability, you create a long-term path of engagement that is both effective and nourishing. Whether you're aiming to support clean energy, education, or climate action. Life Design invites you to begin with self-awareness, then take purposeful, incremental steps.

Connecting Life Design with Inner Development Goals

Parallel to our Life Design work, a global coalition of researchers, educators, and foundations has developed the Inner Development Goals

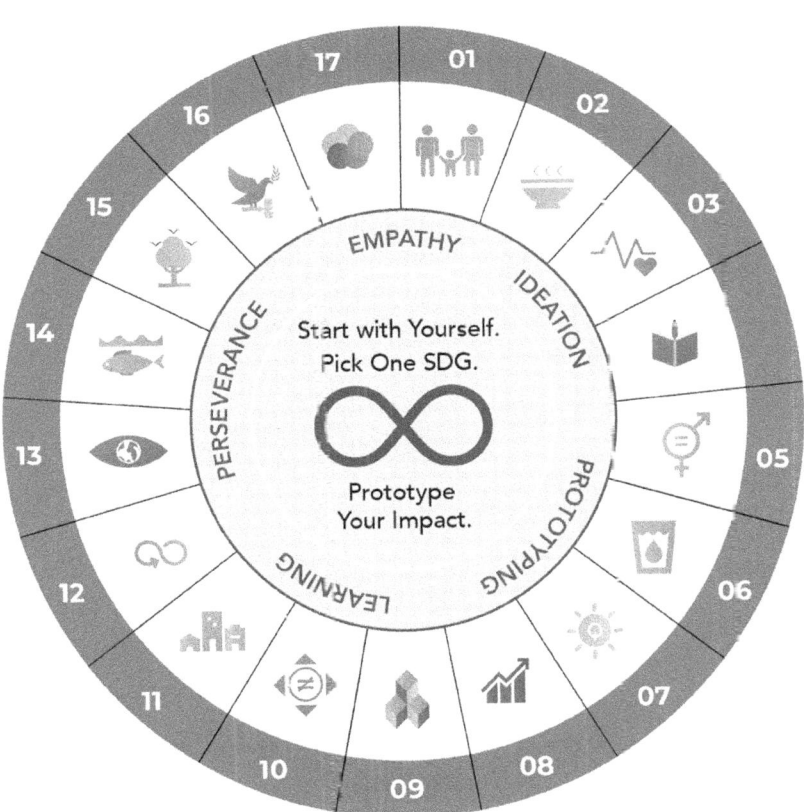

Figure 16.4 Design your sustainable impact.

(IDGs), a framework of five categories and twenty-three essential skills that support personal growth and collective transformation. Designed by the same team that created the visual identity of the SDGs, the IDGs emphasize inner capacities such as presence, empathy, collaboration, and courage as key enablers of sustainable change.

We see strong alignment between the IDGs and Life Design. Both recognize that meaningful external impact begins with internal development. That's why we actively partner with the IDG community – for example, through our collaboration with the IDG Hub at the University of St. Gallen. We've also run Design Your Future workshops with IDG partners and recommend exploring their events, joining local hubs, or even founding your own.

The grand challenge of sustainable development demands not only structural shifts, but also deeply personal engagement. Any activity aiming for systemic change needs to be rooted in personal action. Life Design offers a human-centered approach that helps individuals, teams, and institutions turn good intentions into sustained action. By going through the five Life Design stages and applying the five Life Design abilities, you build the creativity, clarity, and resilience needed to engage meaningfully with the world's most pressing challenges.

At the core, Life Design for sustainable development is a reminder: saving the planet requires sustaining yourself. Start where you are. Pick one goal. Design your path. And let your small, intentional experiments ripple outward into lasting impact.

Conclusion: A Life Design Manifesto

As we stand at the intersection of complexity, longevity, and rapid societal change, Life Design emerges not merely as a method, but as a necessary life competence. Throughout this journey, we have explored how Life Design equips individuals, organizations, and societies to move from passive endurance toward active creation – embracing transition, uncertainty, and possibility. It is not perfection we seek, but progress: through small experiments, courageous iterations, and an ever-renewed commitment to living life as a dynamic, evolving portfolio of meaningful experiences.

What sets Life Design apart is its interdisciplinary foundation and its deep respect for the realities of human life. It integrates creative action with psychological insight, visualization with experimentation, and acknowledges the bumps, doubts, and procrastinations as natural parts of the journey. Far from offering rigid blueprints, Life Design invites a playful yet disciplined way of building lives that are resilient, joyful, and authentically our own. It teaches us not to wait for clarity before we act, but to find clarity through action – through loops of doing, reflecting, and growing.

This is a call to design not just better careers, but better ways of living, learning, and contributing to the world around us. Whether you are an early career explorer, a midlife pivot-seeker, or a seasoned professional shaping your next chapter, Life Design empowers you to move forward – one small prototype, one courageous step at a time. The future is not a fixed point waiting for us; it is a landscape we shape every day by the questions we ask, the experiments we dare, and the possibilities we allow ourselves to imagine.

Now it is your turn. Embrace the loops. Start small. Invite others into your experiments. Remember that designing your future is not a solo performance, but a collective, creative endeavor. The tools are in your hands. The next iteration of your life is waiting – not perfectly mapped, but ready to be shaped with curiosity, courage, and care. Live your life in loops and design a future where more of you – your energy, your talents, your dreams – can come fully alive.

As you close this book, we invite you not only to reflect but to act – to take the ideas, methods, and manifesto you've encountered and begin living them in your own unique way. Life Design is not a theory to admire but a practice to cultivate. It is a mindset, a method, and, above all, a movement: one that encourages you to shape your life with curiosity, intention, and courage.

Through small daily experiments or bold leaps toward your larger vision, you are part of a global shift – changing the world by first changing yourself. By embracing loops over lines, prototypes over perfection, and community over isolation, you not only contribute to your own

---

Box C.1 Manifesto for Proactivity, Growth, and Designing Futures

- **We are not passengers. We are designers.**
  Living on autopilot is easy. But we choose the driver's seat – starting small, dreaming big, and iterating forward.

- **Life is not a problem to solve. It's a portfolio to design.**
  We embrace life's complexity, crafting evolving portfolios that blend meaning, work, creativity, and connection.

- **We move in loops, not lines.**
  Growth is cyclical. We live, experiment, reflect, and redesign. Progress lives in the loop, not the ladder.

- **Action beats perfection.**
  Small experiments lead to big clarity. We act, learn, and adjust – faster than we could plan. Energy is our compass.

- **We track what fuels and drains us.**
  Vitality guides our direction – not just goals, but how it feels to pursue them.

- **We trust prototypes, not assumptions.**
  We test our dreams before we bet the farm. Lived experience is better than untested ideas.

- **Creativity and play are serious strategies.**
  In uncertain times, imagination is a survival skill. Play sparks insight and unlocks possibility.

> **Box C.1 (cont.)**
>
> - **We embrace transitions as features, not bugs.**
>   Change is not a flaw – it's life's primary design challenge. We prepare with creativity and resilience.
> - **Community amplifies design.**
>   We design better, bolder, and more joyfully together. Life Design thrives in teams, circles, communities, and trusted spaces.
> - **We bring more of ourselves into the future.**
>   Authenticity is the ultimate design act. We align our actions with our values, one courageous step at a time.
> - **We design not only for ourselves, but for a thriving planet.**
>   Life Design is not self-centered – it is deeply interconnected. We design for equity, sustainability, and collective well-being.
> - **This is y/our invitation.**
>   To move beyond surviving. To build a future worth living. To design our lives – not by default, but by design. Starting today. Starting with you.

flourishing, but also to healthier organizations, stronger communities, and a more sustainable planet.

To help you begin – or continue – this journey, we offer the Manifesto for Proactivity, Growth, and Designing Futures. It is not a final answer, but a living compass. Let it remind you of what matters. Let it evolve with you. Let it inspire your next steps.

Further Reading

Part I Welcome to Life Design

1 Introduction

Gratton, L., & Scott, A. (2016). *The 100-year life: Living and working in an age of longevity*. Bloomsbury.

Nota, L., & Rossier, J. (Eds.). (2015). *Handbook of life design: From practice to theory and from theory to practice*. Hogrefe Publishing.

Thomke, S. H. (2020). *Experimentation works: The surprising power of business experiments*. Harvard Business Review Press.

2 Life Designer Stories

Bresciani, S., & Kernbach, S. (2020). A design thinking approach for designing careers: Finding authenticity and increasing self-efficacy. *Academy of Management Proceedings*, 19884.

Rehnert, D., & Kernbach, S. (2020). The pathway of a change-maker: Creativity and affect regulation to bridge the intention-action gap. *Academy of Management Proceedings*, 19476.

3 Why Life Design Matters

Bresciani, S., & Kernbach, S. (2020). A design thinking approach for designing careers: Finding authenticity and increasing self-efficacy. *Academy of Management Proceedings*, 2020(1), 19884.

Gratton, L., & Scott, A. (2016). *The 100-year life: Living and working in an age of longevity*. Bloomsbury.

Handy, C. (1989). *The age of unreason*. Business Books.

Ibarra, H. (2023). *Working identity: Unconventional strategies for reinventing your career* (updated edn., with a new preface). Harvard Business Review Press.

Luthans, F., Youssef, C. M., & Avolio, B. J. (2007) *Psychological capital: Developing the human competitive edge*. Oxford University Press.

Perrig-Chiello, P. (2024). *Own your age: Strong and self-determined in the second half of life. Using the psychology of life transitions*. Julius Beltz.

Rehnert, D., & Kernbach, S. (2020). The pathway of a change-maker: Creativity and affect regulation to bridge the intention-action gap. *Academy of Management Proceedings*, 19476.

Part II Life Design Building Blocks

4 Life Design Abilities

Batson, C. D. (2011). *Altruism in humans*. Oxford University Press.

Cooperrider, D. L., & Srivastva, S. (1987). Appreciative inquiry in organizational life. *Research in Organizational Change and Development*, 1(1), 129–169.

Costa, V. D., Tran, V. L., Turchi, J., & Averbeck, B. B. (2014). Dopamine modulates novelty seeking behavior during decision making. *Behavioral Neuroscience*, 128(5), 556–566.

Decety, J., & Jackson, P. L. (2004). The functional architecture of human empathy. *Behavioral and Cognitive Neuroscience Reviews*, 3(2), 71–100.

Dweck, C. S. (2006). *Mindset: The new psychology of success*. Random House.

Eisenberg, N., & Miller, P. A. (1987). The relation of empathy to prosocial and related behaviors. *Psychological Bulletin*, 101(1), 91–119.

Heath, C., & Heath, D. (2010). *Switch: How to change things when change is hard*. Broadway Books.

Heath, C., & Heath, D. (2013). *Decisive: How to make better choices in life and work*. Crown Business.

Kelley, T., & Kelley, D. (2013). *Creative confidence: Unleashing the creative potential within us all*. Crown Business.

Merrill, M. D. (2002). First principles of instruction. *Educational Technology Research and Development*, 50(3), 43–59.

Merrill, M. D. (2009). First principles of instruction. In C. M. Reigeluth & A. Carr (Eds.), *Instructional design theories and models: Building a common knowledge base* (Vol. III). Routledge.

Müller, M. (2019). IBM: Design Thinking adaptation and adoption at scale. This is Design Thinking, July 9. https://thisisdesignthinking.net/2019/07/ibm-design-thinking-adaptation-adoption-at-scale/.

Puccio, G. J., Mance, M., & Switalski, L. B. (2018). *Creativity rising: Creative thinking and creative problem solving in the 21st century*. ICSC Press.

Rehnert, D., & Kernbach, S. (2020). The pathway of a change-maker: Creativity and affect regulation to bridge the intention-action gap. *Academy of Management Proceedings*, 2020, 19476.

Rockliff, H., Gilbert, P., McEwan, K., Lightman, S., & Glover, D. (2008). A pilot exploration of heart rate variability and salivary cortisol responses to compassion-focused imagery. *Clinical Neuropsychiatry*, 5(3), 132–139.

Rosenberg, M. B. (2015). *Nonviolent communication: A language of life* (3rd ed.). PuddleDancer Press.

Shapiro, L. A. (2011). *Embodied cognition*. Routledge.

Whitney, D., & Trosten-Bloom, A. (2010). *The power of appreciative inquiry: A practical guide to positive change*. Berrett-Koehler Publishers.

Wilson, M. (2002). Six views of embodied cognition. *Psychonomic Bulletin & Review*, 9(4), 625–636.

5   Life Loops Framework

Amabile, T. M., & Kramer, S. J. (2011). *The progress principle: Using small wins to ignite joy, engagement, and creativity at work*. Harvard Business Review Press.

Brown, T. (2009). *Change by design: How design thinking creates new alternatives for business and society*. Harvard Business Review Press.

Eppler, M. J., & Mengis, J. (2011). *Management atlas: Management methods for everyday work*. Carl Hanser Verlag.

Kernbach, S., & Eppler, M. J. (2020). *Life Design*. Schäffer-Poeschel.

Kernbach, S., & Eppler, M. J. (2022). *Life-Design-actionbook: Cultivating creativity, curiosity, and initiative. Moving from thinking to acting to proactively shape the future*. Schäffer-Poeschel.

Müller, M. (2019). IBM: Design Thinking adaptation and adoption at scale. This is Design Thinking, July 9. https://thisisdesignthinking.net/2019/07/ibm-design-thinking-adaptation-adoption-at-scale/.

Pfeffer, J., & Sutton, R. I. (2000). *The knowing-doing gap: How smart companies turn knowledge into action*. Harvard Business Review Press.

Pressfield, S. (2012). *The war of art: Break through the blocks and win your inner creative battles*. Black Irish Entertainment.

Riess, H. (2017). The science of empathy. *Journal of Patient Experience*, 4(2), 74–77.

Sniehotta, F. F., Scholz, U., & Schwarzer, R. (2005). Bridging the intention–behaviour gap: Planning, self-efficacy, and action control in the adoption and maintenance of physical exercise. *Psychology and Health*, 20(2), 143–160.

Staats, B. R., Brunner, D. J., & Upton, D. M. (2011). Lean principles, learning, and knowledge work: Evidence from a software services provider. *Journal of Operations Management*, 29(5), 376–390.

6   Life Design Levels

Amabile, T. M., & Kramer, S. J. (2011). The power of small wins. *Harvard Business Review*, 89(5), 70–80.

Arthur, M. B., & Rousseau, D. M. (Eds.). (1996). *The boundaryless career: A new employment principle for a new organizational era*. Oxford University Press.

Clear, J. (2018). *Atomic habits: An easy & proven way to build good habits & break bad ones*. Avery.

Fogg, B. J. (2020). *Tiny habits: The small changes that change everything*. Houghton Mifflin Harcourt.

Peterson, C., & Seligman, M. E. P. (2004). *Character strengths and virtues: A handbook and classification*. Oxford University Press and American Psychological Association.

Platman, K. (2004). Portfolio careers and the search for flexibility in later life. *Work, Employment and Society*, 18(3), 573–599.

Part III Life Design Toolbox

7 Empathy Methods

Emmons, R. A., & McCullough, M. E. (2003). Counting blessings versus burdens: An experimental investigation of gratitude and subjective well-being in daily life. *Journal of Personality and Social Psychology*, 84(2), 377–389.

Handy, C. (1989). *The age of unreason*. Business Books.

Lyubomirsky, S., Sheldon, K. M., & Schkade, D. (2005). Pursuing happiness: The architecture of sustainable change. *Review of General Psychology*, 9(2), 111–131.

Maslow, A. H. (1943). A theory of human motivation. *Psychological Review*, 50(4), 370–396.

Neff, K. D. (2003). The development and validation of a scale to measure self-compassion. *Self and Identity*, 2(3), 223–250.

Peterson, C., & Seligman, M. E. P. (2004). *Character strengths and virtues: A handbook and classification*. Oxford University Press and American Psychological Association.

Seligman, M. E. P. (2011). *Flourish: A visionary new understanding of happiness and well-being*. Free Press.

Seligman, M. E. P., Steen, T. A., Park, N., & Peterson, C. (2005). Positive psychology progress: Empirical validation of interventions. *American Psychologist*, 60(5), 410–421.

8 Ideation Methods

Amabile, T. M. (1996). *Creativity in context: Update to the social psychology of creativity*. Westview Press.

Csikszentmihalyi, M. (1996). *Creativity: Flow and the psychology of discovery and invention*. HarperCollins.

Guilford, J. P. (1950). Creativity. *American Psychologist*, 5(9), 444–454.

Guilford, J. P. (1967). *The nature of human intelligence*. McGraw-Hill.

Guilford, J. P., Christensen, P. R., Merrifield, P. R., & Wilson, R. C. (1978). *Alternate uses: Manual of instructions and interpretation*. Sheridan Psychological Services.

Runco, M. A., & Jaeger, G. J. (2012). The standard definition of creativity. *Creativity Research Journal*, 24(1), 92–96.

Runco, M. A., & Acar, S. (Eds.). (2024). *Handbook of creativity assessment*. Edward Elgar Publishing.

Sawyer, R. K. (2003). *Group creativity: Music, theater, collaboration*. Lawrence Erlbaum Associates.

Schoemaker, P. J. H. (1995). Scenario planning: A tool for strategic thinking. *Sloan Management Review*, 36(2), 25–40.

Wright, S. L., Thompson, R. C., & Galloway, T. S. (2013). The physical impacts of microplastics on marine organisms: A review. *Environmental Pollution*, 178, 483–492.

9   Prototyping Methods

Aristotle. (2009). *Posterior analytics* (J. Barnes, Trans.). Oxford University Press. (Original work published ca. 350 BCE.)

Berg, J. M., Wrzesniewski, A., & Dutton, J. E. (2020). Do the hustle! Empowerment from side-hustles and its effects on full-time work performance. *Academy of Management Journal*, 63(4), 1231–1255.

Brown, T. (2009). *Change by design: How design thinking creates new alternatives for business and society*. Harvard Business Review Press.

Dilts, R. (1994). *Strategies of genius: Volume 1 (Walt Disney, Aristotle, Sherlock Holmes, Wolfgang Amadeus Mozart)*. Meta Publications.

Houde, S., & Hill, C. (1997). What do prototypes prototype? In M. Helander, T. K. Landauer, & P. Prabhu (Eds.), *Handbook of human-computer interaction* (2nd edn., pp. 367–381). Elsevier.

Lally, P., van Jaarsveld, C. H. M., Potts, H. W. W., & Wardle, J. (2010). How are habits formed: Modelling habit formation in the real world. *European Journal of Social Psychology*, 40(6), 998–1009.

Rosen, E. (2019). *The radical sabbatical: The millennial handbook to the quarter life crisis*. John Catt Educational Ltd.

Schrage, M. (1999). *Serious play: How the world's best companies simulate to innovate*. Harvard Business Review Press.

Stickdorn, M., Lawrence, A., Hormess, M. E., & Schneider, J. (2018). *This is service design doing: Applying service design thinking in the real world*. O'Reilly Media.

Thoits, P. A., & Hewitt, L. N. (2001). Volunteer work and well-being. *Journal of Health and Social Behavior*, 42(2), 115–131.

Welch, S. (2009). *10-10-10: A life-transforming idea*. Scribner.

Wu, J. (2022). Staycation: A mysterious power to restore study engagement. *Proceedings of the 9th International Conference on Hospitality and Tourism Management*, 7(1), 52–64.

10 Learning Methods

Beck, A. T. (1976). *Cognitive therapy and the emotional disorders.* International Universities Press.
Dweck, C. S. (2006). *Mindset: The new psychology of success.* Random House.
Fogg, B. J. (2020). *Tiny habits: The small changes that change everything.* Houghton Mifflin Harcourt.
Foucar-Szocki, D., Shephard, B., & Firestien, R. (1980s). PPCO: Plusses, potentials, concerns, overcoming concerns. [Unpublished manuscript.]
Kleist, H. von. (1951). On the gradual construction of thoughts during speech (M. Hamburger, Trans). *German Life and Letters*, 5(1), 42–46.
Mayer, R. E., & Moreno, R. (2003). Nine ways to reduce cognitive load in multimedia learning. *Educational Psychologist*, 38(1), 43–52.
Pollock, R. (2019). *Feedback and reflection in agile teams: Using the start, stop, continue method.* O Reilly Media.
Roth, B. (2015). *The achievement habit: Stop wishing, start doing, and take command of your life.* Harper Business.
Schein, E. H. (1999). *Process consultation revisited: Building the helping relationship.* Addison-Wesley.
Schoen, R. (2012). How to give feedback without shooting ideas down. Innovation Bound, August 2. www.innovationbound.com/articles/how-to-give-feedback-without-shooting-ideas-down

11 Perseverance Methods

Eppler, M. J., & Kernbach, S. (2021). *Meet up! Better meetings through nudging.* Cambridge University Press.
Kahneman, D. (2011). *Thinking, fast and slow.* Farrar, Straus and Giroux.
Khan, A., & Husain, A. (2010). Social support as a moderator of positive psychological strengths and subjective well-being. *Psychological Reports*, 106(2), 534–538.
Kross, E. (2021). *Chatter. The voice in our head, why it matters, and how to harness it.* Crown Publishing Group.
Kross, E., & Ayduk, Ö. (2011). Making meaning out of negative experiences by self-distancing. *Current Directions in Psychological Science*, 20(3), 187–191.
Kross, E., Bruehlman-Senecal, E., Park, J., Burson, A., Dougherty, A., Shablack, H., ... & Ayduk, Ö. (2014). Self-talk as a regulatory mechanism: How you do it matters. *Journal of Personality and Social Psychology*, 106(2), 304–324.
Schulz von Thun, F. (1998). *The inner team and how to work with it: Communication psychology for consulting and everyday life.* Rowohlt.
Sunstein, C. R. (2014). Nudging: A very short guide. *Journal of Consumer Policy*, 37(4), 583–588.
Thaler, R. H., & Sunstein, C. R. (2008). *Nudge: Improving decisions about health, wealth, and happiness.* Yale University Press.
Thaler, R. H., & Sunstein, C. R. (2021). *Nudge: The final edition.* Penguin Books.

Part IV Life Design Secrets: What 10,000+ People Taught Us

12 Method Mix by Transition Type

Bandura, A. (1997). *Self-efficacy: The exercise of control*. W. H. Freeman.

Bridges, W. (2019). *Transitions: Making sense of life's changes* (40th anniversary edn.). Da Capo Press.

Bronson, P. (2002). *What should I do with my life? The true story of people who answered the ultimate question*. Random House.

Maslow, A. H. (1954). *Motivation and personality*. Harper & Row.

Prochaska, J. O., & Velicer, W. F. (1997). The transtheoretical model of health behavior change. *American Journal of Health Promotion*, 12(1), 38–48.

Przybylski, A. K., Murayama, K., DeHaan, C. R., & Gladwell, V. (2013). Motivational, emotional, and behavioral correlates of fear of missing out. *Computers in Human Behavior*, 29(4), 1841–1848.

Runco, M. A. (2007). *Creativity: Theories and themes – research, development, and practice*. Elsevier Academic Press.

Savickas, M. L. (2005). The theory and practice of career construction. In S. D. Brown & R. W. Lent (Eds.), *Career development and counseling: Putting theory and research to work* (pp. 42–70). John Wiley & Sons.

Sawyer, R. K. (2006). *Explaining creativity: The science of human innovation*. Oxford University Press.

Schwartz, B. (2004). *The paradox of choice: Why more is less*. Harper Perennial.

Seligman, M. E. P. (2006). *Learned optimism: How to change your mind and your life*. Vintage.

13 Special Methods: Sustainable Life Design

Adams, J. L. (2001). *Conceptual blockbusting: A guide to better ideas* (4th edn.). Perseus Publishing.

Cannon, M. D., & Edmondson, A. C. (2005). Failing to learn and learning to fail (intelligently): How great organizations put failure to work to improve and innovate. *Long Range Planning*, 38(3), 299–319.

Chen, O., Paas, F., & Sweller, J. (2023). A cognitive load theory approach to defining and measuring task complexity through element interactivity. *Educational Psychology Review*, 35, 63.

Csikszentmihalyi, M. (1990). *Flow: The psychology of optimal experience*. Harper & Row.

Duncombe, S. (2008). *Notes from underground: Zines and the politics of alternative culture* (2nd edn.). Microcosm Publishing.

Edmondson, A. (1999). Psychological safety and learning behavior in work teams. *Administrative Science Quarterly*, 44(2), 350–383.

Edmondson, A. (2019). *The fearless organization: Creating psychological safety in the workplace for learning, innovation, and growth.* Wiley.

Eppler, M. J., & Kernbach, S. (2021). *Meet up! Better meetings through nudging.* Cambridge University Press.

Facer-Childs, E. R., Boiling, S., & Balanos, G. M. (2018). The effects of time of day and chronotype on cognitive and physical performance in healthy volunteers. *Sports Medicine – Open,* 4, 47.

Garvin, D. A., Edmondson, A. C., & Gino, F. (2008). Is yours a learning organization? *Harvard Business Review,* 86(3), 109–116.

Hofstede, G., Hofstede, G. J., & Minkov, M. (2010). *Cultures and organizations: Software of the mind* (3rd edn.). McGraw-Hill.

Horne, J. A., & Östberg, O. (1976). A self-assessment questionnaire to determine morningness-eveningness in human circadian rhythms. *International Journal of Chronobiology,* 4(2), 97–110.

Larkin, J. H., & Simon, H. A. (1987). Why a diagram is (sometimes) worth ten thousand words. *Cognitive Science,* 11(1), 65–100.

Martindale, C., & Hines, D. (1975). Creativity and cortical activation during creative, intellectual, and EEG feedback tasks. *Biological Psychology,* 3(2), 91–100.

Rosenberg, M. B. (2015). *Nonviolent communication: A language of life* (3rd edn.). PuddleDancer Press.

Rozovsky, J. (2015). The five keys to a successful Google team. re:Work with Google. https://rework.withgoogle.com/blog/five-keys-to-a-successful-google-team/.

Schwartz, T., & McCarthy, C. (2007). Manage your energy, not your time. *Harvard Business Review,* 85(10), 63–73.

Shneiderman, B. (1996). The eyes have it: A task by data type taxonomy for information visualizations. *Proceedings of the 1996 IEEE Symposium on Visual Languages,* 336–343.

Sternberg, R. J. (1985). *Beyond IQ: A triarchic theory of human intelligence.* Cambridge University Press.

Sweller, J. (1988). Cognitive load during problem solving: Effects on learning. *Cognitive Science,* 12(2), 257–285.

Sweller, J. (2010). Element interactivity and intrinsic, extraneous, and germane cognitive load. *Educational Psychology Review,* 22(2), 123–138.

Thaler, R. H., & Sunstein, C. R. (2008). *Nudge: Improving decisions about health, wealth, and happiness.* Yale University Press.

Thayer, R. E. (2003). *Calm energy: How people regulate mood with food and exercise.* Oxford University Press.

Tufte, E. R. (2001). *The visual display of quantitative information* (2nd edn.). Graphics Press.

Tversky, B. (2001). Spatial schemas in depictions. In M. Gattis (Ed.), *Spatial schemas and abstract thought* (pp. 79–111). The MIT Press.

Tversky, B., Morrison, J. B., & Betrancourt, M. (2002). Animation: Can it facilitate? *International Journal of Human-Computer Studies,* 57(4), 247–262.

Tversky, B. (2005). Functional significance of visuospatial representations. In P. Shah & A. Miyake (Eds.), *The Cambridge handbook of visuospatial thinking* (pp. 1–34). Cambridge University Press.

Ulibarri, N., Cravens, A. E., Svetina Nabergoj, A., Kernbach, S., & Royalty, A. (2019). *Creativity in research: Cultivate clarity, be innovative, and make progress in your research journey*. Cambridge University Press.

14 Silent Truths: What We Don't Say Out Loud

AARP. (2018). Loneliness and social connections: A national survey of adults 45 and older. www.aarp.org.

Abidin, C. (2016). Visibility labour: Engaging with influencers. Media International Australia.

Ariga, A., & Lleras, A. (2011). Brief and rare mental "breaks" keep you focused: Deactivation and reactivation of task goals preempt vigilance decrements. *Cognition*, 118(3), 439–443.

Arnett, J. J. (2000). Emerging adulthood: A theory of development from the late teens through the twenties. *American Psychologist*, 55(5), 469–480.

Arthur, M. B., & Rousseau, D. M. (Eds.). (1996). *The boundaryless career: A new employment principle for a new organizational era*. Oxford University Press.

Bail, C. A., Argyle, L. P., Brown, T. W., Bumpus, J. P., Chen, H., Hunzaker, M. F., Lee, J., Mann, M., Merhout, F., & Volfovsky, A. (2018). Exposure to opposing views on social media can increase political polarization. *Proceedings of the National Academy of Sciences*, 115(37), 9216–9221.

Baruch, Y., & Lavi-Steiner, O. (2015). The career impact of management education in Israel: Human capital perspective. *Career Development International*, 20(3), 218–237.

Benartzi, S., & Thaler, R. H. (1995). Myopic loss aversion and the equity premium puzzle. *The Quarterly Journal of Economics*, 110(1), 73–92. https://doi.org/10.2307/2118511

Benedek, M., Schickel, R. J., & Neubauer, A. C. (2014). Eye behavior associated with internally versus externally directed cognition. *Frontiers in Psychology*, 5, 886.

Burnett, B., & Evans, D. (2016). *Designing your life: How to build a well-lived, joyful life*. Knopf.

Ekerdt, D. J. (1986). The busy ethic: Moral continuity between work and retirement. *The Gerontologist*, 26(3), 239–244. https://doi.org/10.1093/geront/26.3.239

Folta, T. B., Delmar, F., & Wennberg, K. (2010). Hybrid entrepreneurship. *Strategic Entrepreneurship Journal*, 4(3), 253–269.

Fugate, M., Kinicki, A. J., & Ashforth, B. E. (2004). Employability: A psycho-social construct. *Journal of Vocational Behavior*, 65(1), 14–38.

Goffman, E. (1959). *The presentation of self in everyday life*. Anchor Books.

Hall, D. T. (1996). Protean careers of the 21st century. *Academy of Management Executive*, 10(4), 8–16.

Handy, C. (1994). *The empty raincoat: Making sense of the future*. Hutchinson.

Hawkley, L. C., & Cacioppo, J. T. (2010). Loneliness matters: A theoretical and empirical review of consequences and mechanisms. *Annals of Behavioral Medicine*, 40(2), 218–227. https://doi.org/10.1007/s12160-010-9210-8.

Kim, J. E., & Moen, P. (2002). Retirement transitions, gender, and psychological well-being: A life-course, ecological model. *The Journals of Gerontology Series B: Psychological Sciences and Social Sciences*, 57(3), P212–P222. https://doi.org/10.1093/geronb/57.3.P212.

Kroger, J., Martinussen, M., & Marcia, J. E. (2010). Identity status change during adolescence and young adulthood: A meta-analysis. *Journal of Adolescence*, 33(5), 683–698.

Leaver, T., Highfield, T., & Abidin, C. (2020). *Instagram: Visual social media cultures*. Polity Press.

Lyubomirsky, S., Sheldon, K. M., & Schkade, D. (2005). Pursuing happiness: The architecture of sustainable change. *Review of General Psychology*, 9(2), 111–131. https://doi.org/10.1037/1089-2680.9.2.111.

McAdams, D. P. (2001). The psychology of life stories. *Review of General Psychology*, 5(2), https://doi.org/10.1037/1089-2680.5.2.100.

Michikyan, M., Subrahmanyam, K., & Dennis, J. (2014). Facebook and self-concept clarity: Platform use and self-esteem as predictors of self-concept clarity. *Computers in Human Behavior*, 43, 1–8.

Montag, C., Lachmann, B., Herrlich, M., & Zweig, K. (2019). Social media: Big Five personality traits, and usage patterns. *Behavior and Information Technology*, 38(4), 1–8.

Peterson, C., & Seligman, M. E. P. (2004). *Character strengths and virtues: A handbook and classification*. Oxford University Press.

Pinquart, M., & Schindler, I. (2007). Changes of life satisfaction in the transition to retirement: A latent-class approach. *Psychology and Aging*, 22(3), 442–455. https://doi.org/10.1037/0882-7974.22.3.442.

Raggatt, M., Wright, C. J. C., Carrotte, E., Jenkinson, R., Mulgrew, K., Prichard, I., Lim, M. S. C., & Thornton, L. (2018). "You feel like you've hit rock bottom": A qualitative study of the role of social media in the development and maintenance of eating disorders. *Journal of Eating Disorders*, 6(1), 1–9.

Rowe, J. W., & Kahn, R. L. (1997). Successful aging. *The Gerontologist*, 37(4), 433–440.

Savickas, M. L., Nota, L., Rossier, J., Dauwalder, J.-P., Duarte, M. E., Guichard, J., Soresi, S., Van Esbroeck, R., & Van Vianen, A. E. M. (2009). Life design: A paradigm for career construction in the 21st century. *Journal of Vocational Behavior*, 75(3), 239–250.

Seligman, M. E. P. (2002). *Authentic happiness: Using the new positive psychology to realize your potential for lasting fulfillment*. Free Press.

Sieber, S. D. (1974). Toward a theory of role accumulation. *American Sociological Review*, 39(4), 567–578.

Tang, Y. Y., Ma, Y., Wang, J., Fan, Y., Feng, S., Lu, Q., Yu, Q., Sui, D., Rothbart, M. K., Fan, M., & Posner, M. I. (2007). Short-term meditation training improves attention and self-regulation. *Proceedings of the National Academy of Sciences*, 104(43), 17152–17156.

Von Bonsdorff, M. E., & Rantanen, T. (2011). The impact of retirement on health and well-being. In M. Wang (Ed.), *The Oxford handbook of retirement* (pp. 279–292). Oxford University Press.

Waldinger, R. J., & Schulz, M. S. (2023). *The good life: Lessons from the world's longest scientific study of happiness*. Simon & Schuster.

Wang, M., & Shi, J. (2014). Psychological research on retirement. *Annual Review of Psychology*, 65, 209–233. https://doi.org/10.1146/annurev-psych-010213-115131.

Yang, C.-C., & Brown, B. B. (2016). Online self-presentation on Facebook and self-development during adolescence. *Developmental Psychology*, 52(2), 340–350.

Zaccaro, A., Piarulli, A., Laurino, M., et al. (2018). How breath-control can change your life: A systematic review on psychophysiological correlates of slow breathing. *Frontiers in Human Neuroscience*, 12, 353.

Part V Horizons of Life Design

15 Life Design as a Catalyst for Scaling Change

Batson, C. D., Chang, J., Orr, R., & Rowland, J. (2002). Empathy, attitudes, and action: Can feeling for a member of a stigmatized group motivate one to help the group? *Personality and Social Psychology Bulletin*, 28(12), 1656–1666.

ELDeM YOU consortium. (2023). European life design method for youth (ELDeM YOU) [Project report]. European Union Erasmus+ Programme. Retrieved from www.eldemyou.eu/.

Eppler, M. J., & Kernbach, S. (2021). *Meet up! Better meetings through nudging*. Cambridge University Press.

Gallup. (2024). State of the global workplace: 2024 report with key insights. Gallup. www.gallup.com/workplace/349484/state-of-the-global-workplace.aspx.

Gedeon, S., & Kernbach, S. (2024). Concepts, theories and future directions in career and life design. *CERN IdeaSquare Journal of Experimental Innovation*, 8(3), 5–13.

Kernbach, S. (2022). Towards a science of action: Concepts and theories to reduce procrastination and overcome the intention–action gap. In *European Academy of Management Annual Meeting – EURAM (Conference Paper)*, June.

Kernbach, S., Hall, T., Perry, M., Walsh, N., Lamb, L., Millar, M., & McBride, D. (2023). Assessing Life Design and evaluating its impact on the learning experience: A conceptual overview and emergent framework based on the Designing Futures Programme at University of Galway, Ireland. European Academy of Management (EURAM) Conference, Dublin, Ireland, June.

Luthans, F., Avey, J. B., Avolio, B. J., & Norman, S. M. (2007). Positive psychological capital: Measurement and relationship with performance and satisfaction. *Personnel Psychology*, 60(3), 541–572.

Luthans, F., Youssef, C. M., & Avolio, B. J. (2007). *Psychological capital: Developing the human competitive edge*. Oxford University Press.

Oros, R., Sim, S., Kernbach, S., & Pina e Cunha, M. (2024). Efficacy of career & life design interventions: A systematic review. *European Academy of Management (EURAM) Conference*, Bath, June.

Otte, S., Aggerholm, K., & Raedeke, T. D. (2017). Factors contributing to the quality of transition out of elite sports: A cross-cultural comparison of current and retired professional athletes. *Sport, Exercise, and Performance Psychology*, 6(4), 362–375.

Rehnert, D., & Kernbach, S. (2020). The pathway of a change-maker: Creativity and affect regulation to bridge the intention–action gap. *Academy of Management Annual Meeting*, Vancouver, June.

Stone, A. M., Nelson, M. E., & Kernbach, S. (2023). Life design and design thinking to support individuals to better contribute to achieving the United Nations Sustainable Development Goals (UN SDGs). *European Academy of Management (EURAM) Conference*, Dublin, June.

VIA Institute on Character. (2021). VIA Youth-103 (Age 13–17). VIA Character Strengths. Retrieved from www.viacharacter.org/researchers/assessments/via-youth-103-13-17.

Wylleman, P., & Lavallee, D. (2004). A developmental perspective on transitions faced by athletes. In M. Weiss (Ed.), *Developmental sport and exercise psychology: A lifespan perspective*. Fitness Information Technology, 507–527.

16 Life Design and the Future (of the Planet)

Arthur, M. B., & Rousseau, D. M. (Eds.). (1996). *The boundaryless career: A new employment principle for a new organizational era*. Oxford University Press.

Bienefeld, N. (2025). *Life Design & AI, Executive Education module for Life Design Leadership Training*. St. Gallen.

Eppler, M. J. (2022). *Visual variation: The powerful principle for clear explanations and creative explorations*. MCM Institute, University of St. Gallen.

George, G., Howard-Grenville, J., Joshi, A., & Tihanyi, L. (2016). Understanding and tackling societal grand challenges through management research. *Academy of Management Journal*, 59(6), 1880–1895.

Gratton, L., & Scott, A. (2016). *The 100-year life: Living and working in an age of longevity*. Bloomsbury.

Hawkley, L. C., & Cacioppo, J. T. (2010). Loneliness matters: A theoretical and empirical review of consequences and mechanisms. *Annals of Behavioral Medicine*, 40(2), 218–227.

Inner Development Goals. (2021). *Inner Development Goals (IDGs): Background, method and the Inner Development Goals framework*. Inner Development Goals Initiative. www.innerdevelopmentgoals.org/framework.

Ivcevic, Z., & Grandinetti, M. (2024). Artificial intelligence as a tool for creativity. *Journal of Creativity*, 34(2), Article 100079.

Rowe, J. W., & Kahn, R. L. (1997). Successful aging. *The Gerontologist*, 37(4), 433–440.

Savickas, M. L., Nota, L., Rossier, J., Dauwalder, J. P., Duarte, M. E., Guichard, J., & Van Vianen, A. E. M. (2009). Life design: A paradigm for career construction in the 21st century. *Journal of Vocational Behavior*, 75(3), 239–250.

Smith, J. A., & Lee, K. L. (2023). Artificial intelligence & creativity: A manifesto for collaboration. *Journal of Creative Behavior*, 57(2), 123–140.

Stiglitz, J. E., Sen, A., & Fitoussi, J.-P. (2009). Report by the Commission on the Measurement of Economic Performance and Social Progress. Commission on the Measurement of Economic Performance and Social Progress.

United Nations. (2015). *Transforming our world: The 2030 agenda for sustainable development*. United Nations. https://sdgs.un.org/2030agenda.

Index

action planning
   using guiding questions for, 90, 102
Action Prompts
   first steps, 214, 219
   small shifts, 27, 225
   take the VIA Strengths Survey, 155
   use Opportunity Bingo, 158
   write down Three Good Things, 97, 99, 156
action versus overthinking, 28
actionable clarity, 166
actionable insights, 33
active listening, 204, 259
addressing longevity
   extended retirement phase, 262
   financial pressures, 263
   generational mix, 264
   health management, 263
   identity shifts, 263
   multiple careers, 261
   relationships and community, 264
affect regulation, 8, 52
AI
   as a coach or guide, 258
   as a collaborator or creative partner, 259
   as a companion, 259
   as a Life Design architect, 259
   as a reflective mirror, 258
   as a social simulator, 259
   as a teacher or tutor, 258
AI and human intelligence (HI), 254
AI as Life Design sparring partner, 246
AI Life Design Manifesto, 261
AI, future landscape of, 254
AI, working with, 242, 246
alpha time, Einstein example, 182
Alternative Uses Test (AUT), 53
   as a creative warm-up, 93
ambiguity, 6, 16, 214
analog versus digital
   cognitive capacity, 195

   one eye-span principle, Edward Tufte, 195
   pen and paper, 194, 195
appreciation, 30
authenticity, 90, 224, 225, 271

behavioral economics, 3, 138
   System 1 (fast, automatic, unconscious), 140
   System 2 (slow, deliberate, conscious), 140
   using laziness to advantage, 140
behavior-boosting design, 253
being heard, power of, 37
best-agers, 235
big and small goals, use for, 127
biographical transitions, 20
brainstorming ways, 150

career frameworks
   boundaryless career, 208
   protean career, 208
career transition, 8, 20, 22, 24, 253
   action planning, 214
   guiding questions, 90, 102
   normalize prototyping for adults, 113
   portfolio career, 80, 207, 208, 209, 212, 213, 261, 281
   scenario types and prompts, 153
   Signature Strengths, 218
   stories, 245
   transitions as features, not failures, 253
catalyst for scaling change, Life Design as a, 235
catalysts for redesign, life transitions as, 20
catalyzing momentum, 206
Certificate of Advanced Studies (CAS), 236, 238
challenges, watch out for
   admin load, 213
   energy management, 213
   identity blur, 213
   work creep, 213
character strengths, 80
   curiosity, 80
   gratitude, 80

character strengths (cont.)
   hope, 80
   love, 80
   zest, 80
character strengths and virtues, 80
childhood memories, 218
co-creating through a "Yes, and . . ." mindset, 28
cognitive behavioral therapy (CBT), 259
cognitive load theory, 195
Columbia University, 237
common cognitive biases, 32
community, importance of, 254
company examples (Baloise Insurance, Cambridge University), 120
comparison, three types
   with others, 223
   with ourselves, 223
   with the norm, 223
complementary disciplines, 16
   behavioral economics, 17
   Design Thinking, 16
   knowledge visualization, 17
   positive psychology, 17
complex global transitions, human side of, 248
complexity, 14
concern-overcome combo, essence of the method, 135
concrete versus open-ended wishes, 125
confirmation bias, 32
Connecting the Dots, 86
conscious engagement, 222
convergent thinking (focusing energy), 47
conversation-starters, 195
Core and Optional Methods
   Core Method of creativity (foundational framework), 91
   Future Scenarios (Optional Method), 91
   Opportunity Bingo (Optional Method), 91
Core of Creativity, 91
   procedure and steps, 91
   using convergent thinking, 91, 93, 95
   using divergent thinking, 47
Core of Creativity, procedure and steps for, 91
crafting an environment, elements for, 202
creative collaboration, 27, 32
creative flow, 158
creative mindset, 98
   do it once and learn, 108
creative nudge, need for, 166
creative potential, 91
creative warm-up, 93
Credit Suisse, 24
crime scene, 53
cultivating curiosity, 27
cultural-social environment, 203

curiosity and evolving, 174
curiosity, adaptability, momentum, 106

daily habit, 60
daily practice, 73
deep reflection/rich conversation, 103
deep respect for human realities, 4
deep work, 196
deeper human connection, questions for, 119
demographic data, 19
Design
   Your Home Office, 194
   Your Leadership, 242, 244
   Your Potential, 166, 242, 244
designing transitions, 242
dichotomous thinking, 34, 36
different levels of application, 25, 60
distracting voices
   holding back dialogue, 145
   the Anti-Believer, 145
   the Perfectionist, 145
divergent thinking, 47, 91, 93, 95, 199
diversity, equity, and inclusion (DEI), 242, 244
DJ of the Inner Sound, 143
DJ-style mental "mixer," 145
drastic change, 212
dream in progress
   realizing potential, setting goals, 68
dream job, 22, 32, 208, 213
dream toolkits, 253
driver's seat, mindset for transition, 219, 256

early-career, 269
ELDeM YOU (EU Horizon Project/Erasmus Plus Toolkit), 237
embodied cognition, principle of, 33
embody inner voices, 146
embracing awkwardness/silence, 95
emotional awareness/emotions, 155
emotional connection, 87
emotional resonance, 90
emotional stability, 247
emotional stability, key practices
   empathetic dialogue, 249
   legitimizing language, 249
   visual thinking, 249
empathy prompt, 113
empathy, dimensions of
   behavioral empathy, 47
   cognitive empathy, 47
   emotional empathy, 47
empathy/empathetic listening, 259
empathy-based insights, 76
empowering language, 21
energy competence methods

Index

adjust the strength, 188
choose focus points, 188
color-code the energy, 187
create opportunity statements, 188
describe the energy, 188
list energy elements, 186
make it visual (icons/doodles), 187
set the stage, 186
spot patterns, 188
energy curve, 181
  chronotypes, 181
  natural rhythm, 181
energy curve steps
  alpha time, identify, 182
  chronotype, identify, 181
  Energy Curve, draw, 182
  high time, identify, 182
  intentional change, apply, 184
  prime time, identify, 182
Energy Curve, example of visual tool, 22
energy-givers/-takers, 188
Energy Map, tips and tricks for, 188
energy types
  emotional energy, 111, 182, 185, 188, 192, 221
  mental energy, 182, 185
  physical energy, 98, 185
energy, following the (motivation as fuel), 179
Energy–Tension Matrix, 67, 181, 189, 263
  calm energy, 189
  hyperaggressive energy, 189
  relaxed fatigue, 189
  Robert Thayer, 189
  tense fatigue, 189
  tips and tricks, 192
entry paths
  iterative process, 40, 58
  jumping, 212
  moonlighting, 212
  rejigging, 212
  Strengths Portfolio, 213
environments, 49
episodic memory, 231, 232
existential transition, retirement as, 217
exploration and learning, 30
exploring prototypes, 118

failure celebration example, skateboarding, 203
false empathy, 118
fear of commitment (breaking down), 106
fear of failure, 34, 52, 57, 249
first shitty version, 34, 52
five silent truths, 151, 207
fixed mindset, 33, 56
flow concept, Mihály Csikszentmihalyi, 180
focus shift, 180

focus voices, 146
follow-up sessions, 205
fourth circle, 112
from role to portfolio, 67
from small to big loop, 68
Future Scenarios, 99
  as multioptional thinking, 100
  procedure for creating, 100
  sharing and reflecting on, 102

gallery walk, 197
global institutions (partnerships)
  UN Goals House, i, 8
  World Demographic & Ageing Forum (WDA), xiii, 248
  World Economic Forum (WEF), 8, 24, 248, 249
Global Report, 24
Global Transition Report, 247, 248
good questions, 118, 159
grace points of zero, 20
gratitude journal/gratitude journaling, 67, 204
great Life Design conversations, 117, 118
  curiosity, 118
  empathy, 118
  humility, 118
great questions, more sources for, 119
greater longevity, 14
Growth Journey Map, 128, 130, 131, 132, 157, 158, 245, 266
  energy/challenges/insights, 128
  honouring growth, 128
  individual versus team reflection, 130
  procedure and steps, 131
Growth Journey Map, steps deeper insights, 132
  doing, 131
  implications, 131
  learning, 131
guide your selection, five criteria to, 82
guiding questions, 90, 102
  for reflecting on insights ("What do I want to keep?"), 90

habits and practices, 60, 61, 69
Handy, Charles, 80, 208
helpful dialogue, 118
hidden assumptions, 100
home office, design, 242
hope, 250
human experience, treating as, 138, 230
humble inquiry, 118

288 Index

IBM, Google, International Red Cross, 245
idea generation (individual), 93
idea implementation, 106
   overcoming "forever thinking," 107
   uncovering need behind crazy ideas, 107
ideation
   using Future Scenarios for, 172
identity transformation, 239
increase awareness, 146
informational interviews, 118
initial opportunity statements, 78
inner circle, 203
Inner Development Goals (IDGs), 265, 267, 268
inner dialogue, inner critic, 145, 227
inner reflection (values, strengths, dreams), 20
interdisciplinary, 269
interests, strengths, and values, 91
International Olympic Committee (IOC), xiii, 8, 240, 244
interpersonal communication, 22
interpersonal risk-taking, 204
interview guide, using PPCO as, 135
intimidation, overcoming, 137
intrapersonal communication, 22
iteration
   adjusting features for better fit, 107

keeping visuals alive, 195
key societal contributions, 32
knowledge visualization, 3, 8, 194, 196
Kreatives Unternehmertum (KU), 237

learning and insight, value of, 201
life coaching questions, 119
Life Design
   abilities, 173
   and AI, 254
   and longevity, 261
   and the future, 235, 252
   as an intergenerational playground, 253
   building blocks, 9
   coaching, xiii, 236
   creative skills for, 256
   for individuals, 235
   horizons of, 233
   interventions, 20, 232
   lab, 7, 233
   leadership, xiii, 8, 236, 238
   space (visual tool), 99
   stories on, 65
   sustainability, 267, 271
   teams, 205
   toolbox, 71
Life Design ability
   moving to multioptional thinking, 51

Life Design as a
   compass, 44
   dance, 44
   map, 44
Life Design conversations, 118, 179, 204, 249, 266
   asking open-ended questions, 118
   learning from others' experiences, 118
Life Design for
   best-agers and senior professionals, 236, 238
   experienced professionals, 236, 238
   kids and teenagers, 236
   organizations, 240
   young adults and students, 236, 237
Life Design interventions
   ideation tools, 93, 265
      "Yes, and ... " technique, 95
      Alternative Uses Test (AUT), 93
      Core of Creativity, 91, 265
      Future Scenarios, 266
      Opportunity Bingo, 266
   learning tools, 128
      Growth Journey Map, 128
      PPCO Hollywood Star, 128
      Start–Stop–Continue, 128
   perseverance tools, 138
      Energy Curve steps, 180
      Energy Map, steps for, 181
      Energy-Tension Matrix, 181
      Nudging Nuggets, 266
      Social Support Map, 224
      support categories, 268
   prototyping tools
      Ten Ways of Prototyping, 108, 113
      Magic Circle, 104, 176
      Prototyping Prism, 104, 226
      role-playing, 116
      routine redesign, 160, 161
      Stairway To Heaven, 104, 174
      thirty-day challenge, 116
   reflection tools, 135
      empathy, dimensions of, 175
      Life Portfolio, 155
      Me at My Best, 159, 161
      Signature Strengths, 82
      Strengths Portfolio, 159
      Three Good Things, 83
Life Design tools, 7, 9, 90, 214, 226
   integrating insights into, 121
Life Loops framework, distinctive features of
   from small loops to big changes, 40
   integration of procrastination, 41
   nonlinear design, 40
Life Portfolio, 82, 83, 155
   activities, 84
   analyze the status quo, 84

drivers, 83
realize your activity potential, 85
realize your strengths potential, 84
using the portfolio in different ways, 85
life reboot, 214, 217
life satisfaction, 151, 180, 207, 224, 225, 230
life, not a problem, 270
linear careers, 209, 262
longevity, implications of, 19
long-held creative dream, 67
lost in transition, 20
low-risk experimentation, xiv, 22, 23, 34, 36, 37, 38, 56
low-risk prototypes, 60, 115

Magic Circle, 109
  defining idea, dream, or wish, 109
  exploring motivation, 111
  lowering the threshold, 111
  moving from inspiration to implementation, 108
  selecting top prototypes, 112
  three circles (idea, motivation, prototypes), 109
Map Your Needs (Maslow's hierarchy), 85
Mapping Inner Voices, 57
master plan, 154, 177
matrix procedure, 190
  assess energy, 190
  check tension, 190
  design micro-strategies, 192
  explore your shift, 191
  place yourself on matrix, 191
MBA Programs, xiii, 8, 236, 238
Me at My Best (reflection)
  uncovering energizing moments, 159
mental health, 17, 245, 247, 248
  Deloitte, 245
  DJ of the Inner Sound, 251
  Nudging Nuggets, 245
  Social Support Maps, 245
  Swiss Re, 245
metaphor, playing with, 44, 147
method mixes, 151, 153, 166
methods per phase, 72
micro-prototype, 100 ways to, 226
micro-strategies, examples
  emotional (uplifting song, message friend), 192
  mental (breathing exercise, brain dump), 192
  physical (brisk walk), 192
midlife, 7, 236
mini-sabbatical (intentional small breaks), 95, 108, 124
mini-zine, power of a, 194, 199

momentum, moving forward with, 138
morning routine, example of a, 53
motivation and self-talk, 143
multioptional thinking, 100, 173
multiplicity, bold expression of, 208
myth versus reality of career transitions, 23

naming dilemmas, 63, 238
NASA, i, xiii, 8, 238, 244
need-to-have versus nice-to-have (prioritization), 137
negative affect, 52
negative emotions, 52
negativity, 30, 45
new language and micro-prototyping, prompting as, 256
Nina's journey, 13
nonnormative (e.g., job loss, divorce), 20
nonviolent communication, marshall Rosenberg, 30, 204
normalize prototyping for adults, 113
  legitimacy, 124
  transition programs, 124
normative (e.g., retirement, parenthood), 20
Nudging Nuggets, 138, 141, 165, 170, 266
  changing habits and routines, 140
  concept of nudging, 138
  designing for action (calendar blocks, music cues), 164, 166
  not relying on willpower, 138
  steps, 140

one person-multiple roles (tip), 149
one-on-one conversations, 207
open-ended questions, 118
Opportunity Bingo, 96
  creating the bingo sheet, 97
  group process/team work, 96
  mixing expected with unexpected ideas, 159
  procedure and steps, 96
opportunity statement, as a starting point, 47
optimism, 17, 20, 225, 247, 250
organizational focus table, 242
outplacement transitions, 243
over drama, 36
overcoming blocks, 51
overnight reinvention, myth of, 35
overthinking, 4, 28, 49, 62, 104, 106, 166

paradox of choice, 76
parasympathetic nervous system, activation of, 226
perfection, enemy of progress, 104
perfectionism, 34, 52, 57, 164
personality systems interaction theory (PSI theory), 52

personalization, customizing categories, 150
phases of the Life Loops, 57
  empathy, 55
  ideation, 55
  learning, 56
  perseverance, 57
  prototyping, 56
portfolio
  anchor job, 208
  benefits, 213
  challenges, 213
  coined by Charles Handy (*The age of Unreason*), 208
  diversified/adaptive, 208
  flexibility/evolving portfolio, 208
  versatility, 212
portfolio activities, 60, 64, 211, 212
portfolio careers, benefits of, 213
portfolio of activities, 4, 21, 59, 60, 63, 68
portfolio thinking, 19, 21, 263
portfolios, types of, 210
  balanced portfolio, 210
  encore portfolio, 210
  entrepreneurial portfolio, 210
  hybrid portfolio, 210
  patchwork portfolio, 210
  transition portfolio, 210
positive affect, 53
positive moments, 87
power of language (staycation effect), 124
power of meaning (routines versus rituals), 205
Powerful Identity Learning Laboratories (PILL), 20
PPCO acronym, 128, 132, 133, 134, 135
  concern, 133
  overcome, 133
  plus, 133
  potential, 133
PPCO Hollywood Star, feedback method, 128
practical intelligence, 180
predictability, 100
preretirement transitions, 243
proactivity, xii, 3, 186, 270, 271
procrastination
  finite, 247
  infinite, 247
procrastination, overcoming, 237, 247
productivity and well-being, fuel for, 85, 180
prototype conversations, 49
prototyping
  goal of (movement over overthinking), 104
  low-risk experiments, 56
  methods for, 104
  turning ideas into movement, 104
prototyping low-risk experiments, 49

Prototyping Prism, 104
  dual approach of, 106
  strategy 1 (feasible ideas), 106
  strategy 2 (crazy ideas), 107
  use of adjustable features/dimensions, 107
psychological capital (hope, optimism, resilience, and self-efficacy), 20
psychological capital (PsyCap), elements of, 250
  hope, 250
  optimism, 250
  resilience, 250
  self-efficacy, 250
psychological safety, 179, 203, 204, 205, 238
psychological well-being, 30
psychological/social transformation, 216
psychological-emotional safety, 202, 203
purposeful action, 36

questions, three types of, 118
  confrontational inquiries, 119
  diagnostic inquiries, 119
  pure humble inquiries, 119

Radical Sabbatical, The, Emma Rosen, 122
reactive habits, 10
real-life application, 151
real-life situations, 153
redesigning the end of the day, 67
  changing routines, habit formation, 67
reducing mismatched expectations, benefits for, 120
refinements, examples of, 78
reflection
  depth, maximizing, 90
  linking insights to Life Design tools, 90
  use of childhood memories in, 90
retirement, 214
  action prompt, 214
  boredom, 214
  identity shifts, 216
  negative surprises, 216
  positive surprises, 217
  reflection prompt, 214
  uncertainty, 214
  unhelpful myths, 214
return on investment (ROI), 74
reverse bucket list, 232
rhythms and rituals, 202, 204
  examples, 204
  habit formation/behavior change, 204
  relying on repetition/structure (not just motivation), 204
Robert Sternberg's model, 199

Index

role-playing, 116
   "If I were you" variation, 116
   Walt Disney method (dreamer, critic, realist), 116
romanticized ideas, 37
routine redesign, 160, 161
   intentional change (morning/evening), 161
   reclaiming sense of agency, 20

scaffolding, 95, 203, 204, 216, 242, 250
scenario planning
   personal application in Life Design, 25
scenario thinking (strategic planning), 10, 100
scenario types and prompts
   scenario 1 (most likely path/realistic) 100
   scenario 2 (complete career switch), 100
   scenario 3 (no constraints/dream), 102
   scenario 4 (optional/blended vision), 102
science-based approach, 14, 16
scientific support, benefits of
   psychological resilience, 208
   skill development/employability, 208
   stronger sense of purpose, 208
   well-being/cognitive health, 208
SDGs along the Life Loops framework, 265
   empathy, 265
   ideation, 265
   learning, 266
   perseverance, 266
   prototyping, 266
self-compassion, energy as a, 185
self-compassion/self-support, 21, 53, 145, 240
self-discovery, travel as a path to, 232
self-empathy, 30, 45, 47, 73
self-judgment, 36
self-reflection, 9, 133, 134, 258
self-responsibility, 20
self-sabotage to self-support, shifting from, 145
self-sabotaging narratives, 32
self-talk, power of, 143
short-term emotional reactions, 52
Signature Strengths
   activate and expand your use of Signature Strengths, 83
   character strengths survey, 82
   core traits/compass, 155
   identify your Signature Strengths, 82
   take the test, 82
   using as a filter for choices/opportunities, 163
   view your strengths ranking, 82
silent truths, 151, 230, 231
skepticism, 36, 45, 259
small adjustments, 135
small daily habits and practices, 60

small loop, 40, 41
small prototypes, 36, 38
social biases, against evening types, 185
social jet lag, 186
social media impact, 220
social media, effects of, 220
   behavioral consequences, 221
   cognitive distortions, 221
   developmental and identity challenges, 222
   psychological distress, 221
Social Support Map, 147
   activating network, 147
   life transitions (support for), 147
   procedure and steps, 147
   visualizing network, 147
space-holder, role of life designer, 204
spark curiosity, 13, 76
Stairway to Heaven, 104
   breaking prototypes, 106
Stanford professor example, 184
Stanford University, i, 3, 237, 239
start small, 12, 32, 65, 86, 160, 212, 269
Start–Stop–Continue, vii, 136
   procedure and steps, 136
   tips and concepts, 137
Start–Stop–Continue, reflection tool, 128, 135, 136, 171
Stellenbosch University, 24, 237
stories
   dream in progress, 68
   from role to portfolio, 67
   from small to big loop, 68
   redesigning the end of the day, 67
storytelling, 10, 68, 69, 87, 90, 104, 164, 171, 177, 231, 247
Strengths Portfolio, 82, 90, 156
   active ingredients, 159
   life portfolio (broader landscape), 164
   part 1 (Signature Strengths), 82
   part 2 (life portfolio use), 82, 83
subtle observations, giving feedback on, 135
support categories
   cheerleaders (moral support), 148
   connectors (resource linking), 149
   draw your map, 148
   GKITBs (accountability/nudge), 149
   joiners (action partners), 149
   take action, 149
supportive social environment, 151, 179, 202
supportive voices, the chill voice, the Life Designer, 145
sustainable Life Design, pillars of energy
   competence, 179
   supportive social environment, 179
   tangible output, 179

sustainable success
  connection to Inner Development Goals
    (IDGs), 265
  core reminder, 268
  key, 266
sustained action, 202, 268
Swiss Stock Exchange, 24, 99, 244
symbolic zones (brain, heart, gut), 145

tangible output, 192
  shifts perspective, 192
  sparks creativity, 192
  supports action, 192
task intensity levels
  demanding tasks, 185
  proactive/novel tasks, 185
  routine tasks, 185
task–energy matching, 185
Ten Ways of Prototyping, 104, 108, 109, 113, 123,
    125, 173, 174, 176, 226
  desk research, 113
  internship, 121
  Life Design conversations, 117
  observation, 115
  role-playing, 116
  sabbatical, 122
  shadowing, 119
  side hustle, 121
  thirty-day challenge, 116
  volunteering, 120
Ten-Ten-Ten framework, 124
The 100-Year Life, 18
the Nexel Collaborative, 8, 24, 236, 239, 248
The Science of Action, 138
thirty-day challenge, 116
  constraints, power of, 117
  time limited experiment, 117
Three Good Things, 154
  building emotional awareness, 155
  noticing patterns/joy, 155
Three Good Things, method, 62, 67, 73, 74, 76,
    78, 83, 155, 161, 162, 165, 201, 218, 225,
    243, 244
three methods
  one key method, 71
  two additional methods, 71
tiny experiments, 22
transition competence
  addressing longevity, 18, 261
  life design ability, 261
  prototyping phase, 20
  transition type a/b/c/d, 153
transition type a, the Unsettled Starter, 154
  foggy in-between space, 154
  lack of clarity/confidence, 154

main challenge, 153
  method mixes 1, 2, 3, 155
  scenarios and methods, 153
transition type b, the Overwhelmed
    Navigator, 153
  decision fatigue, 160
  main challenge, 160
  method mixes 4, 5, 6, 161
  paralysis, 160
  scenarios and methods, 160
  stuckness, 160
transition type c, the Stuck Creative, 166
  escaping overthinking loop, 166
  main challenge, 166
  method mixes 7, 8, 9, 168
  paralyzed by options, 166
  scenarios and methods, 166
    Connecting the dots, 166
    DJ of the Inner Sound, 169
    Future Scenarios, 171
    Nudging Nuggets, 170
    Opportunity Bingo, 168
    Social Support Map, 169
    Start–Stop–Continue, 171
    Strengths Portfolio, 171
transition type d, the Meaning-Maker, 172
  bridging aspiration and action, 172
  finding purpose/relevance, 154
  main challenge, 154
  mix 10, 11, 12, 176
  scenarios and methods, 154
    Ten Ways of Prototyping, 173
    Ten-Minute Prototype, 176
    cultivating empathy, 175, 176
    existential question, 178
    five Life Design abilities, 174
    lifelong learning (staying in growth
        mode), 178
    Magic Circle, 173, 176
transitions, as features, 242
travel map, 232

UN General Assembly, 261
UN Goals House, i, 8, 24, 248
UN Sustainable Development Goals (SDGs),
    238, 247, 265, 268
un/supportive (sub)cultures, risk-averse
    cultures, 203
use solo or in conversation, 134
UX design, 9, 211

VIA Character Strengths Survey, 80, 155, 163
VIA Institute on Character, 79, 82
visual strategies, 192
  Life Design Space, 194

visual artifacts, 194
visual thinking, 194
visual tools, xi, 194, 249
   two-by-two matrix, 196
   making scenarios visual, 187
   scenario d as a vision board, 103
   sketches, diagrams, maps, frameworks, 194
visualization examples, 197
volatility, 14, 208

well-being layer (perma), 85
well-being practice, 179
wishful thinking, 36
work smarter, not longer, 185
work–life rhythms, 254
World Demographic & Ageing Forum (WDA), xiii, 8, 248

"Yes, and ... " technique, 95

For EU product safety concerns, contact us at Calle de José Abascal, 56–1°, 28003 Madrid, Spain or eugpsr@cambridge.org.

www.ingramcontent.com/pod-product-compliance
Ingram Content Group UK Ltd.
Pitfield, Milton Keynes, MK11 3LW, UK
UKHW020051040426
469672UK00019B/399